AVENGERS
MILLENNIUM

AVENGERS (1963) #56
WRITER: ROY THOMAS
PENCILER: JOHN BUSCEMA
INKER: GEORGE KLEIN
LETTERER: SAM ROSEN
EDITOR: STAN LEE

AVENGERS (1963) #71
WRITER: ROY THOMAS
PENCILER: SAL BUSCEMA
INKER: SAM GRAINGER
LETTERER: SAM ROSEN
EDITOR: STAN LEE

AVENGERS CREATED BY **STAN LEE** & **JACK KIRBY**

COLLECTION EDITOR: JENNIFER GRÜNWALD
ASSISTANT EDITOR: SARAH BRUNSTAD
ASSOCIATE MANAGING EDITOR: ALEX STARBUCK
EDITOR, SPECIAL PROJECTS: MARK D. BEAZLEY
SENIOR EDITOR, SPECIAL PROJECTS: JEFF YOUNGQUIST
SVP PRINT, SALES & MARKETING: DAVID GABRIEL
BOOK DESIGNER: ADAM DEL RE

EDITOR IN CHIEF: AXEL ALONSO
CHIEF CREATIVE OFFICER: JOE QUESADA
PUBLISHER: DAN BUCKLEY
EXECUTIVE PRODUCER: ALAN FINE

AVENGERS: MILLENNIUM. Contains material originally published in magazine form as AVENGERS: MILLENNIUM #1-4, and AVENGERS #56 and #71. First printing 2015. ISBN# 978-0-7851-9166-7. Published by MARVEL WORLDWIDE, INC., a subsidiary of MARVEL ENTERTAINMENT, LLC. OFFICE OF PUBLICATION: 135 West 50th Street, New York, NY 10020. Copyright © 2015 MARVEL No similarity between any of the names, characters, persons, and/or institutions in this magazine with those of any living or dead person or institution is intended, and any such similarity which may exist is purely coincidental. **Printed in the U.S.A.** ALAN FINE, President, Marvel Entertainment; DAN BUCKLEY, President, TV, Publishing and Brand Management; JOE QUESADA, Chief Creative Officer; TOM BREVOORT, SVP of Publishing; DAVID BOGART, SVP of Operations & Procurement, Publishing; C. CEBULSKI, VP of International Development & Brand Management; DAVID GABRIEL, SVP Print, Sales & Marketing; JIM O'KEEFE, VP of Operations & Logistics; DAN CARR, Executive Director of Publishing Technology; SUSAN CRESPI, Editorial Operations Manager; ALEX MORALES, Publishing Operations Manager; STAN LEE, Chairman Emeritus. For information regarding advertising in Marvel Comics or on Marvel.com, please contact Jonathan Rheingold, VP of Custom Solutions & Ad Sales, at jrheingold@marvel.com. For Marvel subscription inquiries, please call 800-217-9158. **Manufactured between 4/3/2015 and 5/18/2015 by SOLISCO PRINTERS, SCO**

AVENGERS
MILLENNIUM

WRITER
MIKE COSTA

STORYBOARD ARTISTS
MAST & GEOFFO

PENCILERS/INKERS
CARMINE DI GIANDOMENICO (#1-2, #4)
& PACO DIAZ (#3)
WITH ENIS CISIC (#4)

COLORIST
ANDRES MOSSA

LETTERER
VC's TRAVIS LANHAM

COVER ART
LEINIL YU & MATT MILLA (#1)
AND MIKE DEODATO & FRANK MARTIN (#2-4)

ASSISTANT EDITORS: JON MOISAN WITH ALANNA SMITH
EDITORS: TOM BREVOORT WITH WIL MOSS

PRODUCTION- ARLIN ORTIZ   PRODUCTION MANAGER- TIM SMITH 3

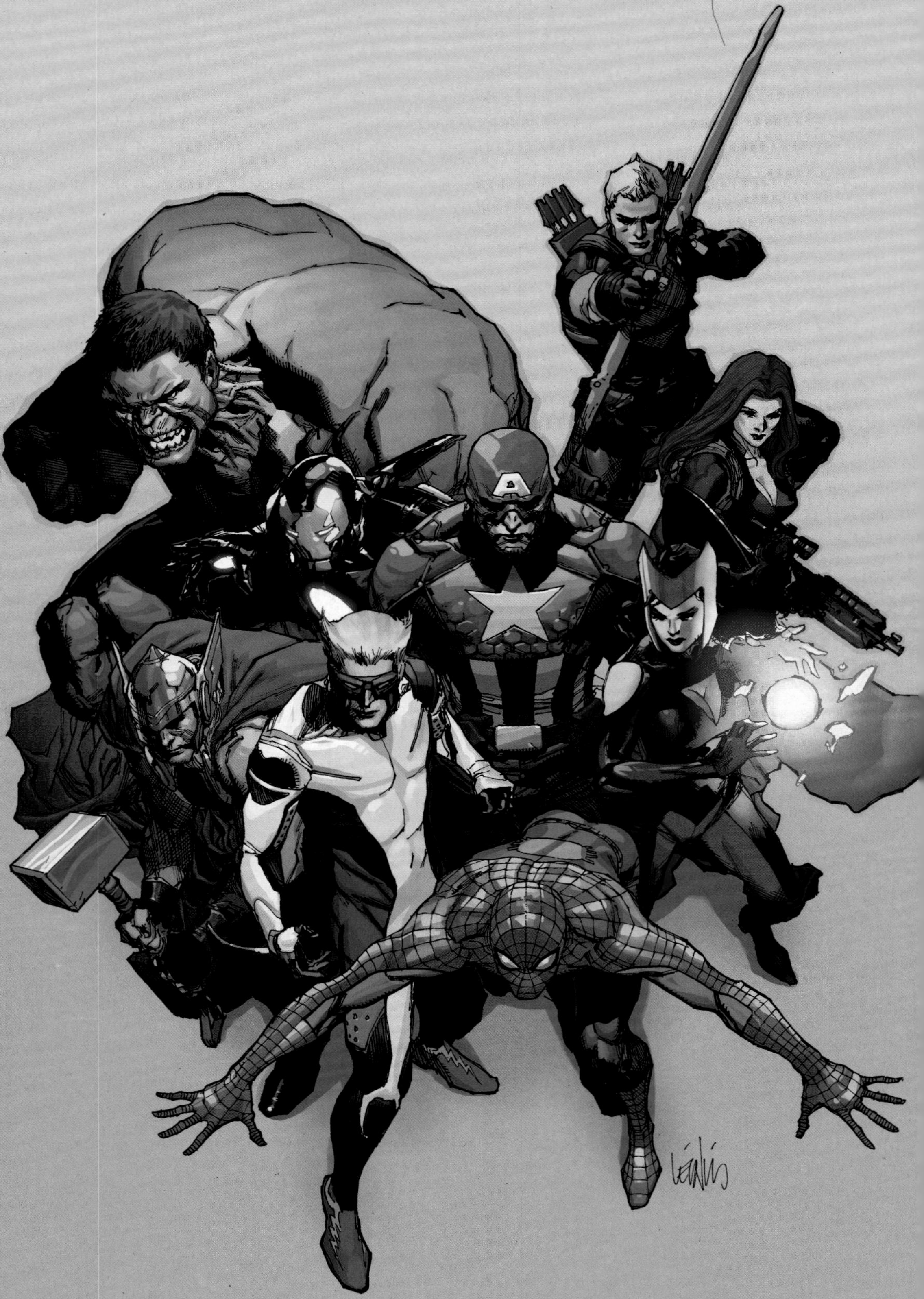

CHAPTER 1

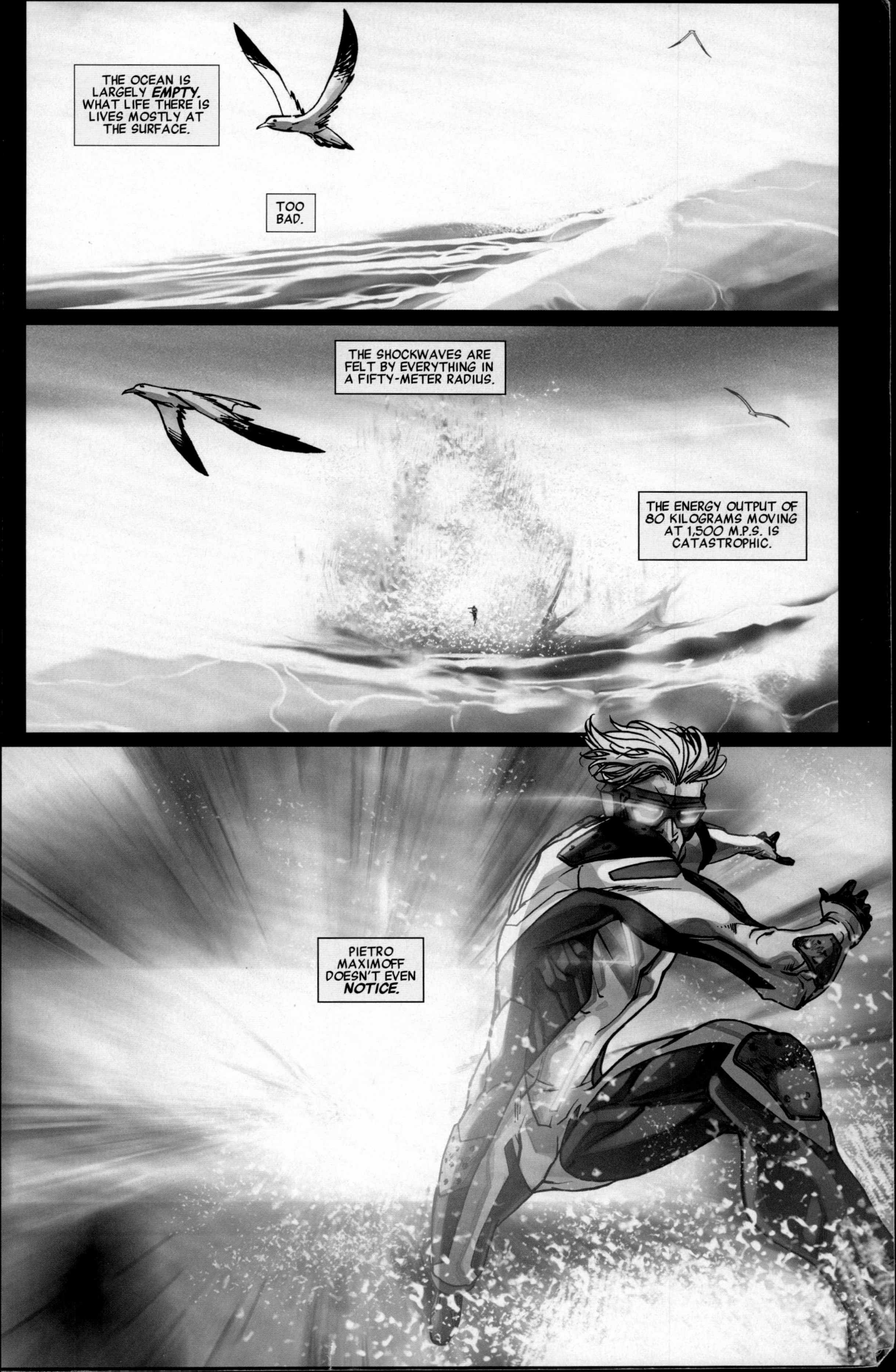
THE OCEAN IS LARGELY EMPTY. WHAT LIFE THERE IS LIVES MOSTLY AT THE SURFACE.
TOO BAD.
THE SHOCKWAVES ARE FELT BY EVERYTHING IN A FIFTY-METER RADIUS.
THE ENERGY OUTPUT OF 80 KILOGRAMS MOVING AT 1,500 M.P.S. IS CATASTROPHIC.
PIETRO MAXIMOFF DOESN'T EVEN NOTICE.

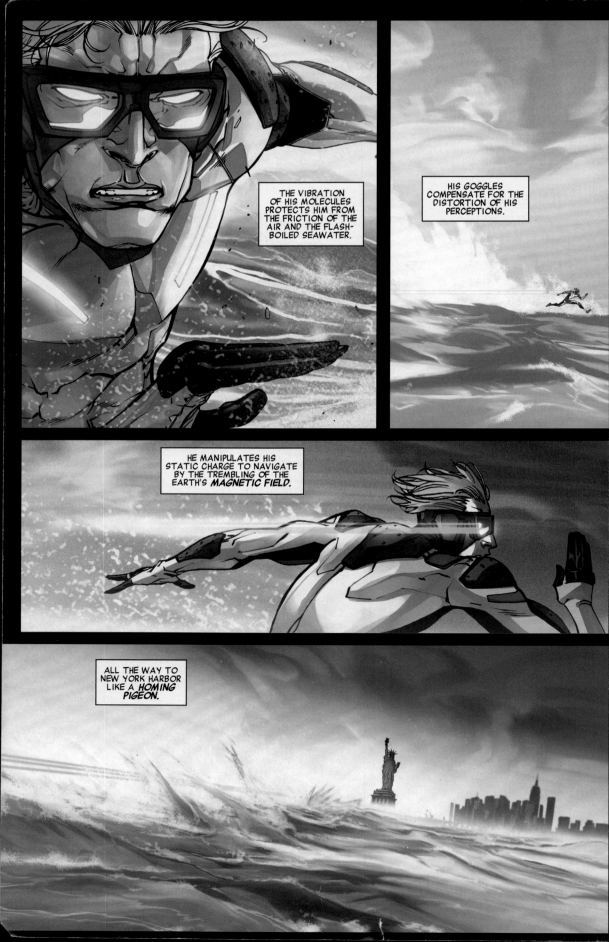

THE VIBRATION OF HIS MOLECULES PROTECTS HIM FROM THE FRICTION OF THE AIR AND THE FLASH-BOILED SEAWATER.

HIS GOGGLES COMPENSATE FOR THE DISTORTION OF HIS PERCEPTIONS.

HE MANIPULATES HIS STATIC CHARGE TO NAVIGATE BY THE TREMBLING OF THE EARTH'S *MAGNETIC FIELD.*

ALL THE WAY TO NEW YORK HARBOR LIKE A *HOMING PIGEON.*

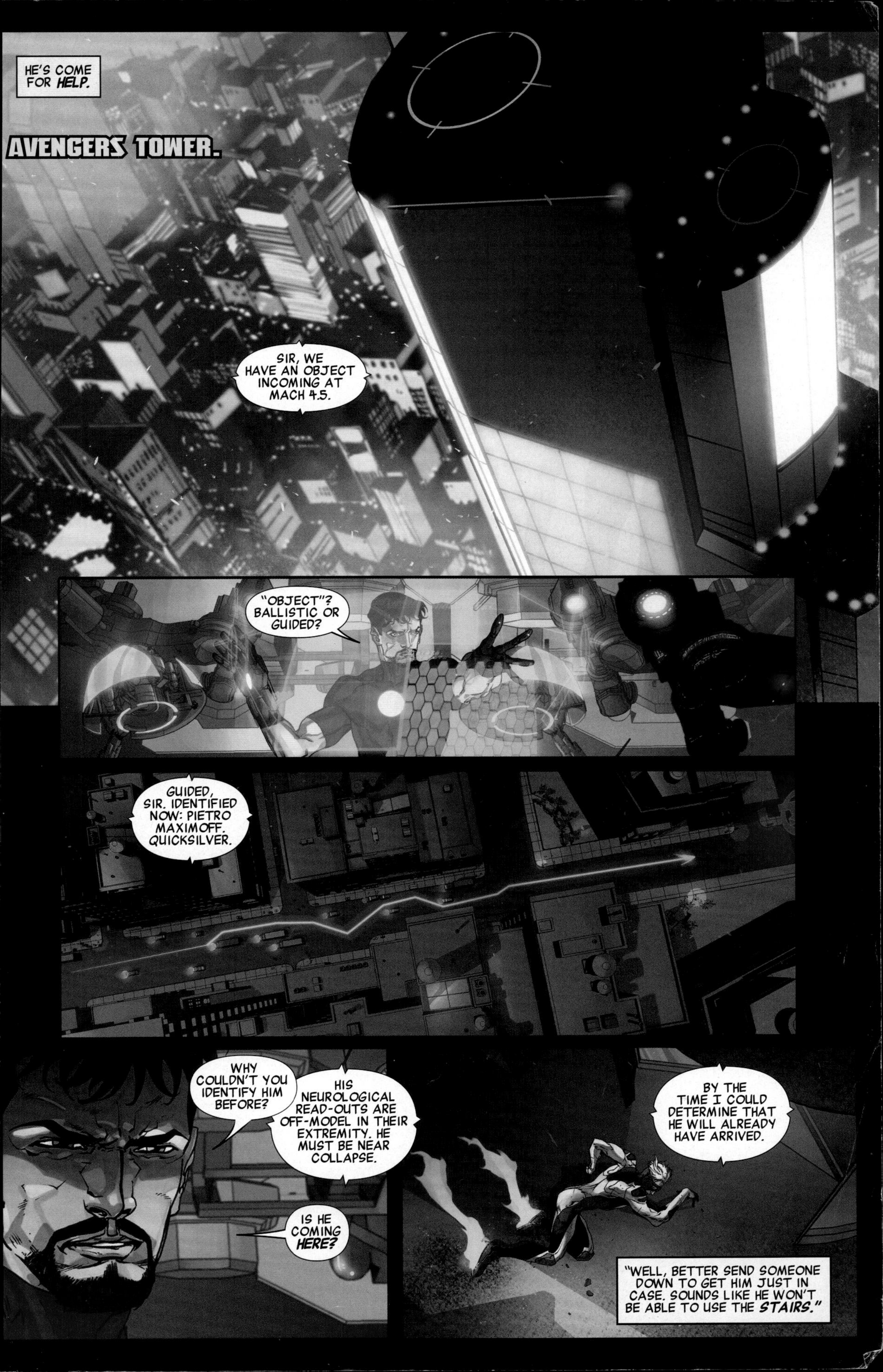
HE'S COME FOR HELP.
AVENGERS TOWER.
SIR, WE HAVE AN OBJECT INCOMING AT MACH 4.5.
"OBJECT"? BALLISTIC OR GUIDED?
GUIDED, SIR. IDENTIFIED NOW: PIETRO MAXIMOFF. QUICKSILVER.
WHY COULDN'T YOU IDENTIFY HIM BEFORE?
HIS NEUROLOGICAL READ-OUTS ARE OFF-MODEL IN THEIR EXTREMITY. HE MUST BE NEAR COLLAPSE.
IS HE COMING HERE?
BY THE TIME I COULD DETERMINE THAT HE WILL ALREADY HAVE ARRIVED.
"WELL, BETTER SEND SOMEONE DOWN TO GET HIM JUST IN CASE. SOUNDS LIKE HE WON'T BE ABLE TO USE THE STAIRS."

AVENGERS MILLENNIUM

CHAPTER ONE

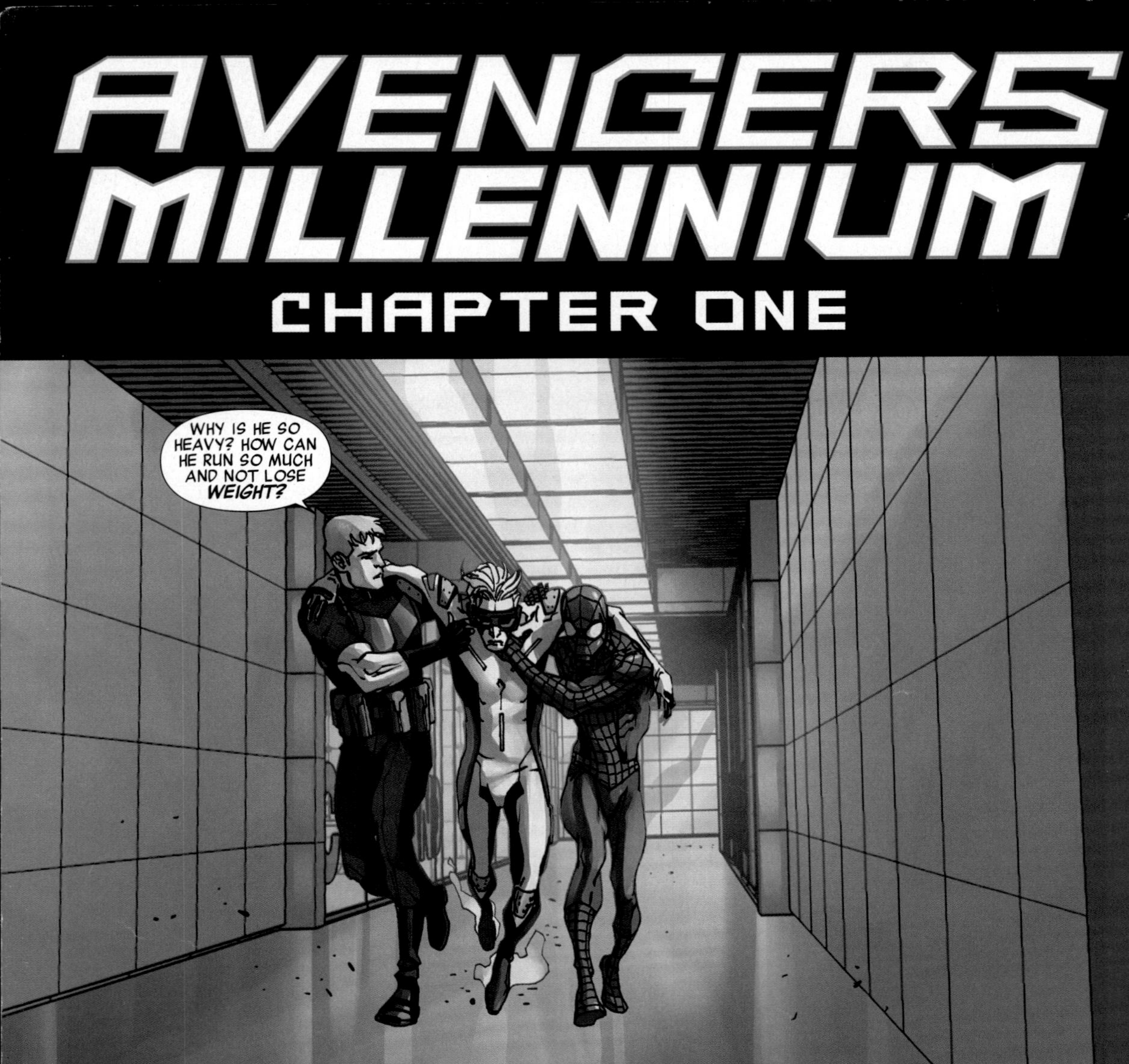
WHY IS HE SO HEAVY? HOW CAN HE RUN SO MUCH AND NOT LOSE *WEIGHT?*

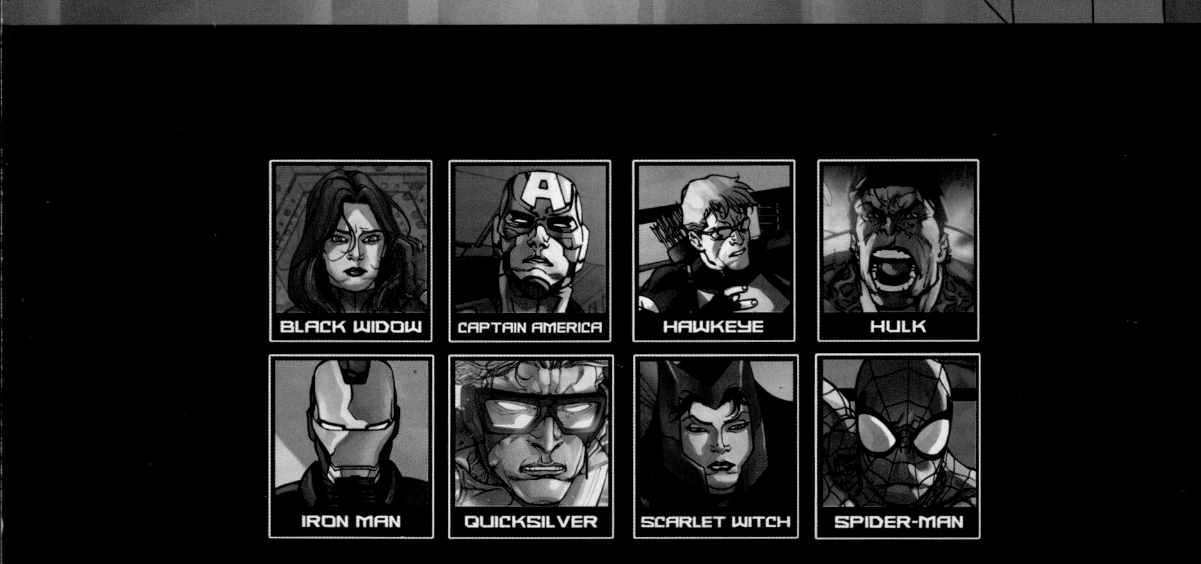
BLACK WIDOW
CAPTAIN AMERICA
HAWKEYE
HULK
IRON MAN
QUICKSILVER
SCARLET WITCH
SPIDER-MAN

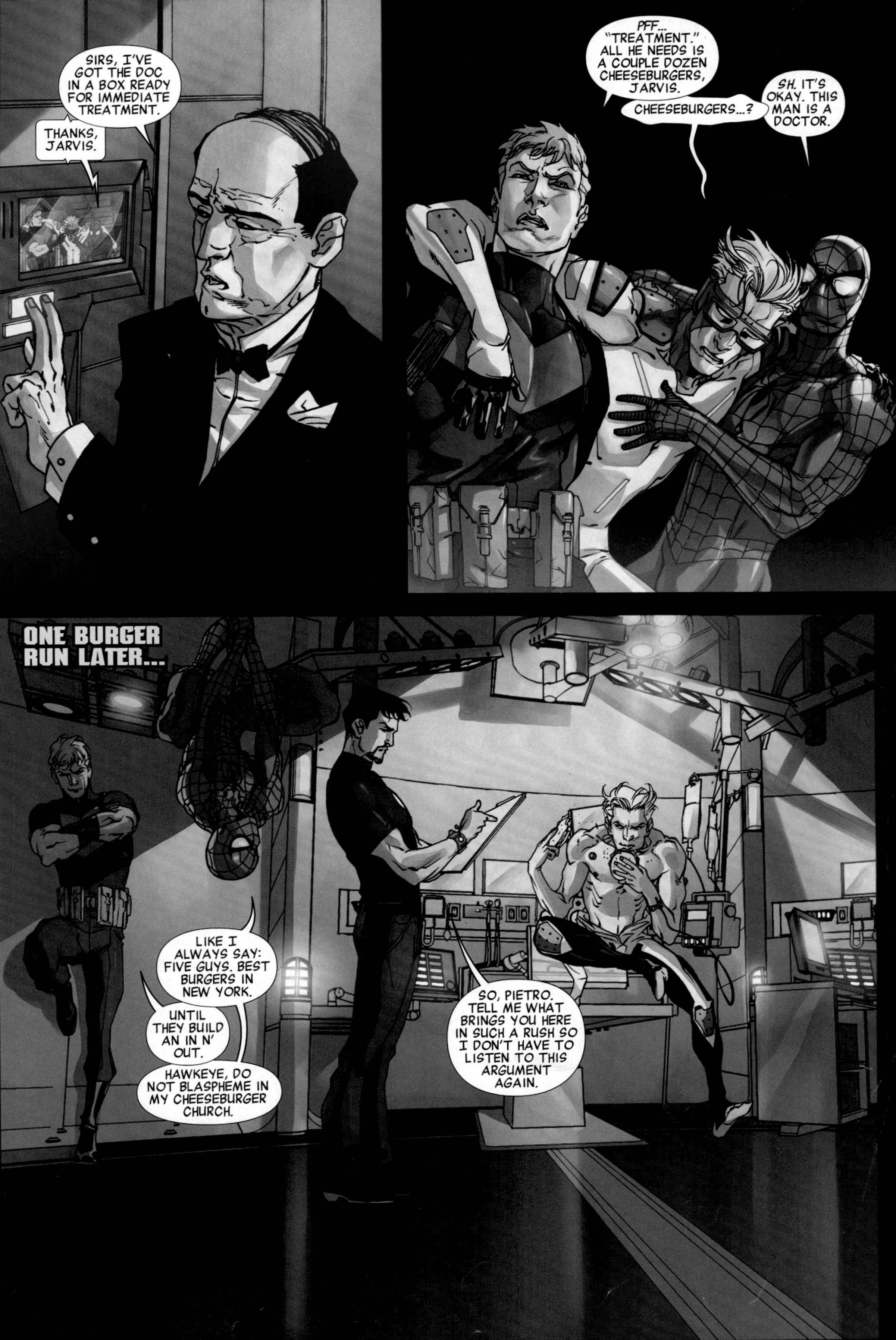
SIRS, I'VE GOT THE DOC IN A BOX READY FOR IMMEDIATE TREATMENT.
THANKS, JARVIS.
PFF... "TREATMENT." ALL HE NEEDS IS A COUPLE DOZEN CHEESEBURGERS, JARVIS.
CHEESEBURGERS...?
SH. IT'S OKAY. THIS MAN IS A DOCTOR.
ONE BURGER RUN LATER...
LIKE I ALWAYS SAY: FIVE GUYS. BEST BURGERS IN NEW YORK.
UNTIL THEY BUILD AN IN N' OUT.
HAWKEYE, DO NOT BLASPHEME IN MY CHEESEBURGER CHURCH.
SO, PIETRO. TELL ME WHAT BRINGS YOU HERE IN SUCH A RUSH SO I DON'T HAVE TO LISTEN TO THIS ARGUMENT AGAIN.

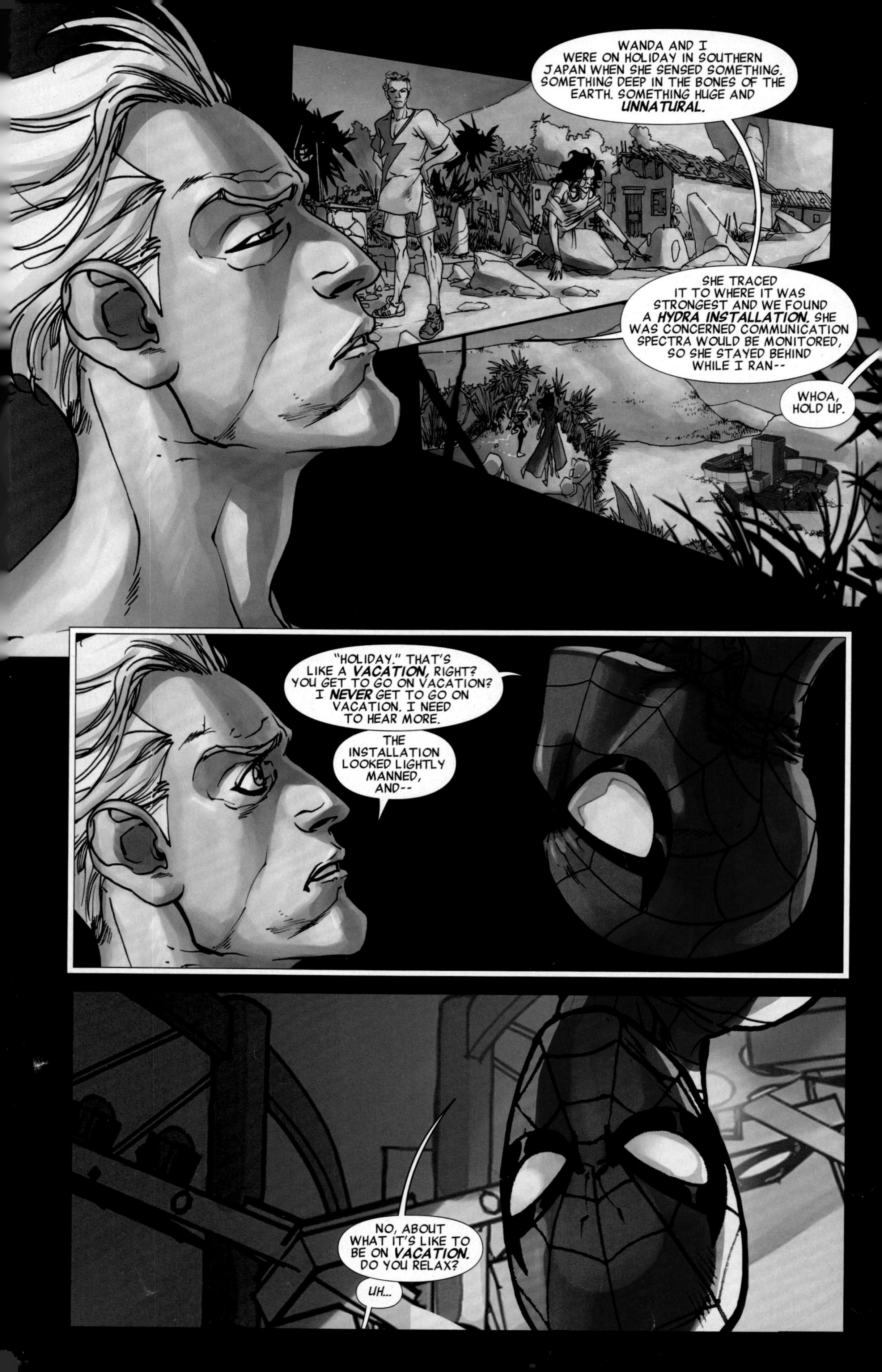
WANDA AND I WERE ON HOLIDAY IN SOUTHERN JAPAN WHEN SHE SENSED SOMETHING. SOMETHING DEEP IN THE BONES OF THE EARTH. SOMETHING HUGE AND UNNATURAL.
SHE TRACED IT TO WHERE IT WAS STRONGEST AND WE FOUND A HYDRA INSTALLATION. SHE WAS CONCERNED COMMUNICATION SPECTRA WOULD BE MONITORED, SO SHE STAYED BEHIND WHILE I RAN--
WHOA, HOLD UP.
"HOLIDAY." THAT'S LIKE A VACATION, RIGHT? YOU GET TO GO ON VACATION? I NEVER GET TO GO ON VACATION. I NEED TO HEAR MORE.
THE INSTALLATION LOOKED LIGHTLY MANNED, AND--
NO, ABOUT WHAT IT'S LIKE TO BE ON VACATION. DO YOU RELAX?
UH...

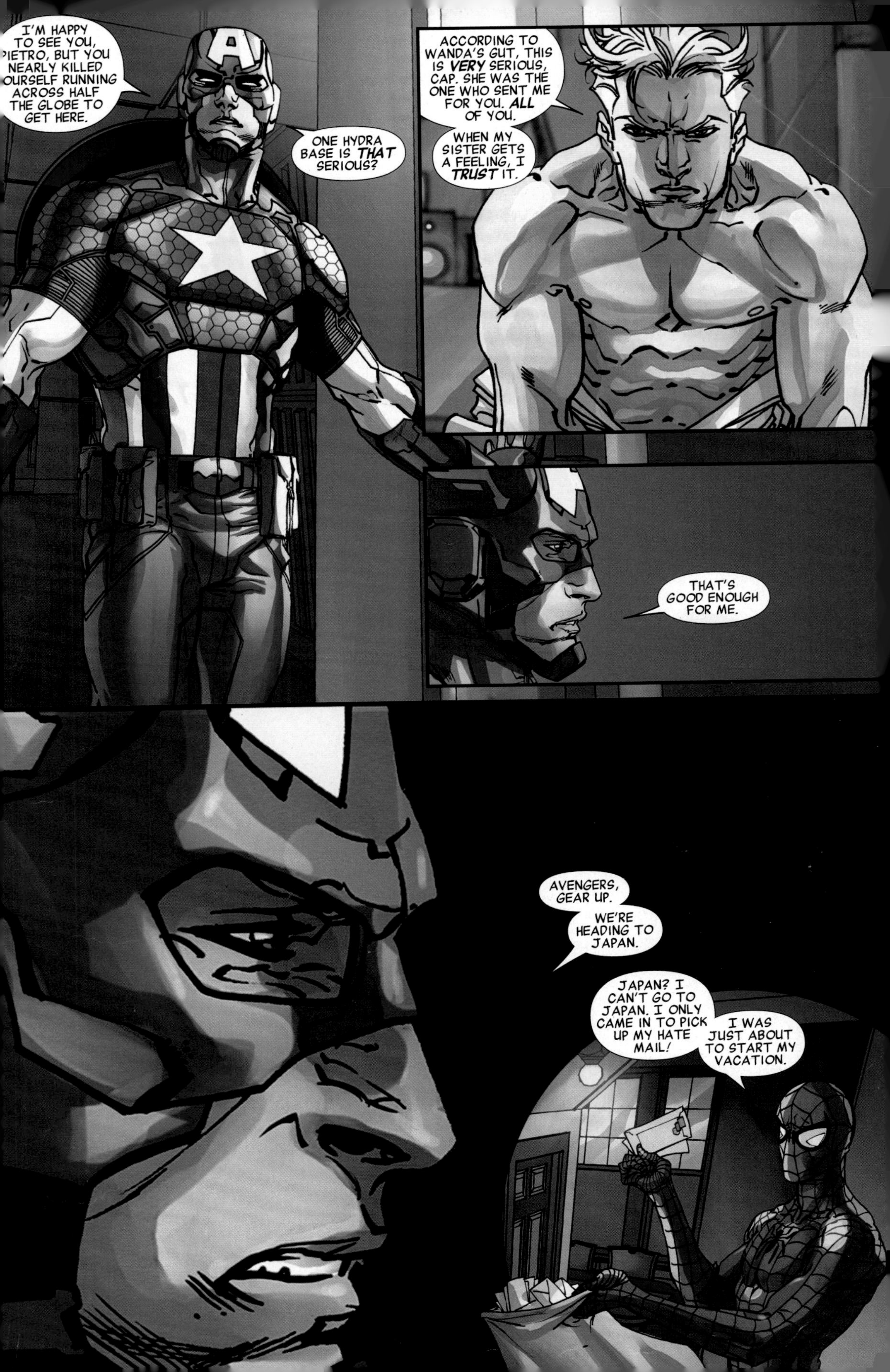
I'M HAPPY TO SEE YOU, PIETRO, BUT YOU NEARLY KILLED YOURSELF RUNNING ACROSS HALF THE GLOBE TO GET HERE.
ONE HYDRA BASE IS THAT SERIOUS?
ACCORDING TO WANDA'S GUT, THIS IS VERY SERIOUS, CAP. SHE WAS THE ONE WHO SENT ME FOR YOU. ALL OF YOU.
WHEN MY SISTER GETS A FEELING, I TRUST IT.
THAT'S GOOD ENOUGH FOR ME.
AVENGERS, GEAR UP.
WE'RE HEADING TO JAPAN.
JAPAN? I CAN'T GO TO JAPAN. I ONLY CAME IN TO PICK UP MY HATE MAIL!
I WAS JUST ABOUT TO START MY VACATION.

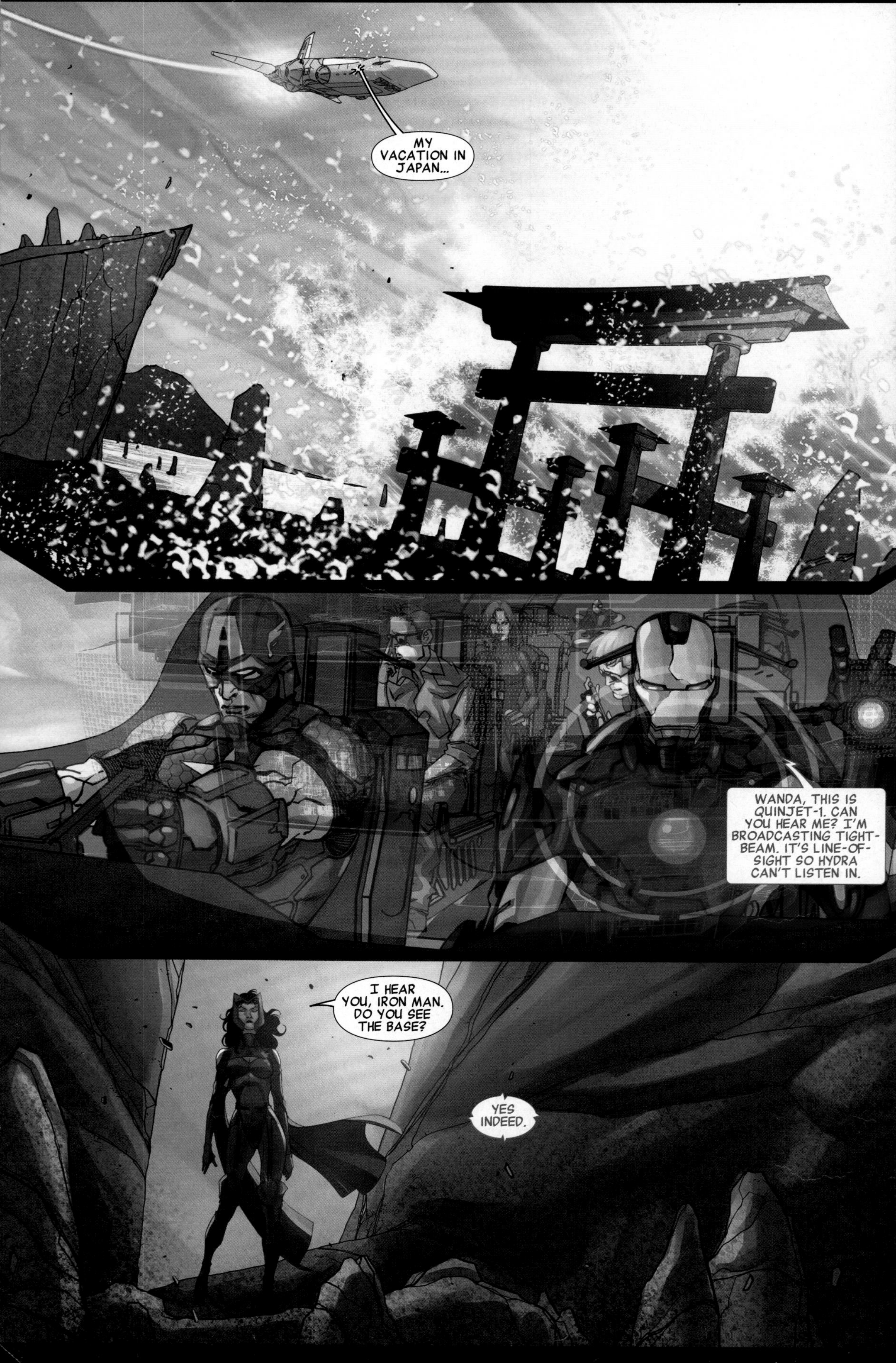

MY VACATION IN JAPAN...
WANDA, THIS IS QUINJET-1. CAN YOU HEAR ME? I'M BROADCASTING TIGHT-BEAM. IT'S LINE-OF-SIGHT SO HYDRA CAN'T LISTEN IN.
I HEAR YOU, IRON MAN. DO YOU SEE THE BASE?
YES INDEED.

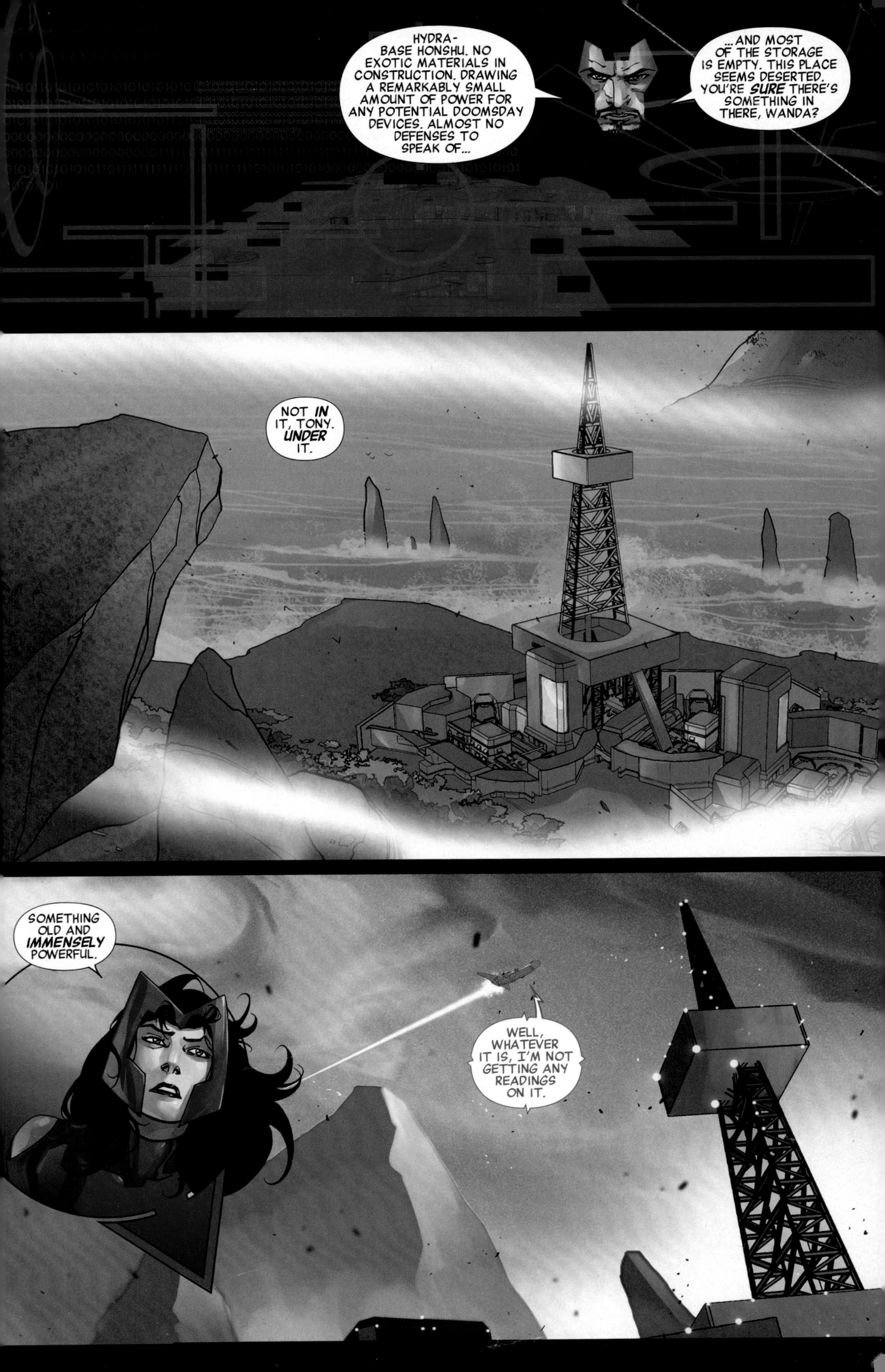
HYDRA-BASE HONSHU. NO EXOTIC MATERIALS IN CONSTRUCTION. DRAWING A REMARKABLY SMALL AMOUNT OF POWER FOR ANY POTENTIAL DOOMSDAY DEVICES. ALMOST NO DEFENSES TO SPEAK OF...
...AND MOST OF THE STORAGE IS EMPTY. THIS PLACE SEEMS DESERTED. YOU'RE SURE THERE'S SOMETHING IN THERE, WANDA?
NOT IN IT, TONY. UNDER IT.
SOMETHING OLD AND IMMENSELY POWERFUL.
WELL, WHATEVER IT IS, I'M NOT GETTING ANY READINGS ON IT.

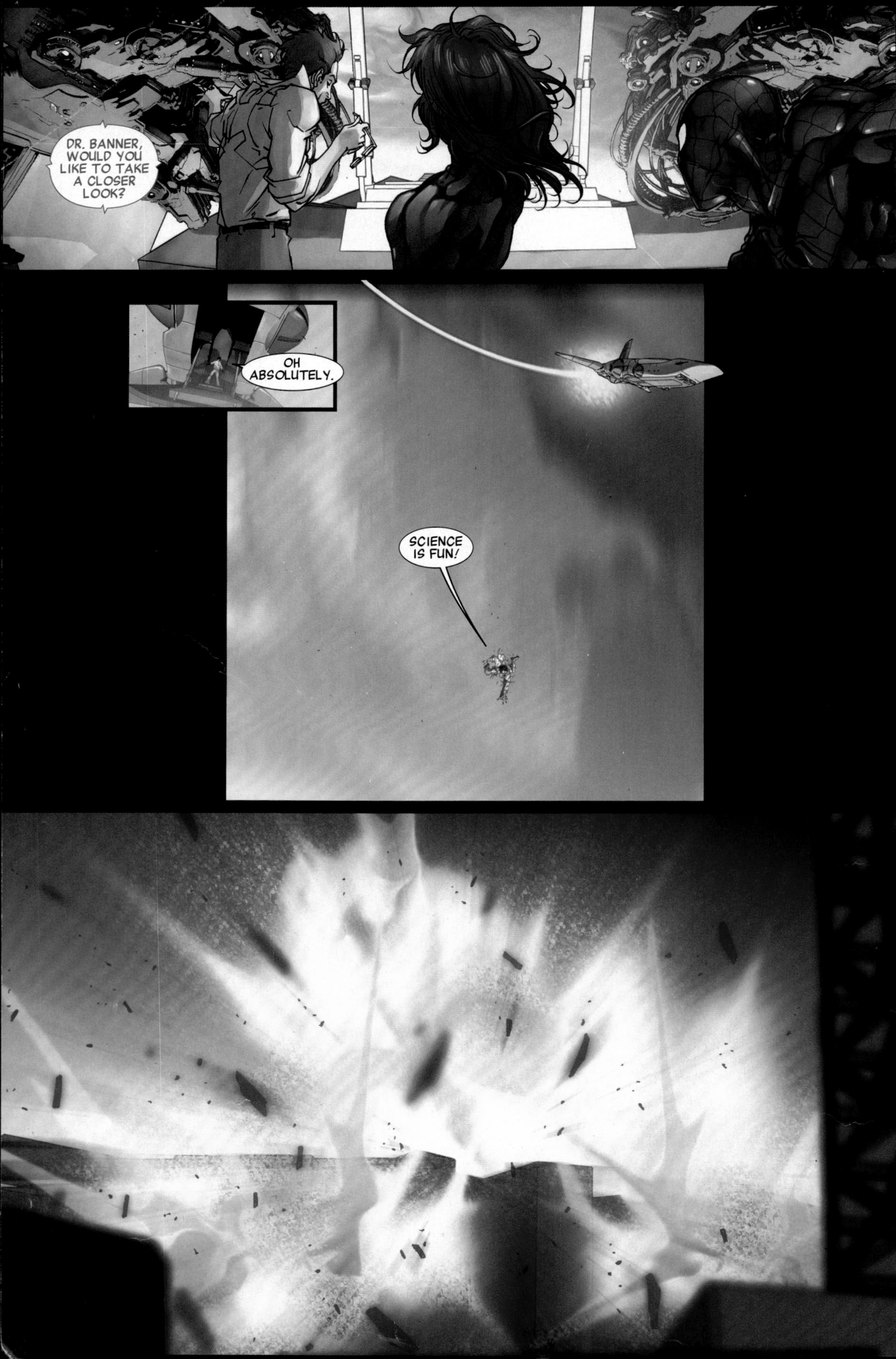
DR. BANNER, WOULD YOU LIKE TO TAKE A CLOSER LOOK?
OH ABSOLUTELY.
SCIENCE IS FUN!

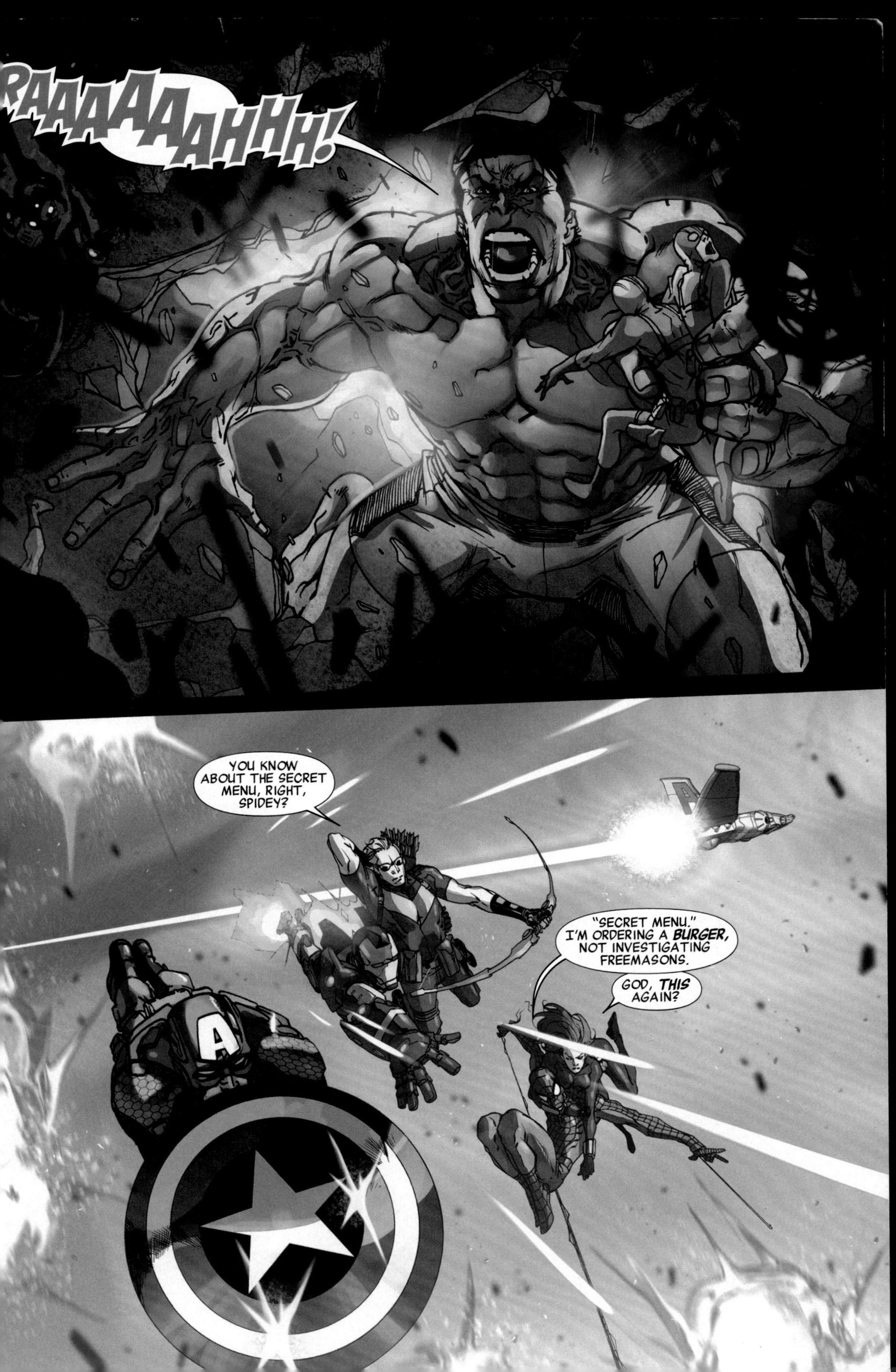
RAAAAAAHHHH!
YOU KNOW ABOUT THE SECRET MENU, RIGHT, SPIDEY?
"SECRET MENU." I'M ORDERING A BURGER, NOT INVESTIGATING FREEMASONS.
GOD, THIS AGAIN?

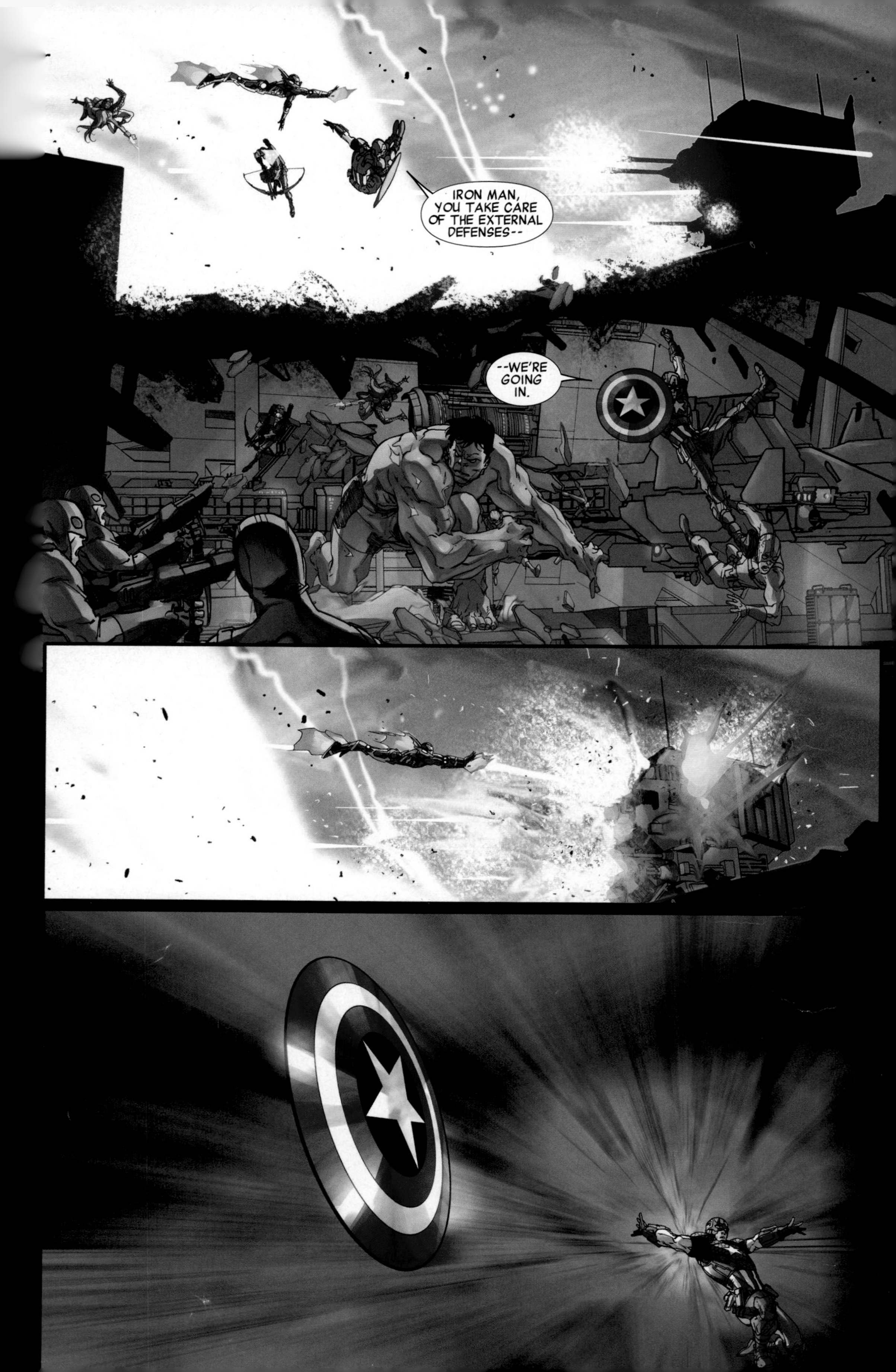
IRON MAN, YOU TAKE CARE OF THE EXTERNAL DEFENSES--
--WE'RE GOING IN.

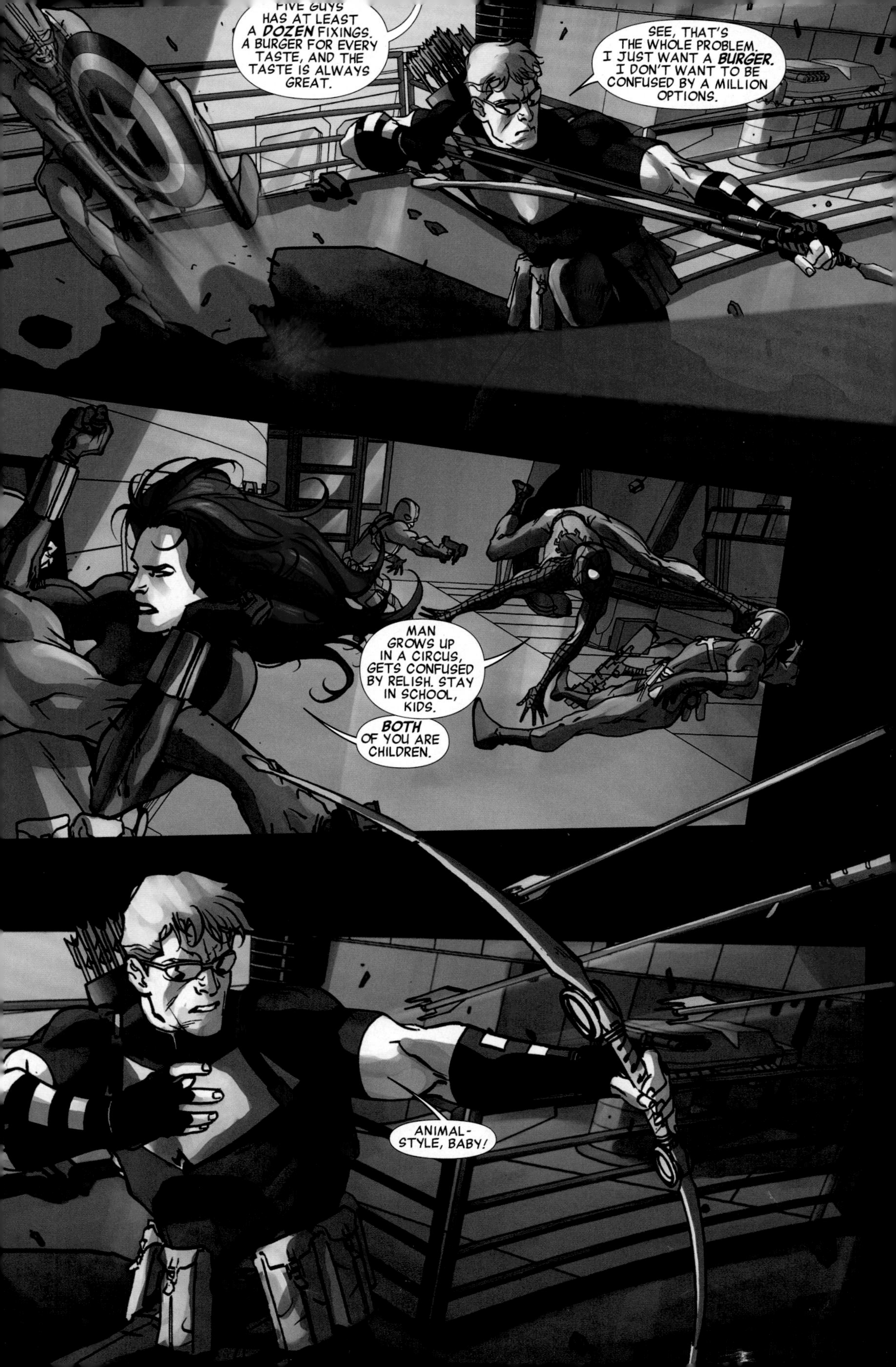
FIVE GUYS HAS AT LEAST A DOZEN FIXINGS. A BURGER FOR EVERY TASTE, AND THE TASTE IS ALWAYS GREAT.
SEE, THAT'S THE WHOLE PROBLEM. I JUST WANT A BURGER. I DON'T WANT TO BE CONFUSED BY A MILLION OPTIONS.
MAN GROWS UP IN A CIRCUS, GETS CONFUSED BY RELISH. STAY IN SCHOOL, KIDS.
BOTH OF YOU ARE CHILDREN.
ANIMAL-STYLE, BABY!

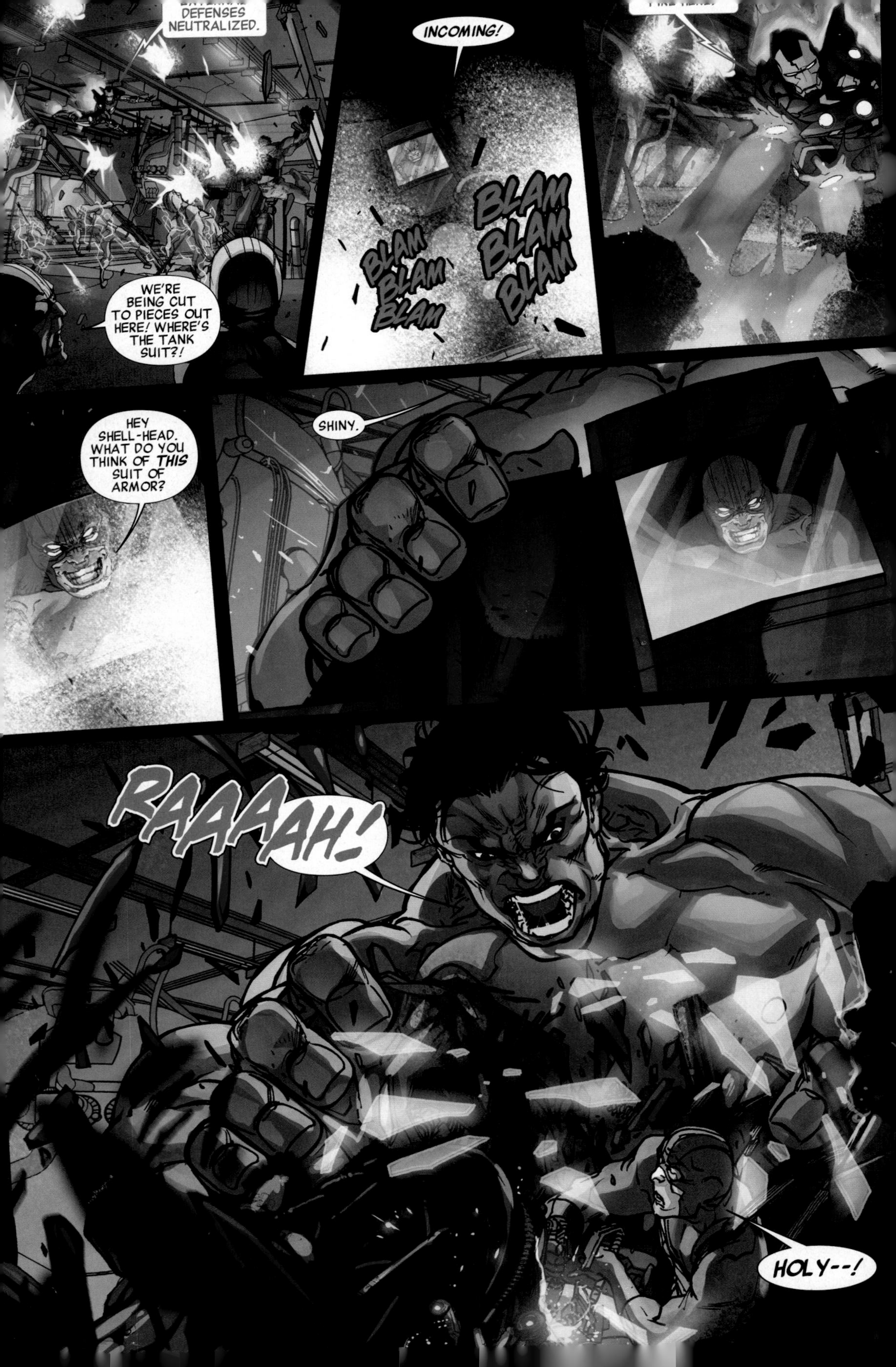
DEFENSES NEUTRALIZED.
WE'RE BEING CUT TO PIECES OUT HERE! WHERE'S THE TANK SUIT?!
INCOMING!
BLAM BLAM BLAM
BLAM BLAM BLAM
HEY SHELL-HEAD. WHAT DO YOU THINK OF THIS SUIT OF ARMOR?
SHINY.
RAAAAH!
HOLY--!

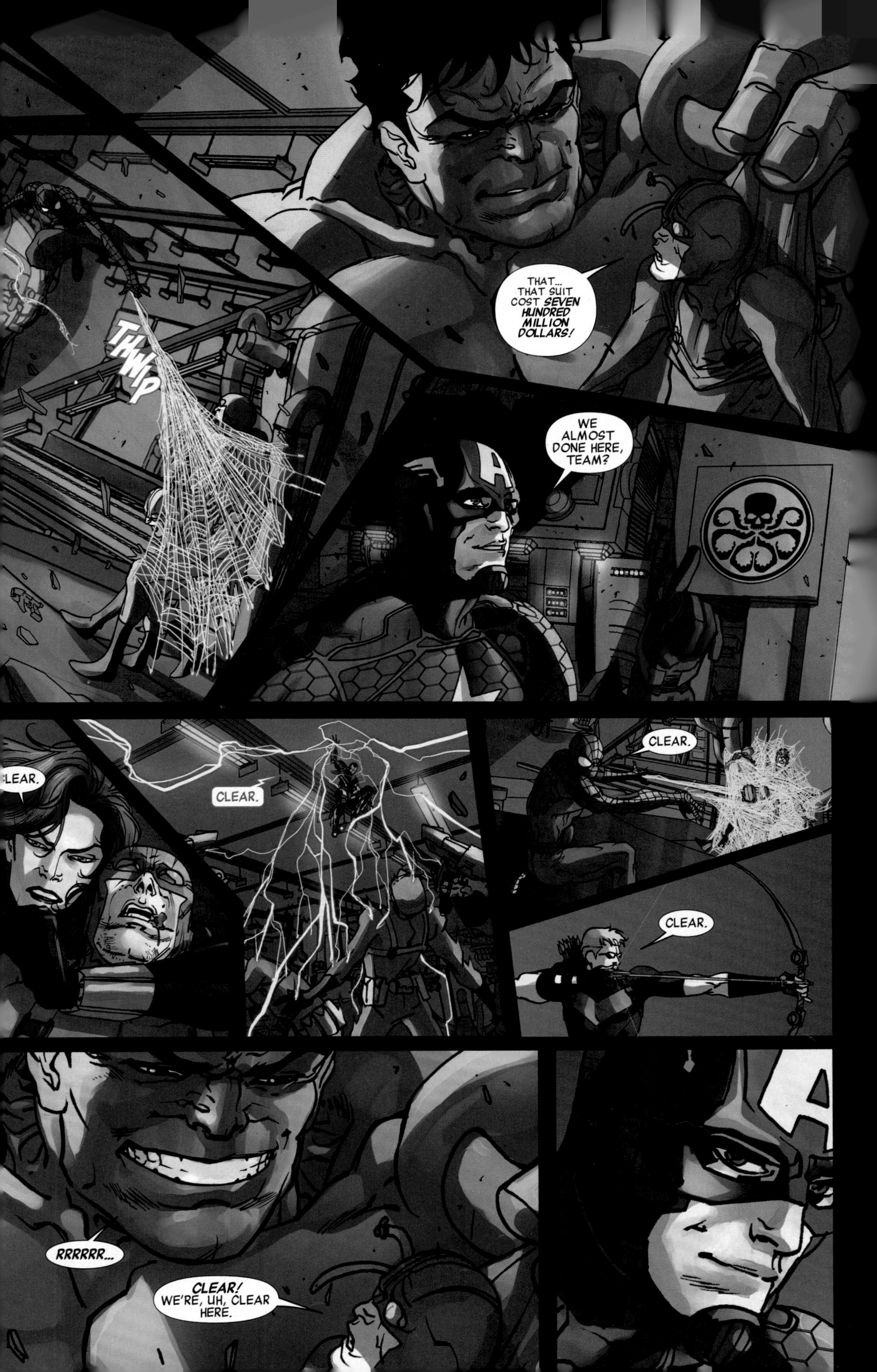
THWIP
THAT... THAT SUIT COST SEVEN HUNDRED MILLION DOLLARS!
WE ALMOST DONE HERE, TEAM?
CLEAR.
CLEAR.
CLEAR.
CLEAR.
RRRRRR...
CLEAR! WE'RE, UH, CLEAR HERE.

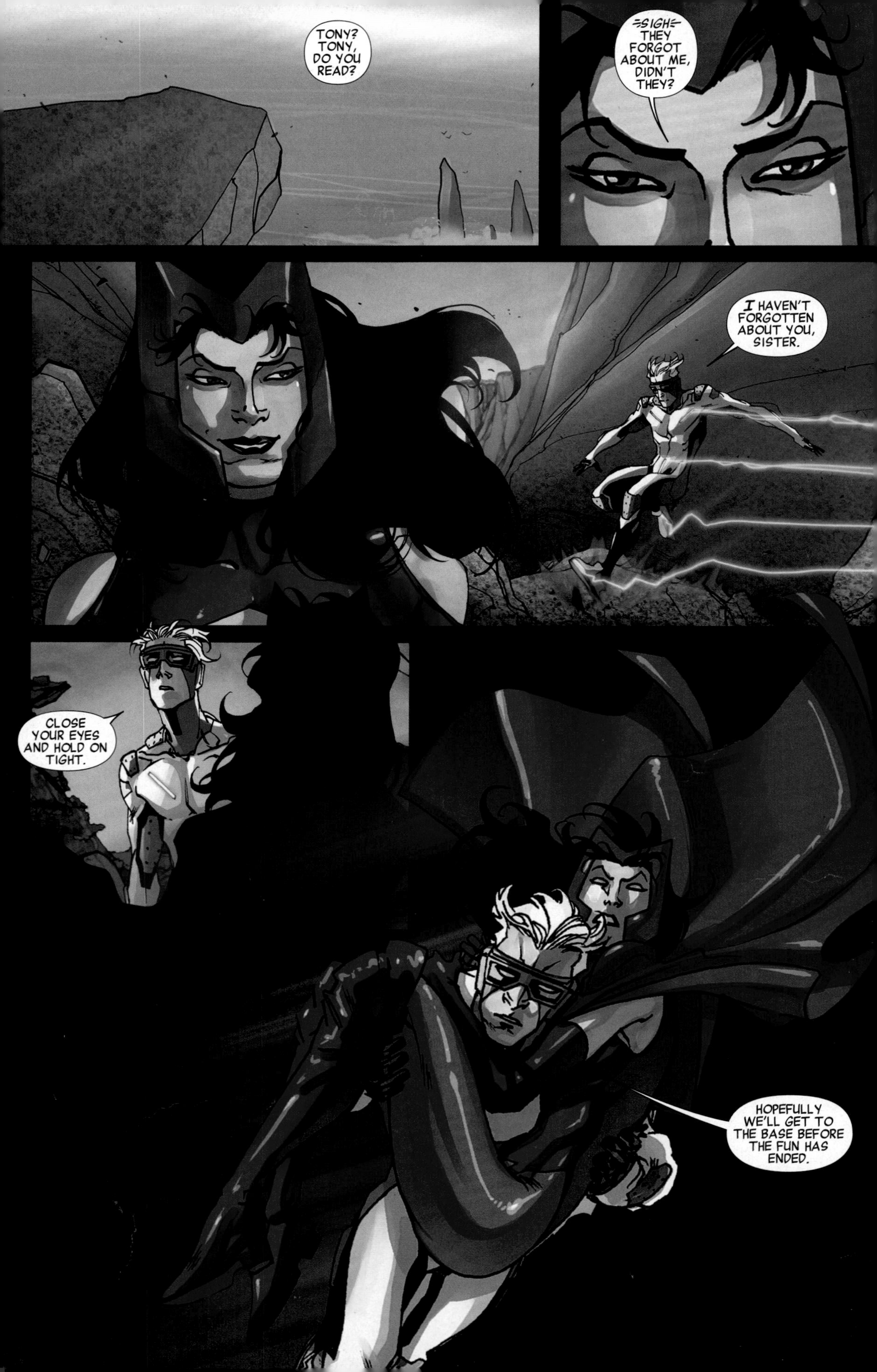
TONY? TONY, DO YOU READ?
=SIGH= THEY FORGOT ABOUT ME, DIDN'T THEY?
I HAVEN'T FORGOTTEN ABOUT YOU, SISTER.
CLOSE YOUR EYES AND HOLD ON TIGHT.
HOPEFULLY WE'LL GET TO THE BASE BEFORE THE FUN HAS ENDED.

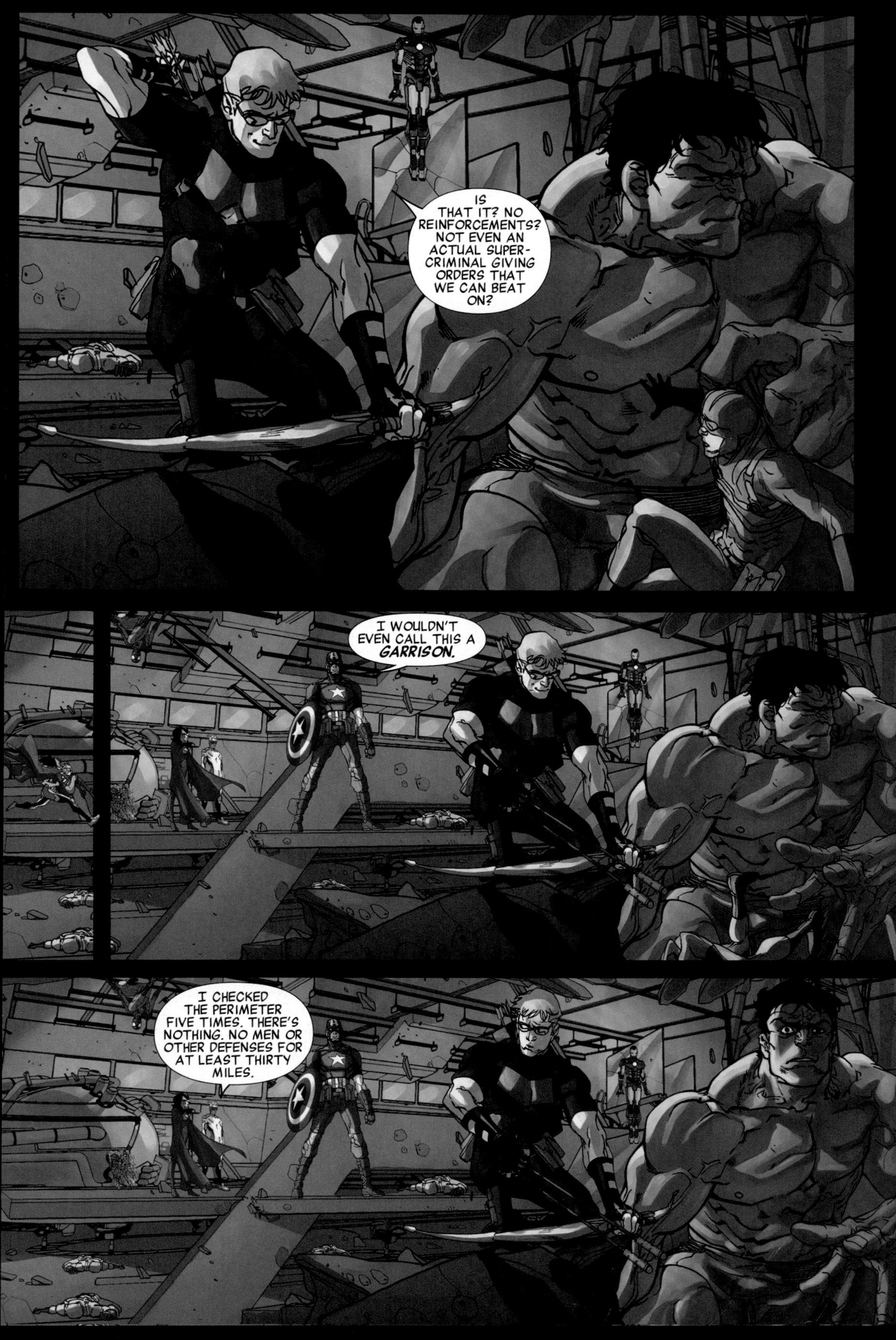
IS THAT IT? NO REINFORCEMENTS? NOT EVEN AN ACTUAL SUPER-CRIMINAL GIVING ORDERS THAT WE CAN BEAT ON?
I WOULDN'T EVEN CALL THIS A GARRISON.
I CHECKED THE PERIMETER FIVE TIMES. THERE'S NOTHING. NO MEN OR OTHER DEFENSES FOR AT LEAST THIRTY MILES.

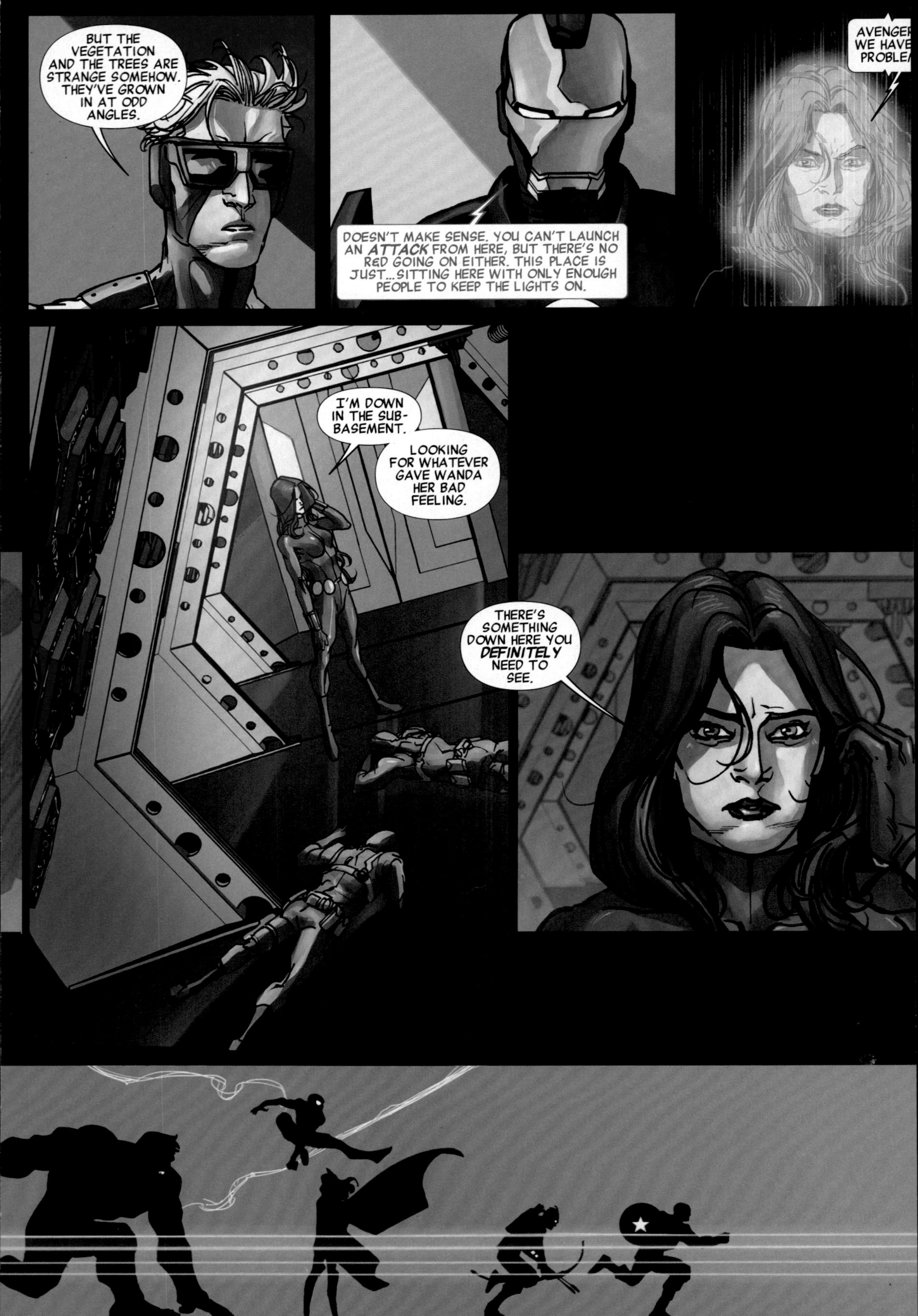
BUT THE VEGETATION AND THE TREES ARE STRANGE SOMEHOW. THEY'VE GROWN IN AT ODD ANGLES.
DOESN'T MAKE SENSE. YOU CAN'T LAUNCH AN ATTACK FROM HERE, BUT THERE'S NO R&D GOING ON EITHER. THIS PLACE IS JUST...SITTING HERE WITH ONLY ENOUGH PEOPLE TO KEEP THE LIGHTS ON.
AVENGER WE HAVE PROBLE
I'M DOWN IN THE SUB-BASEMENT.
LOOKING FOR WHATEVER GAVE WANDA HER BAD FEELING.
THERE'S SOMETHING DOWN HERE YOU DEFINITELY NEED TO SEE.

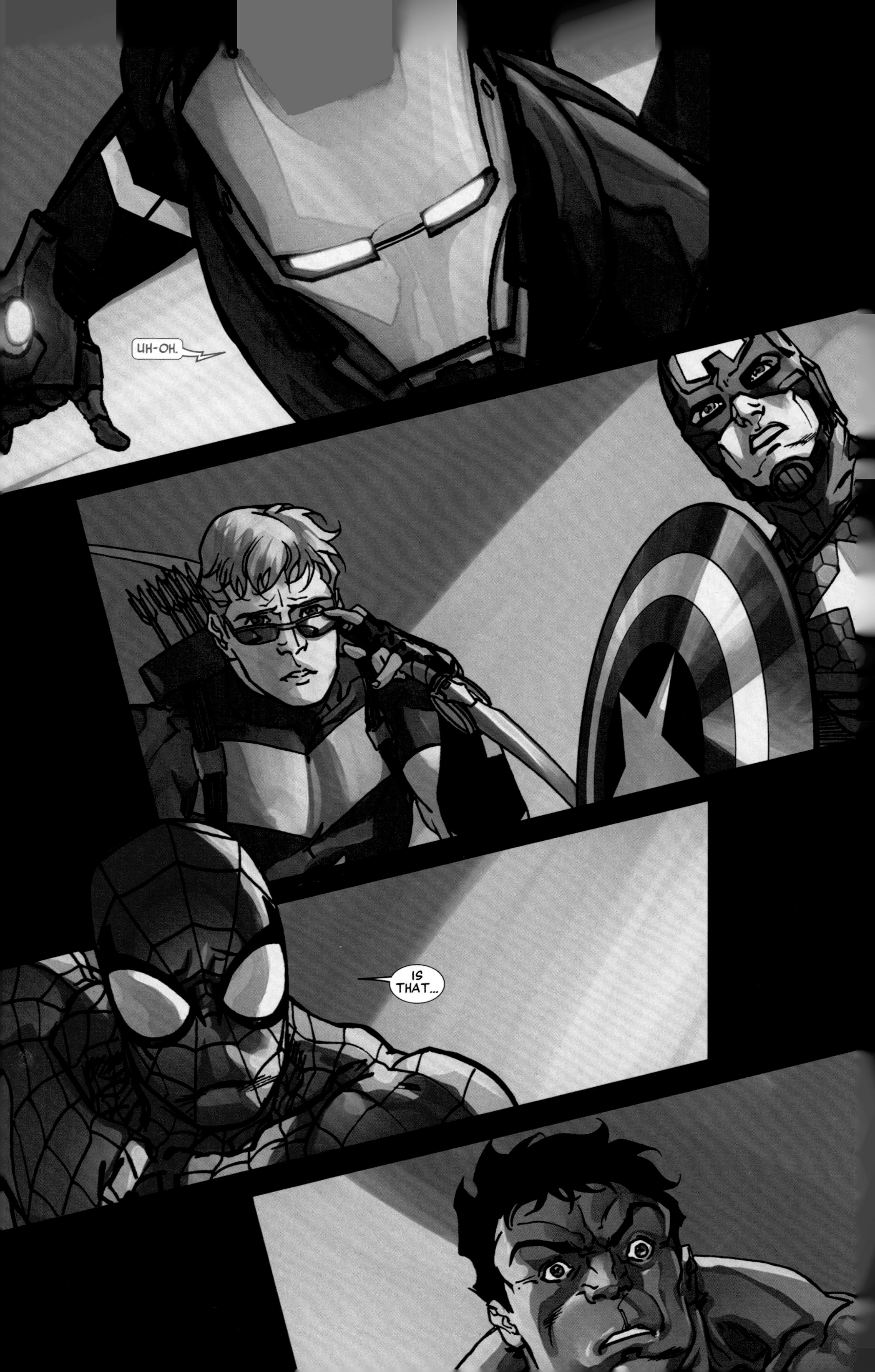
UH-OH.
IS THAT...

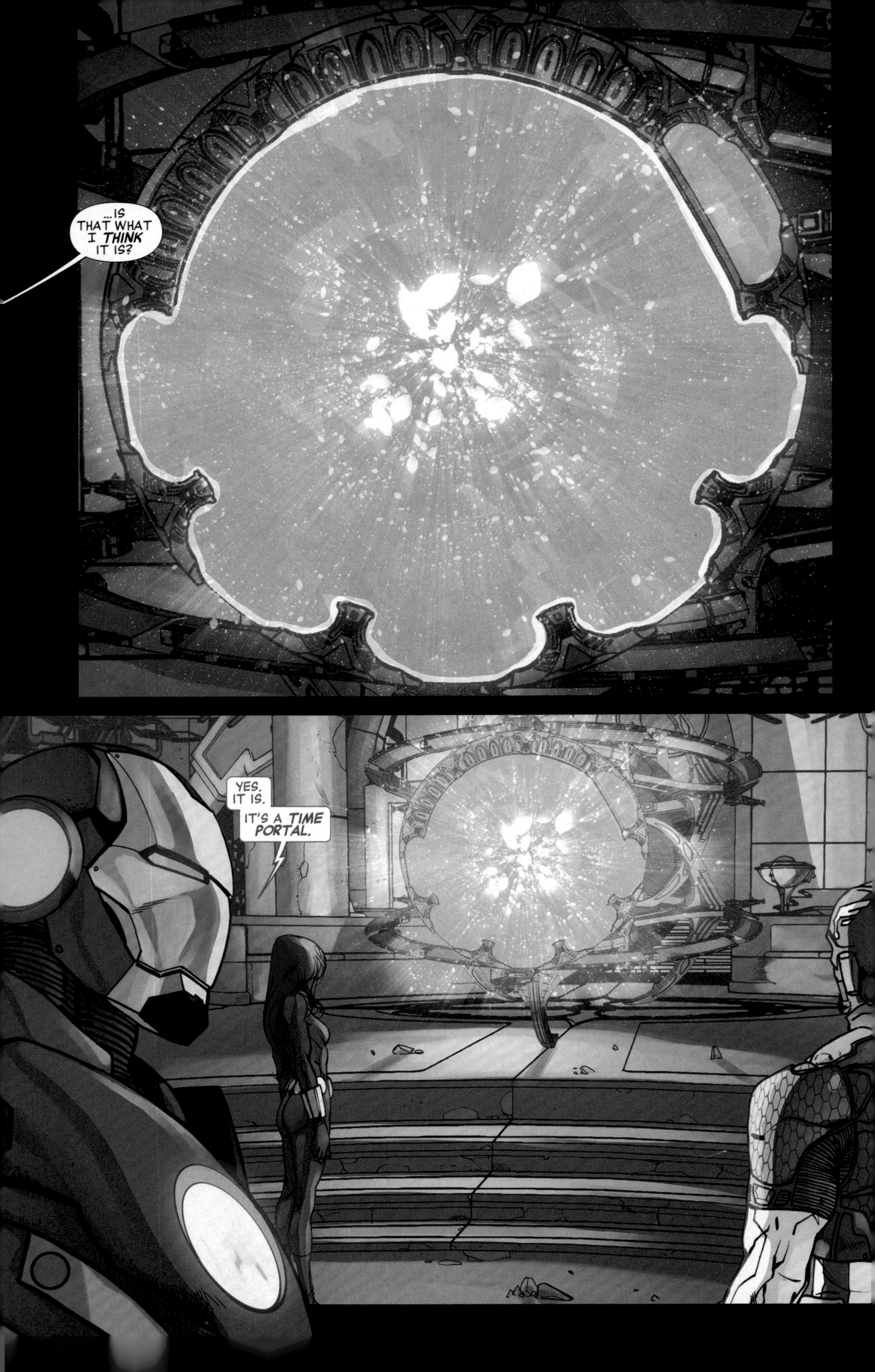
...IS THAT WHAT I *THINK* IT IS?
YES. IT IS.
IT'S A *TIME PORTAL.*

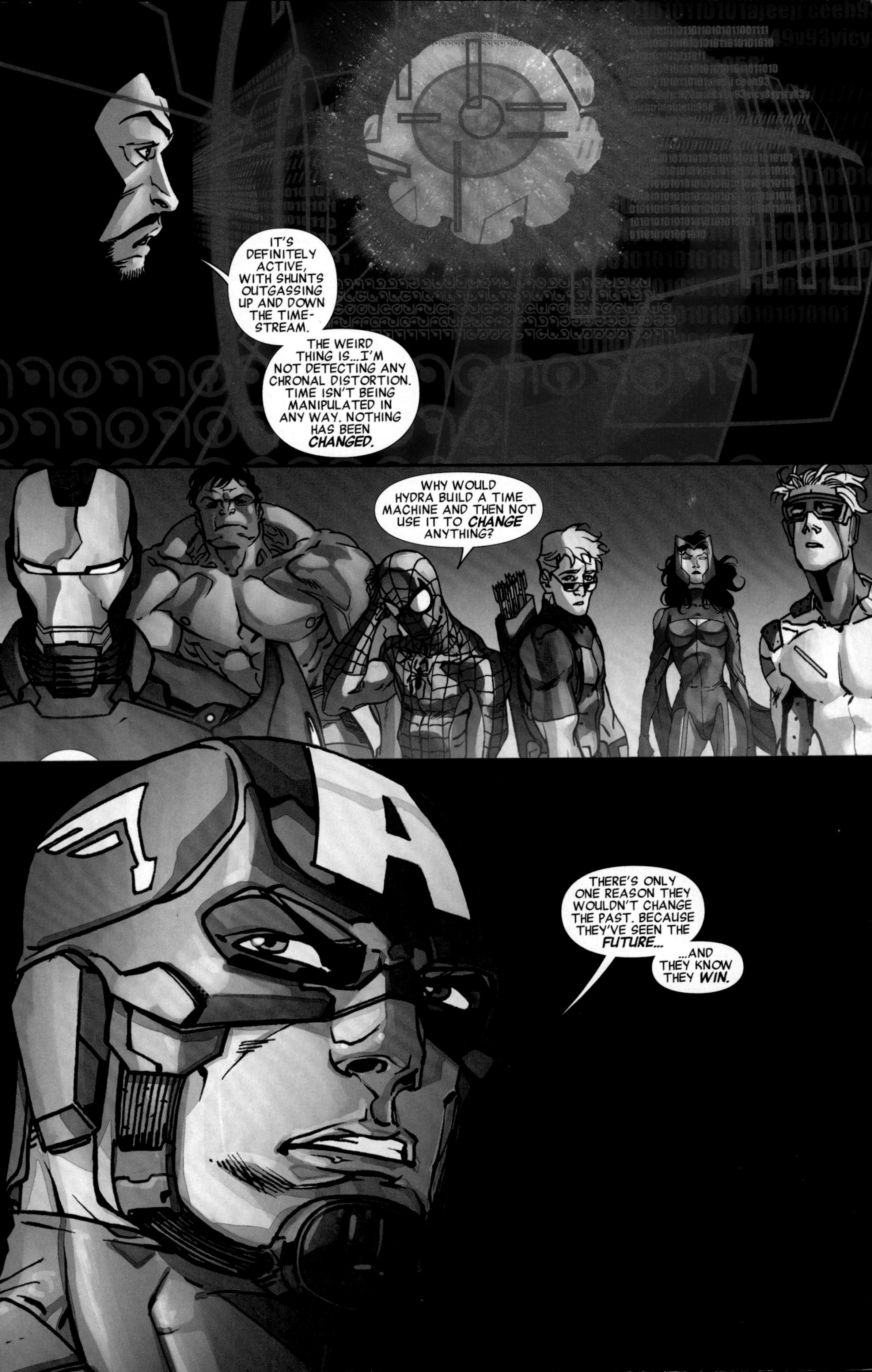
IT'S DEFINITELY ACTIVE, WITH SHUNTS OUTGASSING UP AND DOWN THE TIME-STREAM.
THE WEIRD THING IS...I'M NOT DETECTING ANY CHRONAL DISTORTION. TIME ISN'T BEING MANIPULATED IN ANY WAY. NOTHING HAS BEEN CHANGED.
WHY WOULD HYDRA BUILD A TIME MACHINE AND THEN NOT USE IT TO CHANGE ANYTHING?
THERE'S ONLY ONE REASON THEY WOULDN'T CHANGE THE PAST. BECAUSE THEY'VE SEEN THE FUTURE...
...AND THEY KNOW THEY WIN.

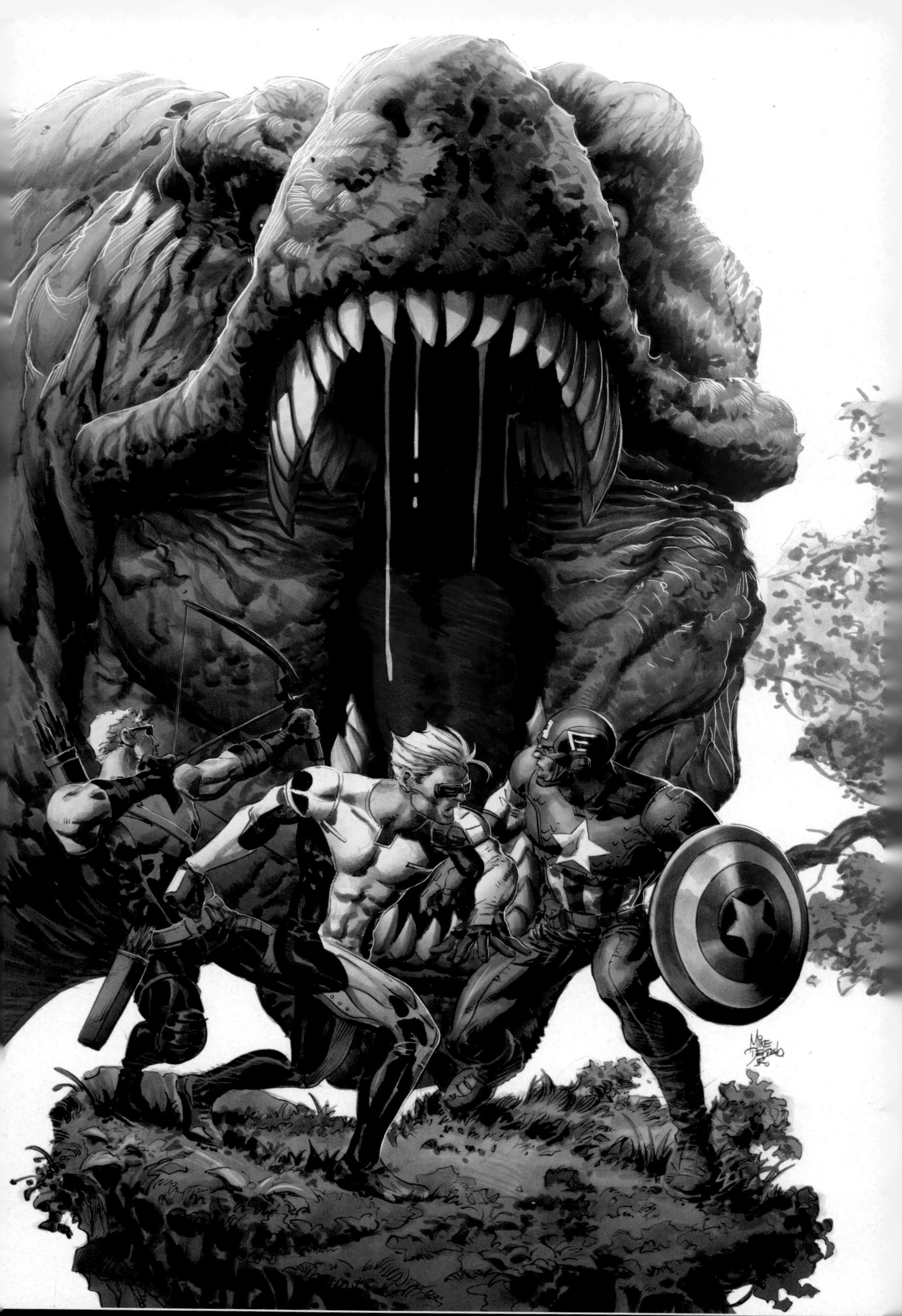

CHAPTER 2

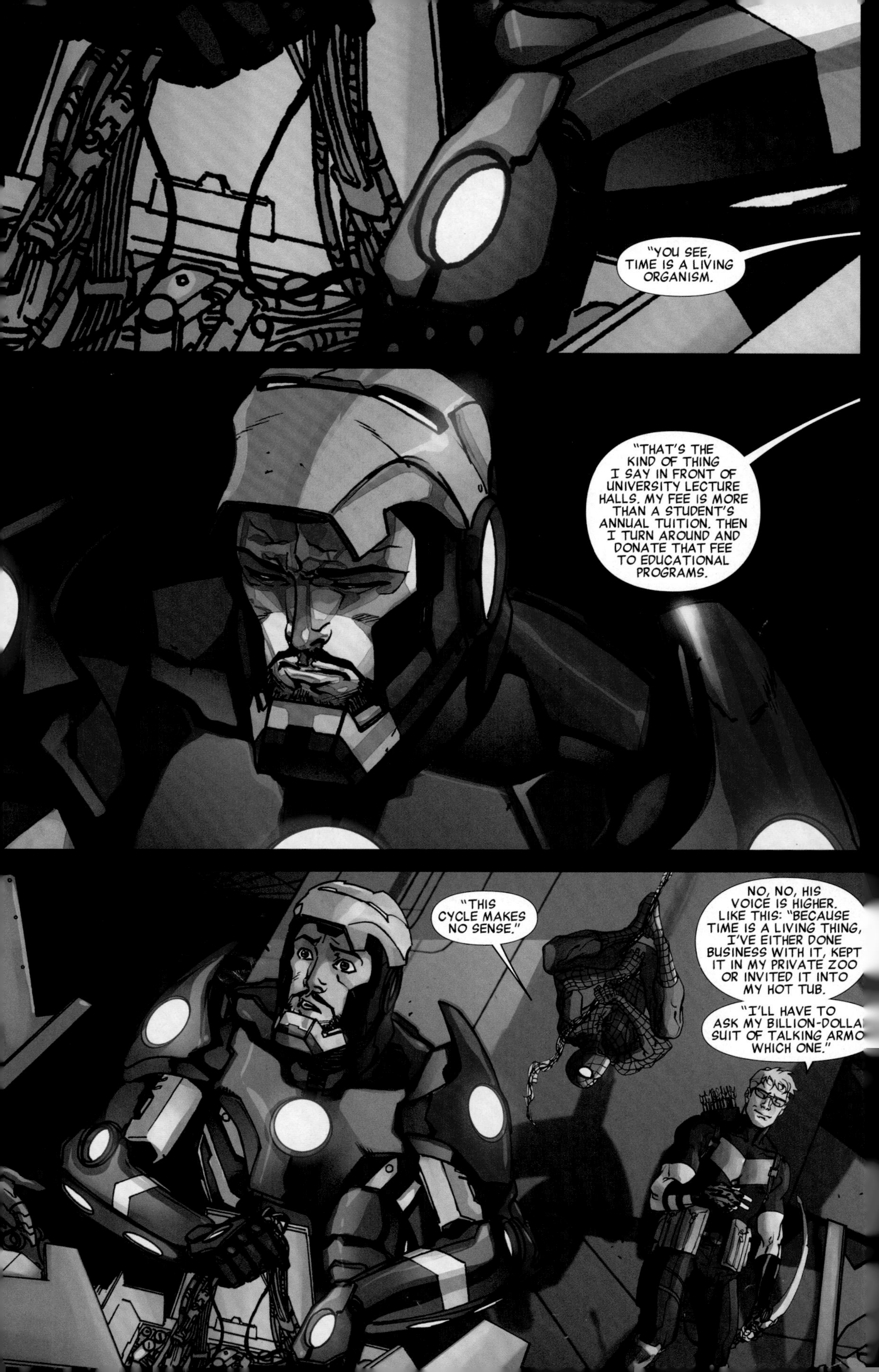
"YOU SEE, TIME IS A LIVING ORGANISM.
"THAT'S THE KIND OF THING I SAY IN FRONT OF UNIVERSITY LECTURE HALLS. MY FEE IS MORE THAN A STUDENT'S ANNUAL TUITION. THEN I TURN AROUND AND DONATE THAT FEE TO EDUCATIONAL PROGRAMS.
"THIS CYCLE MAKES NO SENSE."
NO, NO, HIS VOICE IS HIGHER. LIKE THIS: "BECAUSE TIME IS A LIVING THING, I'VE EITHER DONE BUSINESS WITH IT, KEPT IT IN MY PRIVATE ZOO OR INVITED IT INTO MY HOT TUB.
"I'LL HAVE TO ASK MY BILLION-DOLLA SUIT OF TALKING ARMO WHICH ONE."

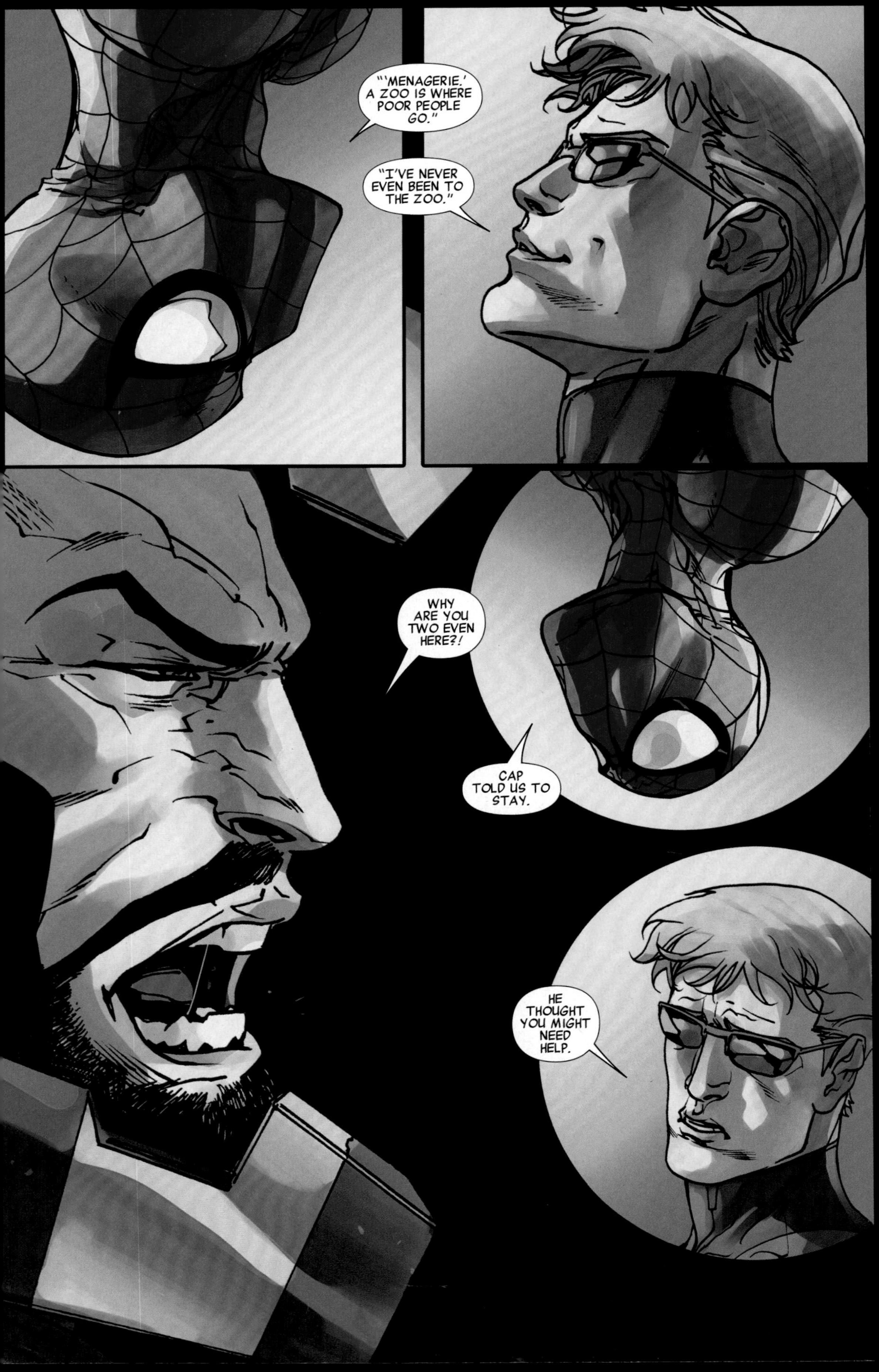
"'MENAGERIE.' A ZOO IS WHERE POOR PEOPLE GO."
"I'VE NEVER EVEN BEEN TO THE ZOO."
WHY ARE YOU TWO EVEN HERE?!
CAP TOLD US TO STAY.
HE THOUGHT YOU MIGHT NEED HELP.

AVENGERS MILLENNIUM
CHAPTER TWO

> WE'VE BEEN ALL OVER THIS INSTALLATION AND QUICKSILVER HAS SEARCHED THE SURROUNDING VALLEY. THERE'S NO ONE ELSE HERE. NOTHING.

QUICKSILVER, PIETRO MAXIMOFF, CAME TO THE AVENGERS AFTER HIS SISTER, WANDA, THE SCARLET WITCH, SENSED SOMETHING SINISTER DEEP IN THE BONES OF THE EARTH--DIRECTLY UNDER A HYDRA BASE IN JAPAN. WHEN THE AVENGERS WENT TO INVESTIGATE, THE BASE WAS BARELY STAFFED...UNUSUAL FOR A BUILDING THAT HOUSES A FULLY OPERATIONAL TIME PORTAL. THEIR CONFUSION ONLY GREW AS IT BECAME CLEAR THAT THERE HAD BEEN NO DISTURBANCES IN THE TIME STREAM. THAT IS, UNTIL THEY REALIZED THAT WHOEVER USED IT DIDN'T HAVE TO CHANGE THE FUTURE--BECAUSE THEIR TRIUMPH HAD ALREADY BEEN ENSURED!

BLACK WIDOW | CAPTAIN AMERICA | HAWKEYE | HULK | IRON MAN | QUICKSILVER | SCARLET WITCH | SPIDER-MAN

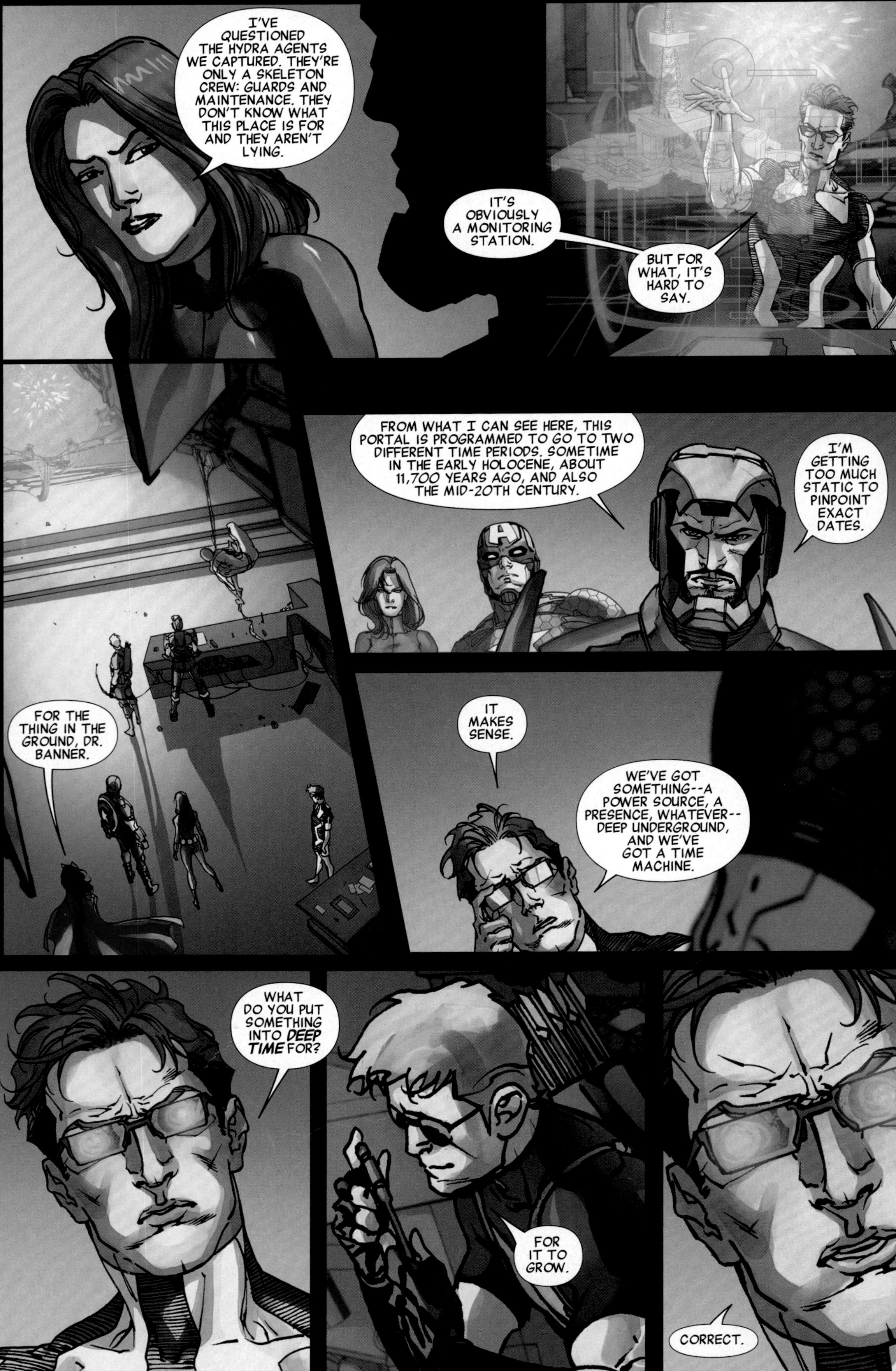
I'VE QUESTIONED THE HYDRA AGENTS WE CAPTURED. THEY'RE ONLY A SKELETON CREW: GUARDS AND MAINTENANCE. THEY DON'T KNOW WHAT THIS PLACE IS FOR AND THEY AREN'T LYING.
IT'S OBVIOUSLY A MONITORING STATION.
BUT FOR WHAT, IT'S HARD TO SAY.
FOR THE THING IN THE GROUND, DR. BANNER.
FROM WHAT I CAN SEE HERE, THIS PORTAL IS PROGRAMMED TO GO TO TWO DIFFERENT TIME PERIODS. SOMETIME IN THE EARLY HOLOCENE, ABOUT 11,700 YEARS AGO, AND ALSO THE MID-20TH CENTURY.
I'M GETTING TOO MUCH STATIC TO PINPOINT EXACT DATES.
IT MAKES SENSE.
WE'VE GOT SOMETHING--A POWER SOURCE, A PRESENCE, WHATEVER--DEEP UNDERGROUND, AND WE'VE GOT A TIME MACHINE.
WHAT DO YOU PUT SOMETHING INTO DEEP TIME FOR?
FOR IT TO GROW.
CORRECT.

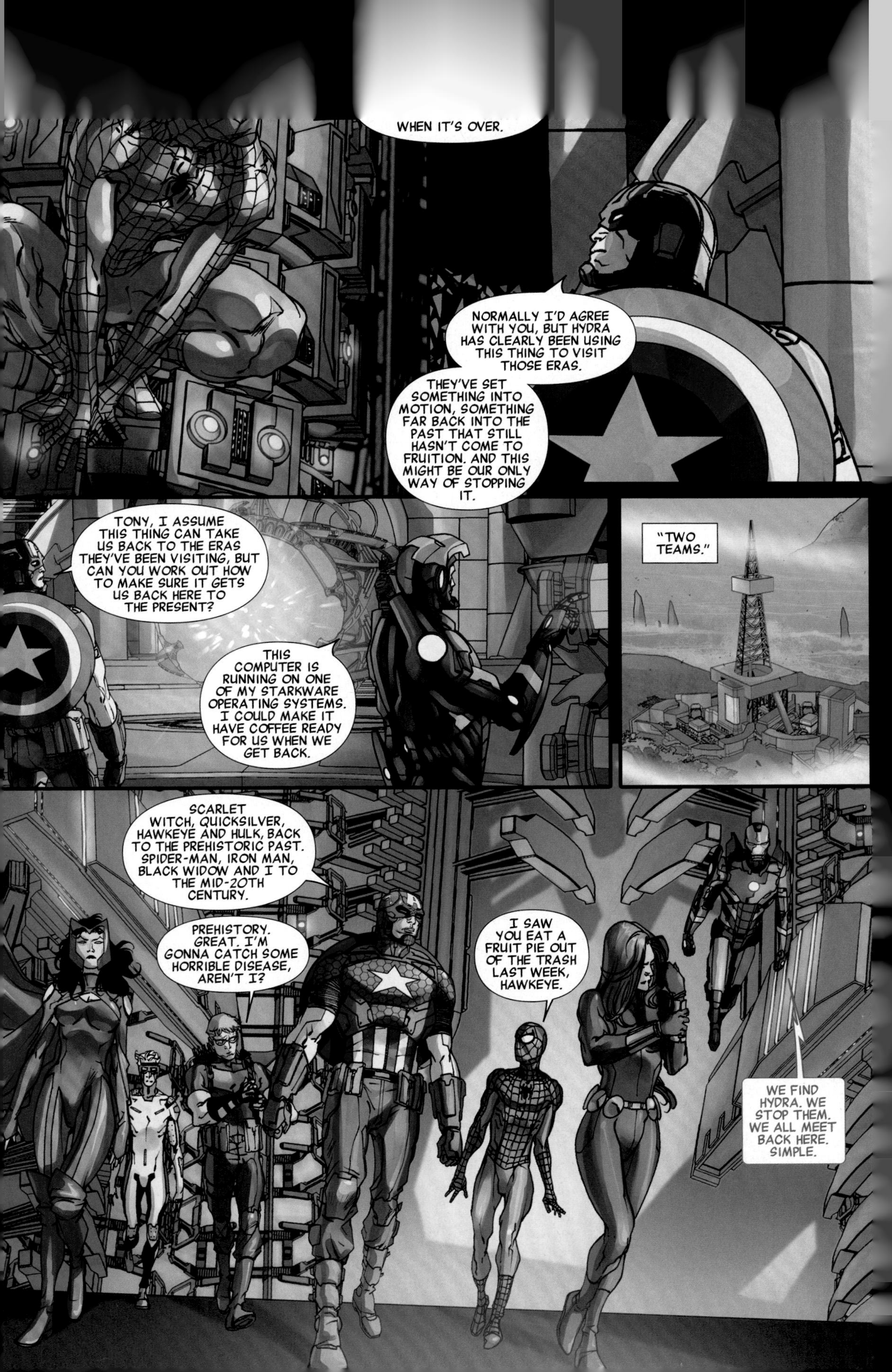
WHEN IT'S OVER.
NORMALLY I'D AGREE WITH YOU, BUT HYDRA HAS CLEARLY BEEN USING THIS THING TO VISIT THOSE ERAS.
THEY'VE SET SOMETHING INTO MOTION, SOMETHING FAR BACK INTO THE PAST THAT STILL HASN'T COME TO FRUITION. AND THIS MIGHT BE OUR ONLY WAY OF STOPPING IT.
TONY, I ASSUME THIS THING CAN TAKE US BACK TO THE ERAS THEY'VE BEEN VISITING, BUT CAN YOU WORK OUT HOW TO MAKE SURE IT GETS US BACK HERE TO THE PRESENT?
THIS COMPUTER IS RUNNING ON ONE OF MY STARKWARE OPERATING SYSTEMS. I COULD MAKE IT HAVE COFFEE READY FOR US WHEN WE GET BACK.
"TWO TEAMS."
SCARLET WITCH, QUICKSILVER, HAWKEYE AND HULK, BACK TO THE PREHISTORIC PAST. SPIDER-MAN, IRON MAN, BLACK WIDOW AND I TO THE MID-20TH CENTURY.
PREHISTORY. GREAT. I'M GONNA CATCH SOME HORRIBLE DISEASE, AREN'T I?
I SAW YOU EAT A FRUIT PIE OUT OF THE TRASH LAST WEEK, HAWKEYE.
WE FIND HYDRA. WE STOP THEM. WE ALL MEET BACK HERE. SIMPLE.

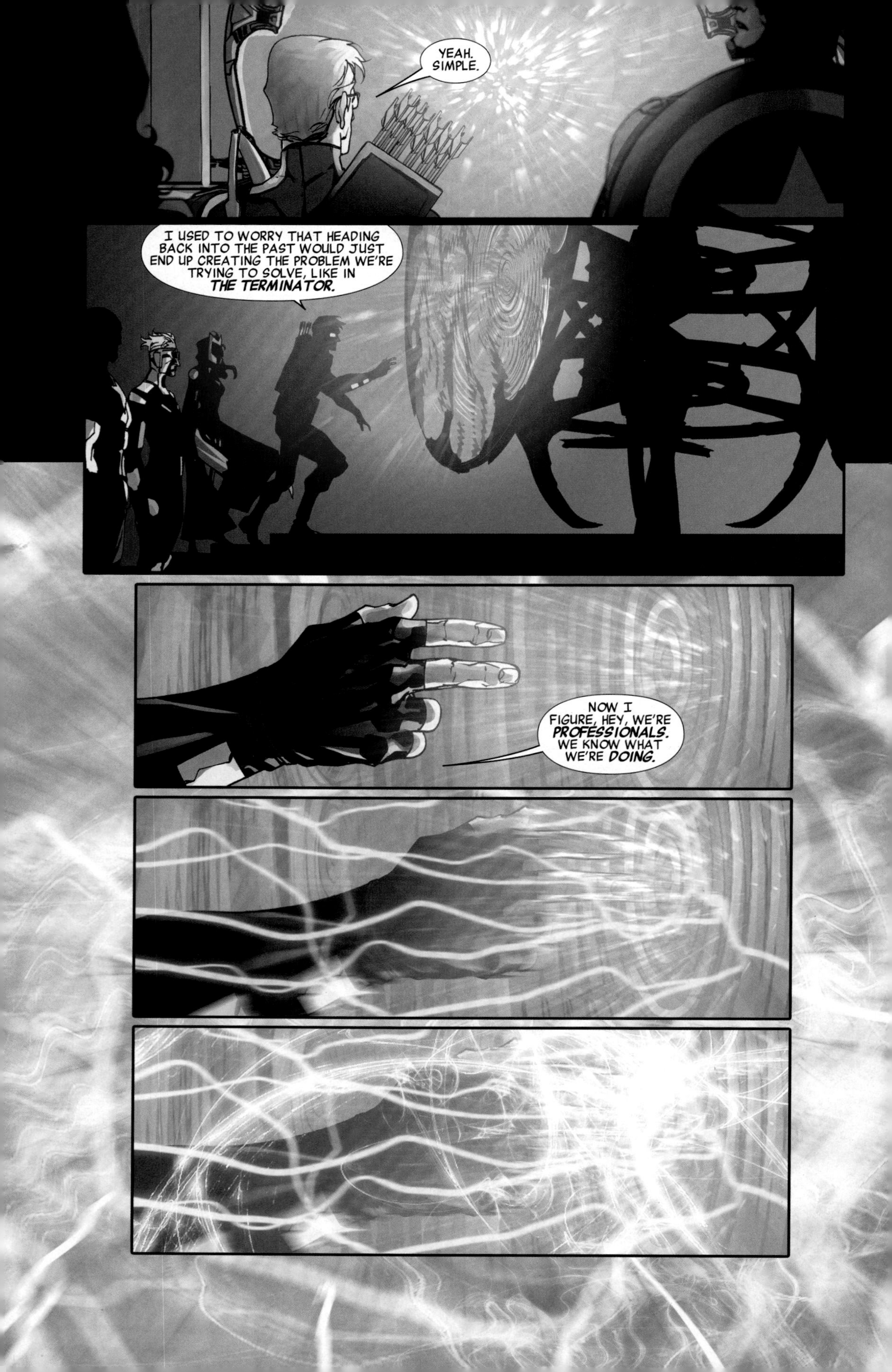
YEAH. SIMPLE.
I USED TO WORRY THAT HEADING BACK INTO THE PAST WOULD JUST END UP CREATING THE PROBLEM WE'RE TRYING TO SOLVE, LIKE IN ***THE TERMINATOR.***
NOW I FIGURE, HEY, WE'RE ***PROFESSIONALS.*** WE KNOW WHAT WE'RE ***DOING.***

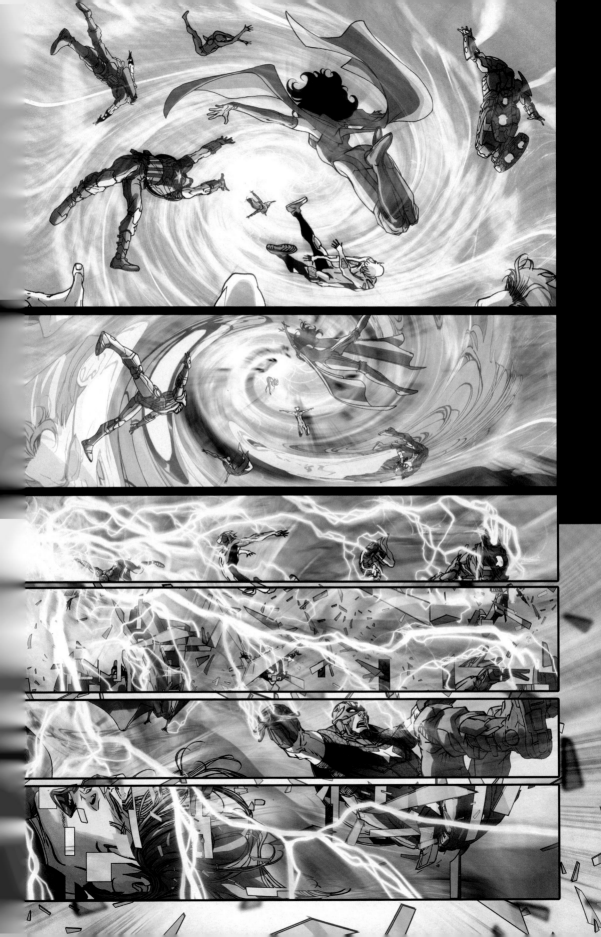

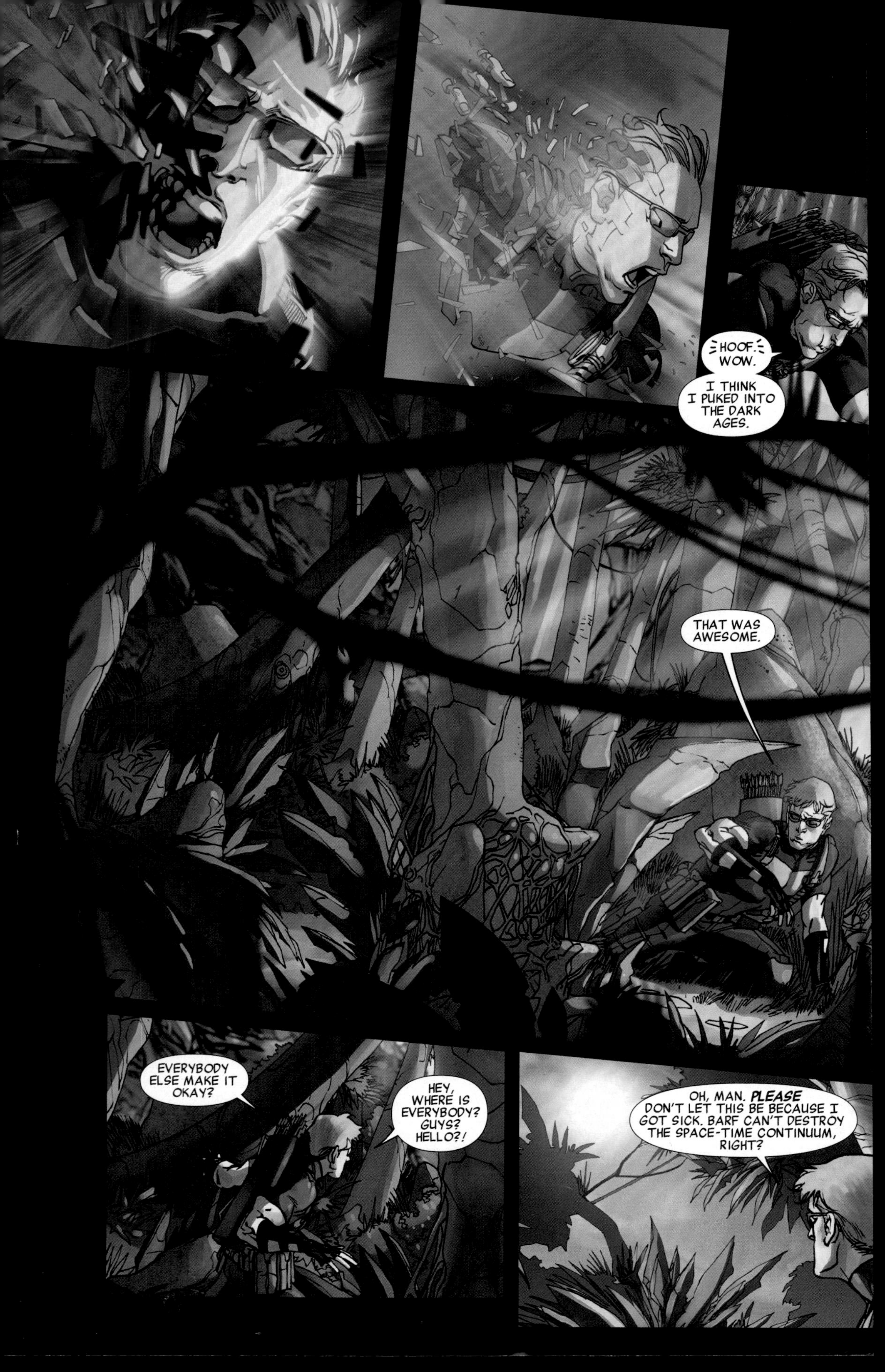
HOOF. WOW.
I THINK I PUKED INTO THE DARK AGES.
THAT WAS AWESOME.
EVERYBODY ELSE MAKE IT OKAY?
HEY, WHERE IS EVERYBODY? GUYS? HELLO?!
OH, MAN. PLEASE DON'T LET THIS BE BECAUSE I GOT SICK. BARF CAN'T DESTROY THE SPACE-TIME CONTINUUM, RIGHT?

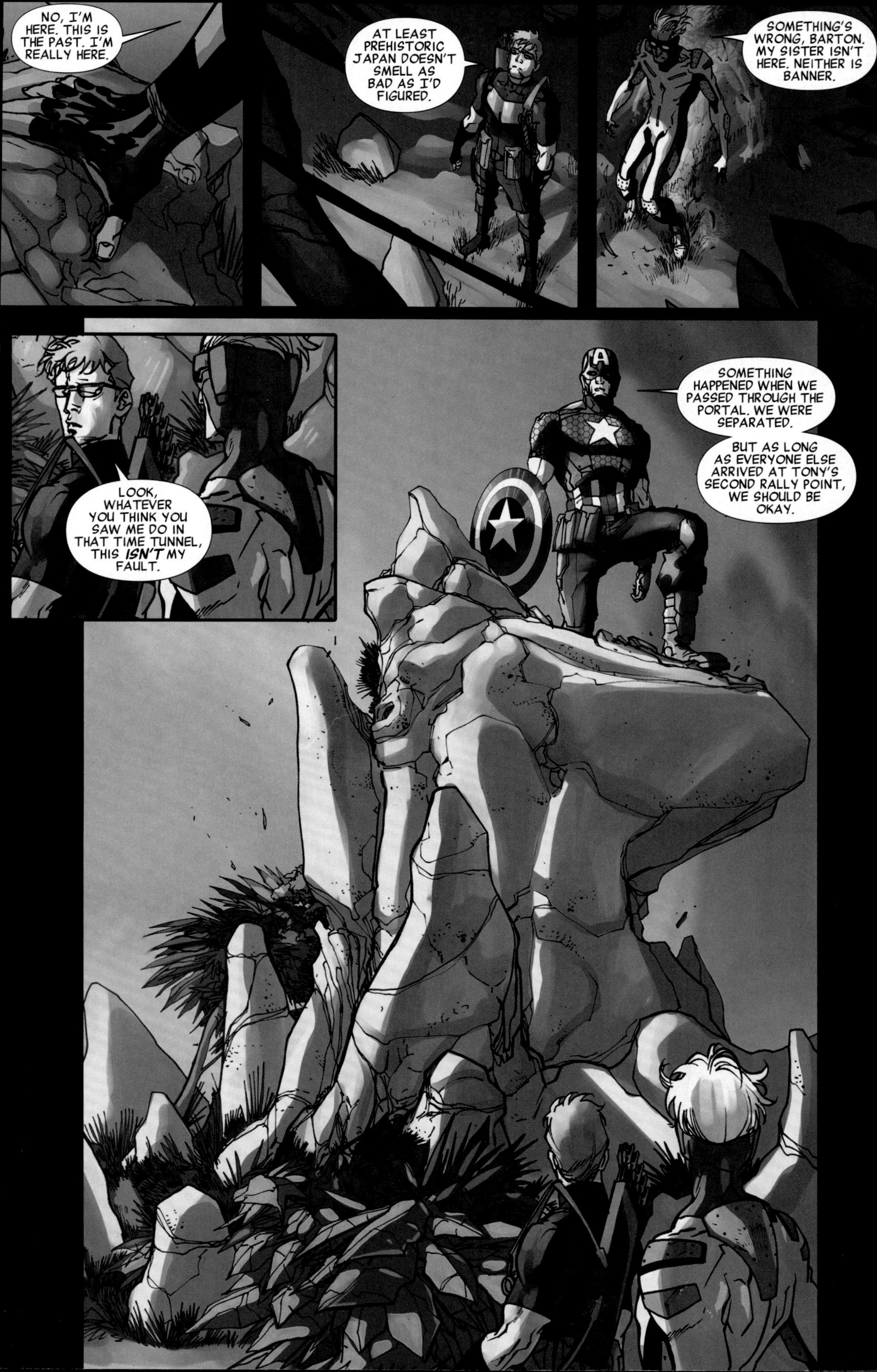
NO, I'M HERE. THIS IS THE PAST. I'M REALLY HERE.
AT LEAST PREHISTORIC JAPAN DOESN'T SMELL AS BAD AS I'D FIGURED.
SOMETHING'S WRONG, BARTON. MY SISTER ISN'T HERE. NEITHER IS BANNER.
LOOK, WHATEVER YOU THINK YOU SAW ME DO IN THAT TIME TUNNEL, THIS ISN'T MY FAULT.
SOMETHING HAPPENED WHEN WE PASSED THROUGH THE PORTAL. WE WERE SEPARATED.
BUT AS LONG AS EVERYONE ELSE ARRIVED AT TONY'S SECOND RALLY POINT, WE SHOULD BE OKAY.

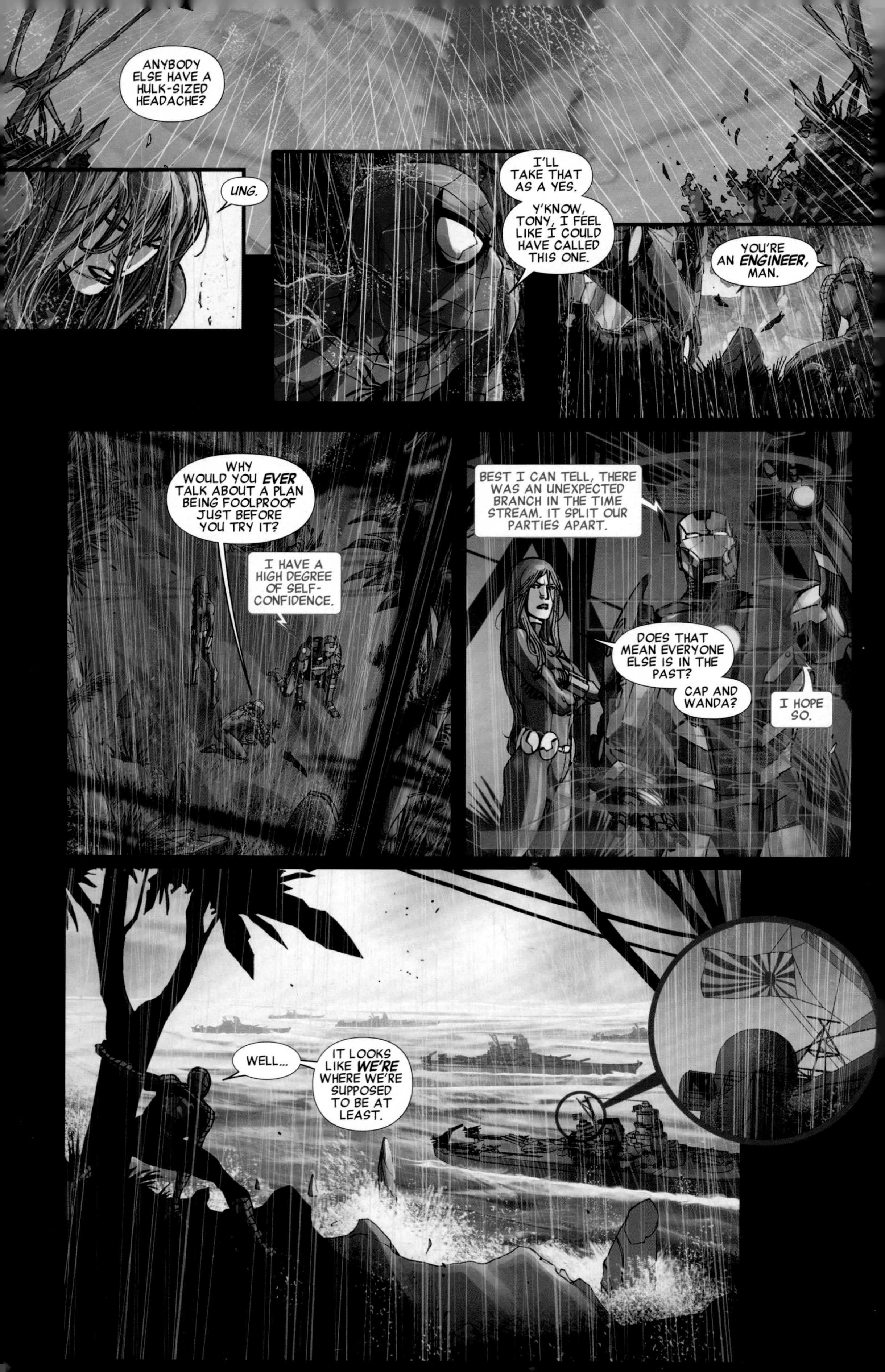
ANYBODY ELSE HAVE A HULK-SIZED HEADACHE?
UNG.
I'LL TAKE THAT AS A YES.
Y'KNOW, TONY, I FEEL LIKE I COULD HAVE CALLED THIS ONE.
YOU'RE AN ENGINEER, MAN.
WHY WOULD YOU EVER TALK ABOUT A PLAN BEING FOOLPROOF JUST BEFORE YOU TRY IT?
I HAVE A HIGH DEGREE OF SELF-CONFIDENCE.
BEST I CAN TELL, THERE WAS AN UNEXPECTED BRANCH IN THE TIME STREAM. IT SPLIT OUR PARTIES APART.
DOES THAT MEAN EVERYONE ELSE IS IN THE PAST?
CAP AND WANDA?
I HOPE SO.
WELL...
IT LOOKS LIKE WE'RE WHERE WE'RE SUPPOSED TO BE AT LEAST.

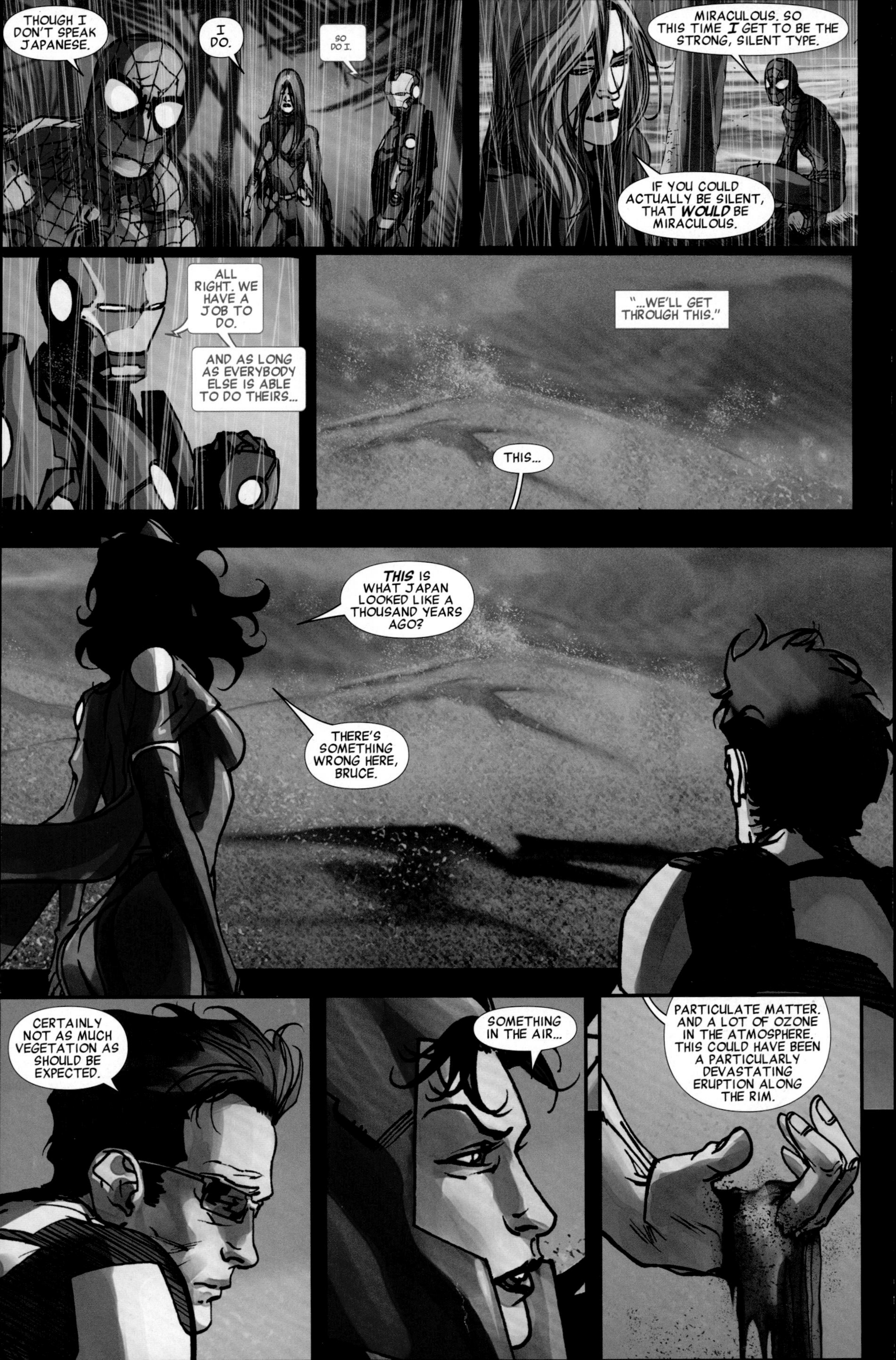

THOUGH I DON'T SPEAK JAPANESE.
I DO.
SO DO I.
MIRACULOUS. SO THIS TIME I GET TO BE THE STRONG, SILENT TYPE.
IF YOU COULD ACTUALLY BE SILENT, THAT WOULD BE MIRACULOUS.
ALL RIGHT. WE HAVE A JOB TO DO.
AND AS LONG AS EVERYBODY ELSE IS ABLE TO DO THEIRS...
"...WE'LL GET THROUGH THIS."
THIS...
THIS IS WHAT JAPAN LOOKED LIKE A THOUSAND YEARS AGO?
THERE'S SOMETHING WRONG HERE, BRUCE.
CERTAINLY NOT AS MUCH VEGETATION AS SHOULD BE EXPECTED.
SOMETHING IN THE AIR...
PARTICULATE MATTER. AND A LOT OF OZONE IN THE ATMOSPHERE. THIS COULD HAVE BEEN A PARTICULARLY DEVASTATING ERUPTION ALONG THE RIM.

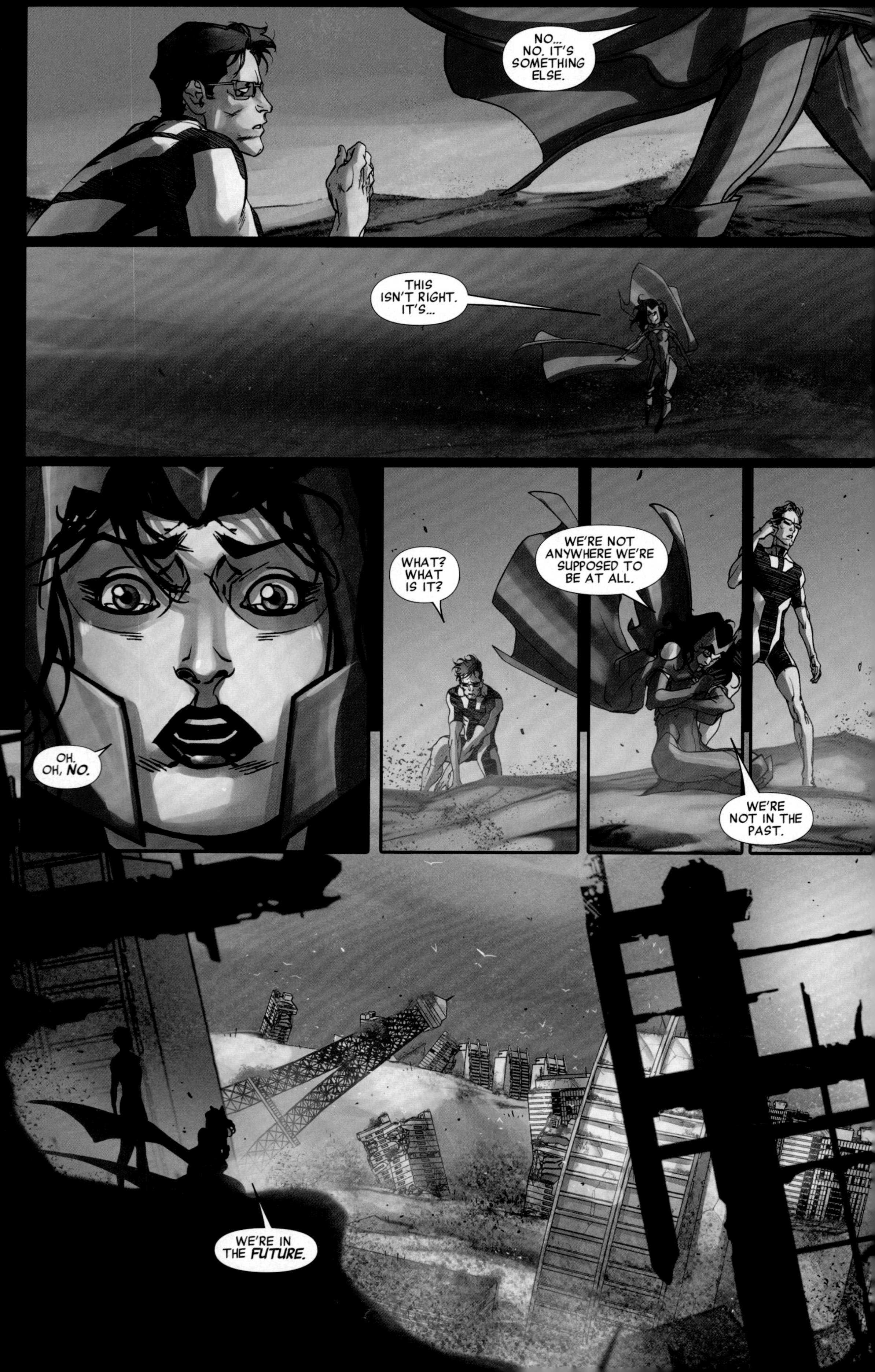

NO... NO. IT'S SOMETHING ELSE.
THIS ISN'T RIGHT. IT'S...
OH. OH, **NO.**
WHAT? WHAT IS IT?
WE'RE NOT ANYWHERE WE'RE SUPPOSED TO BE AT ALL.
WE'RE NOT IN THE PAST.
WE'RE IN THE ***FUTURE.***

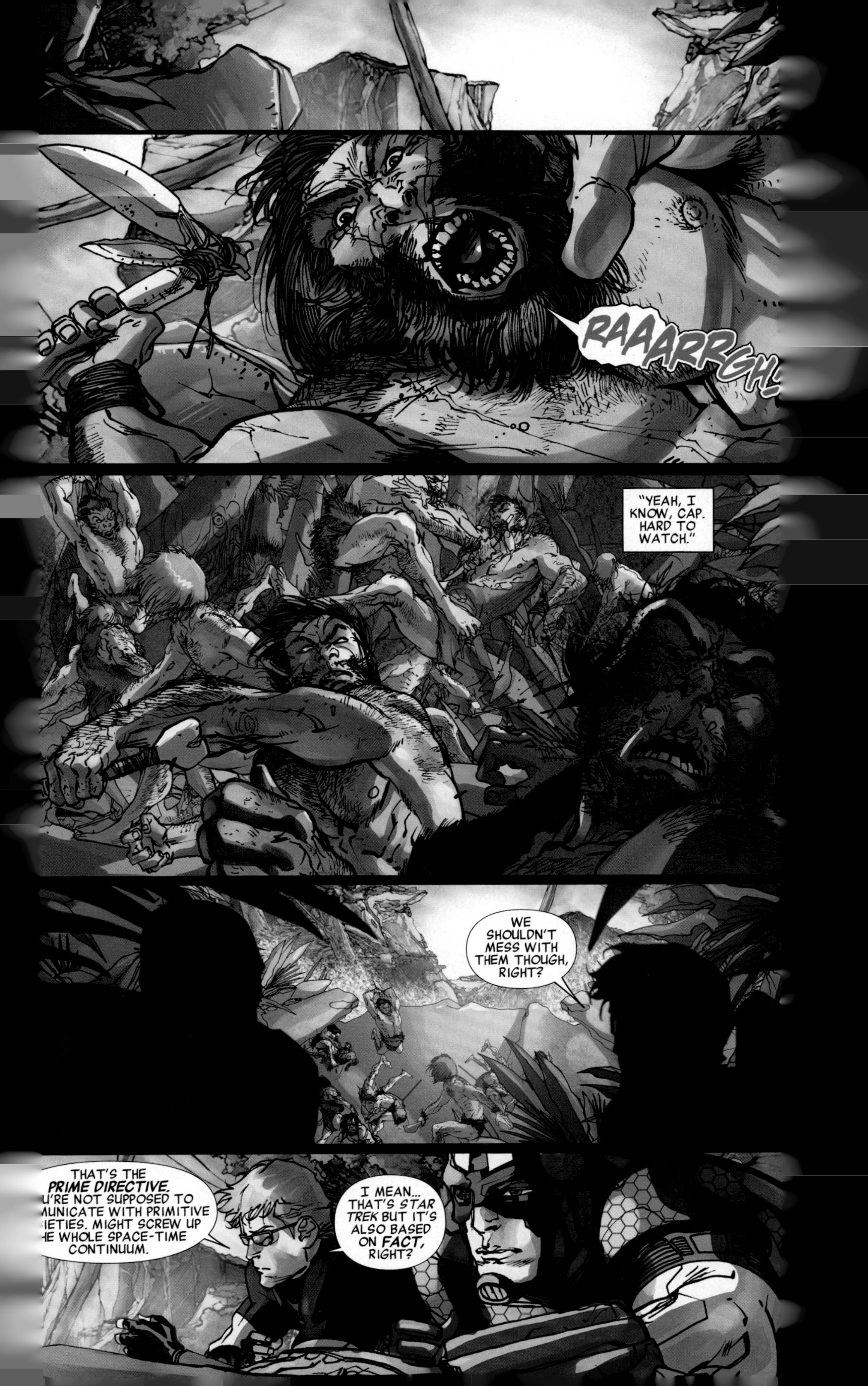
RAAARRRGH!
"YEAH, I KNOW, CAP. HARD TO WATCH."
WE SHOULDN'T MESS WITH THEM THOUGH, RIGHT?
THAT'S THE PRIME DIRECTIVE. U'RE NOT SUPPOSED TO MUNICATE WITH PRIMITIVE CIETIES. MIGHT SCREW UP HE WHOLE SPACE-TIME CONTINUUM.
I MEAN... THAT'S STAR TREK BUT IT'S ALSO BASED ON FACT, RIGHT?

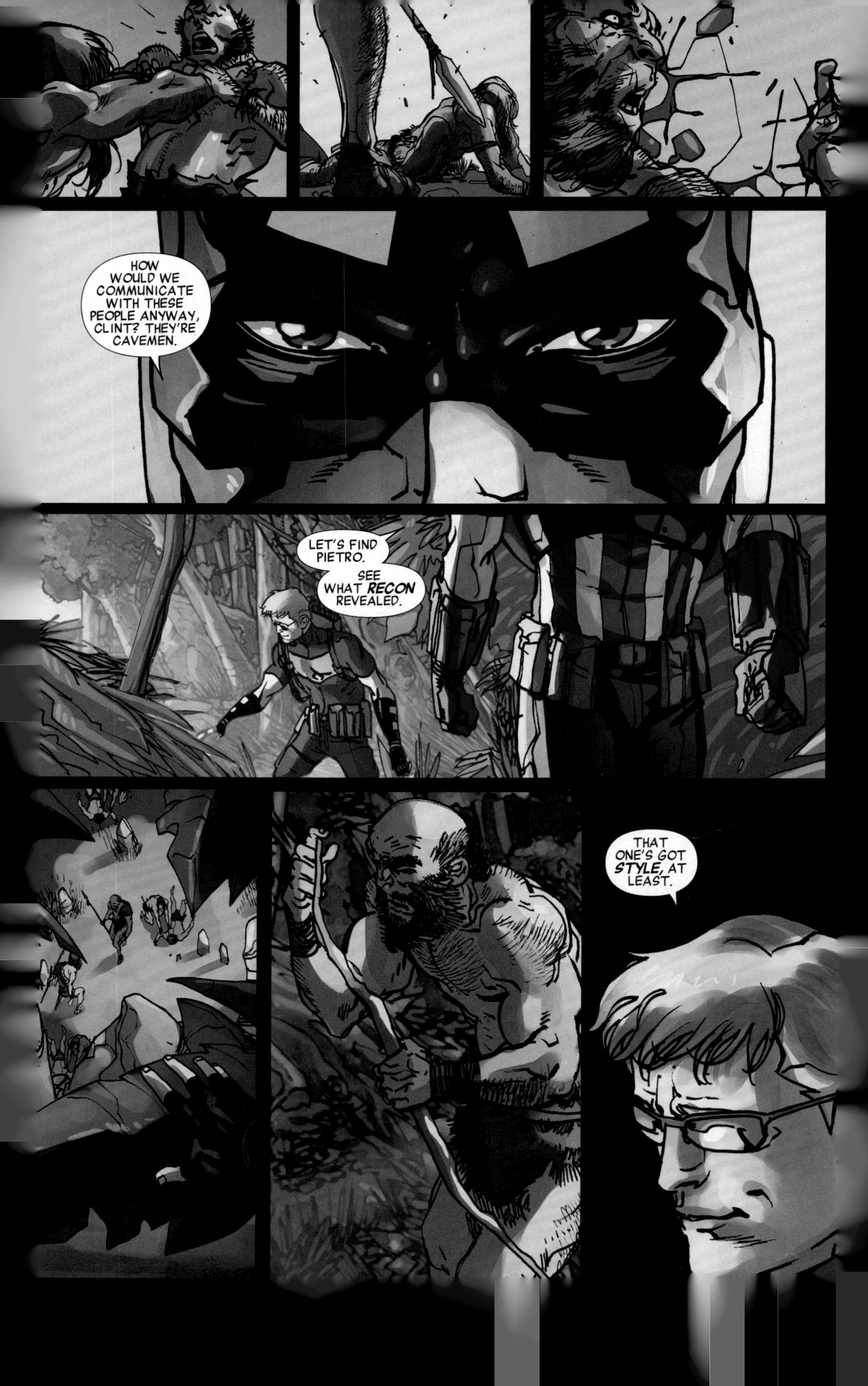
HOW WOULD WE COMMUNICATE WITH THESE PEOPLE ANYWAY, CLINT? THEY'RE CAVEMEN.
LET'S FIND PIETRO.
SEE WHAT RECON REVEALED.
THAT ONE'S GOT STYLE, AT LEAST.

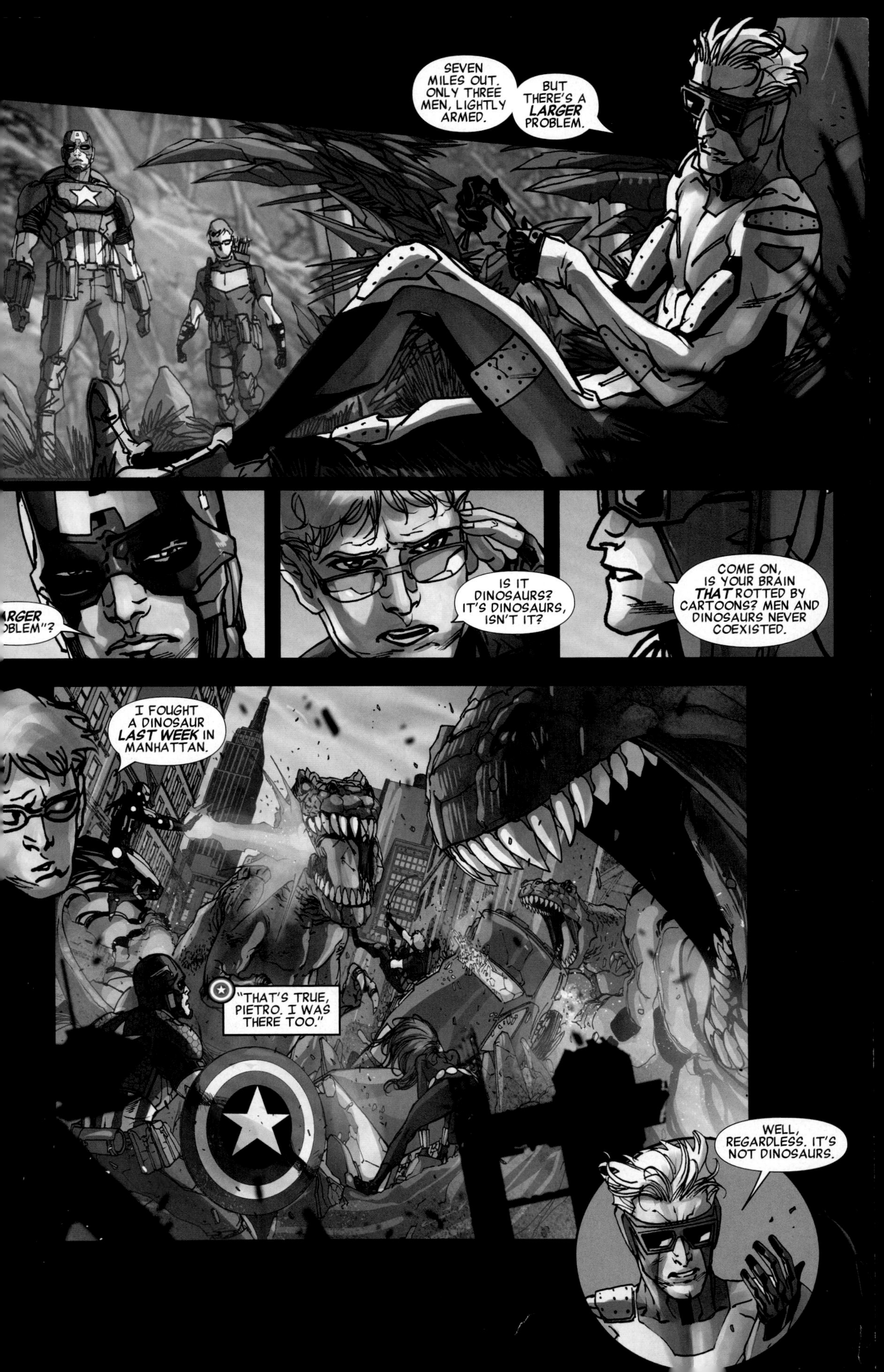
SEVEN MILES OUT. ONLY THREE MEN, LIGHTLY ARMED.
BUT THERE'S A LARGER PROBLEM.
"LARGER PROBLEM"?
IS IT DINOSAURS? IT'S DINOSAURS, ISN'T IT?
COME ON, IS YOUR BRAIN THAT ROTTED BY CARTOONS? MEN AND DINOSAURS NEVER COEXISTED.
I FOUGHT A DINOSAUR LAST WEEK IN MANHATTAN.
"THAT'S TRUE, PIETRO. I WAS THERE TOO."
WELL, REGARDLESS. IT'S NOT DINOSAURS.

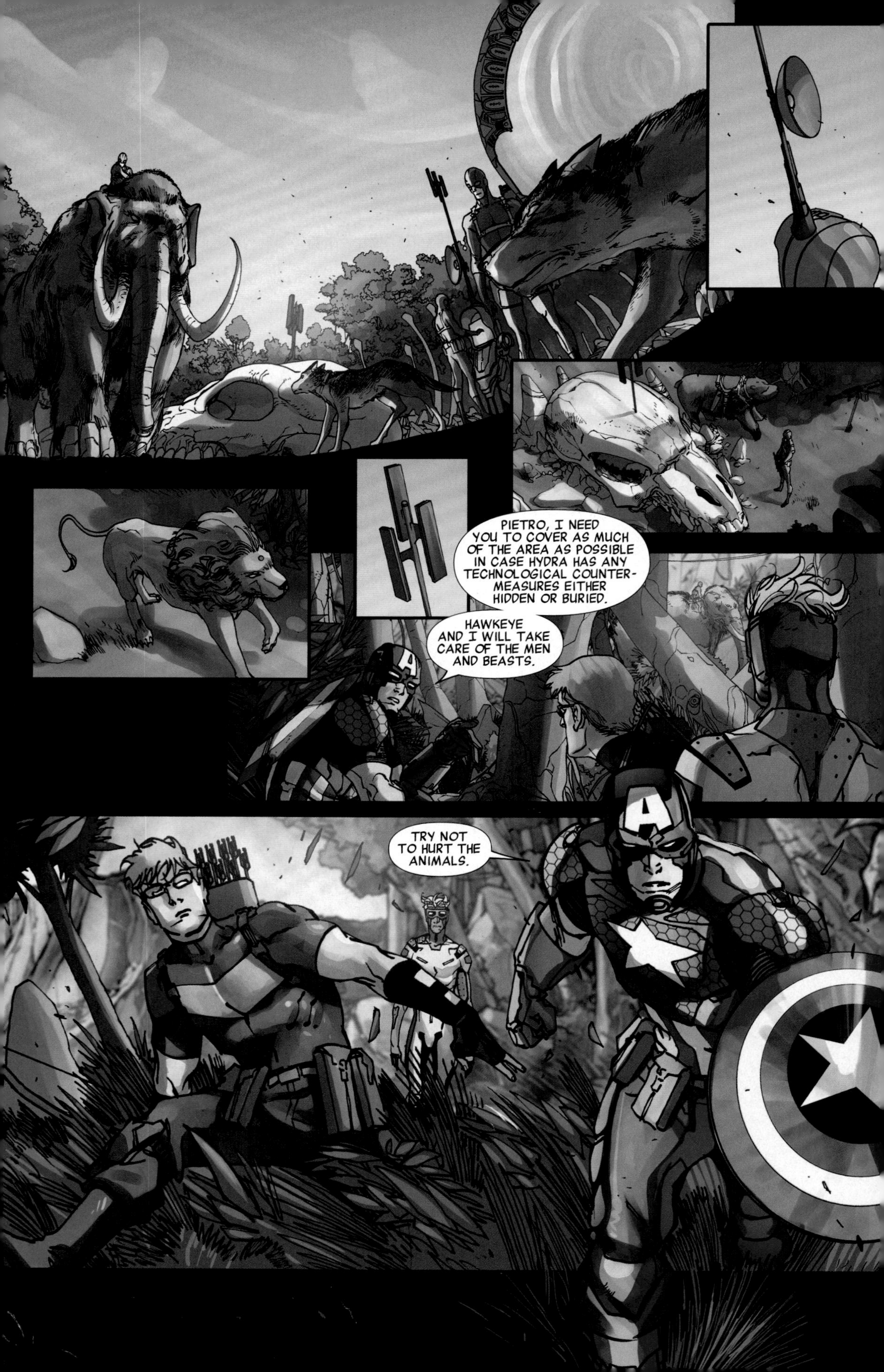
PIETRO, I NEED YOU TO COVER AS MUCH OF THE AREA AS POSSIBLE IN CASE HYDRA HAS ANY TECHNOLOGICAL COUNTER-MEASURES EITHER HIDDEN OR BURIED.
HAWKEYE AND I WILL TAKE CARE OF THE MEN AND BEASTS.
TRY NOT TO HURT THE ANIMALS.

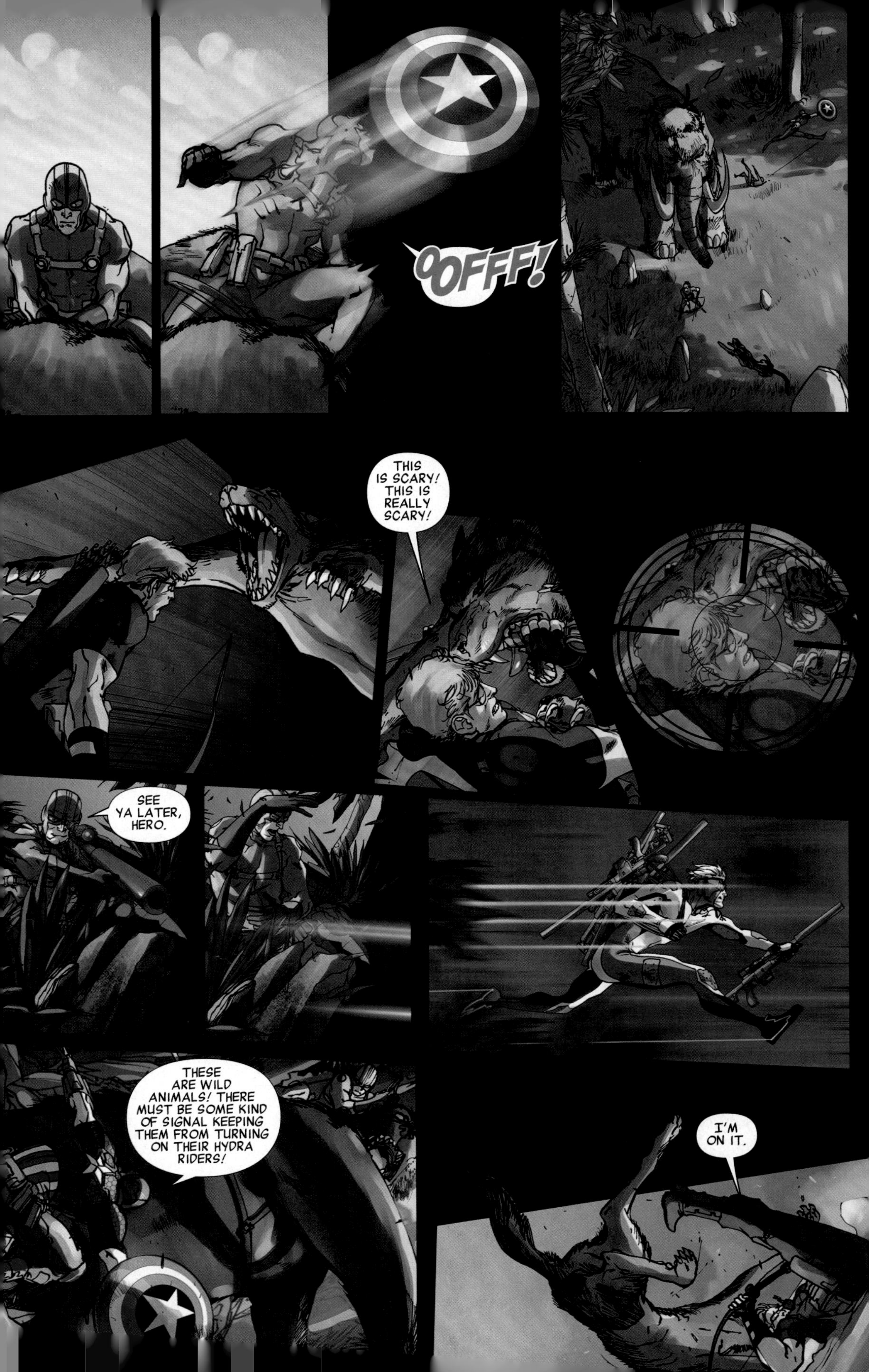
OOFFF!
THIS IS SCARY! THIS IS REALLY SCARY!
SEE YA LATER, HERO.
THESE ARE WILD ANIMALS! THERE MUST BE SOME KIND OF SIGNAL KEEPING THEM FROM TURNING ON THEIR HYDRA RIDERS!
I'M ON IT.

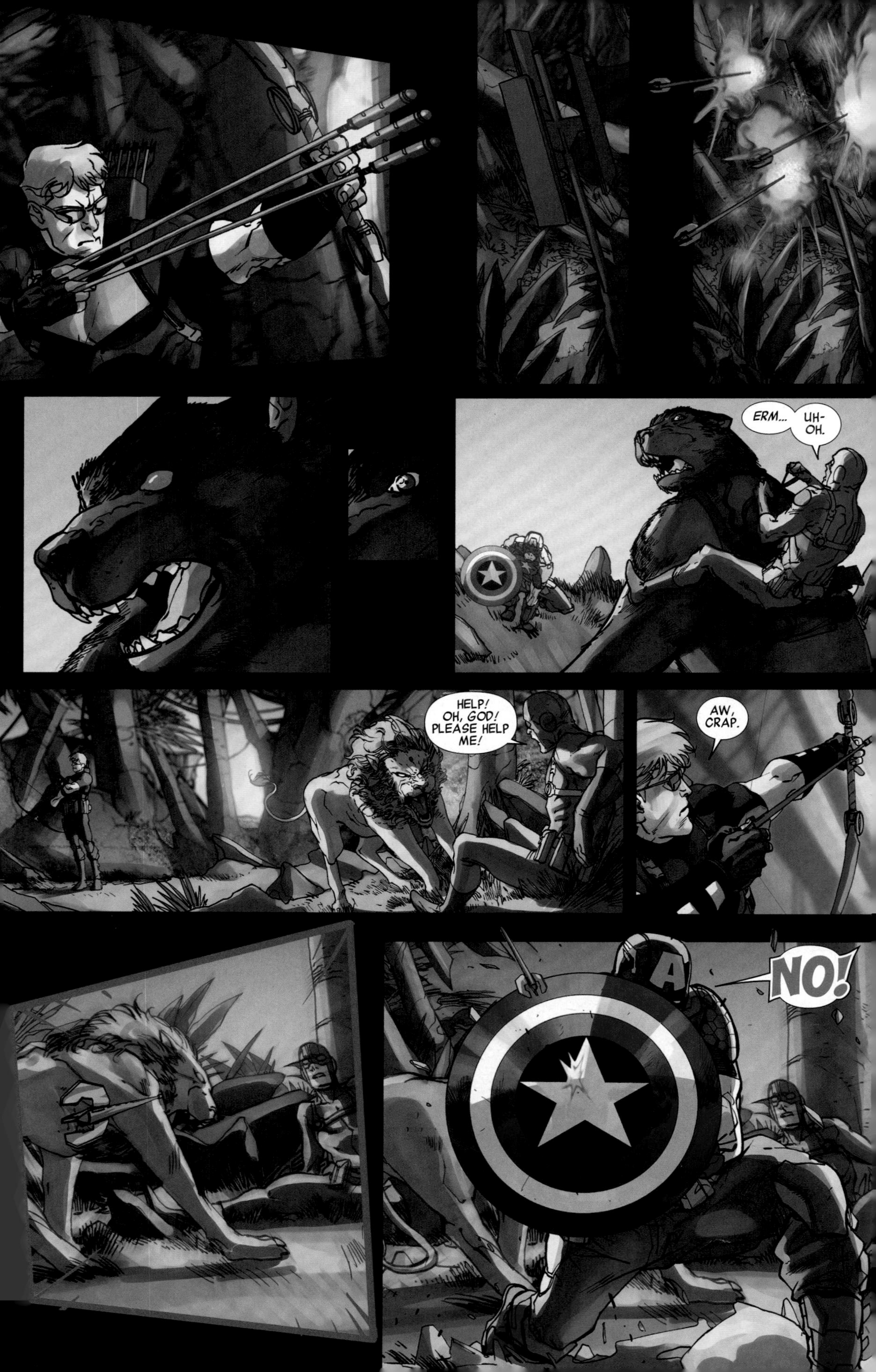
ERM...
UH-OH.
HELP! OH, GOD! PLEASE HELP ME!
AW, CRAP.
NO!

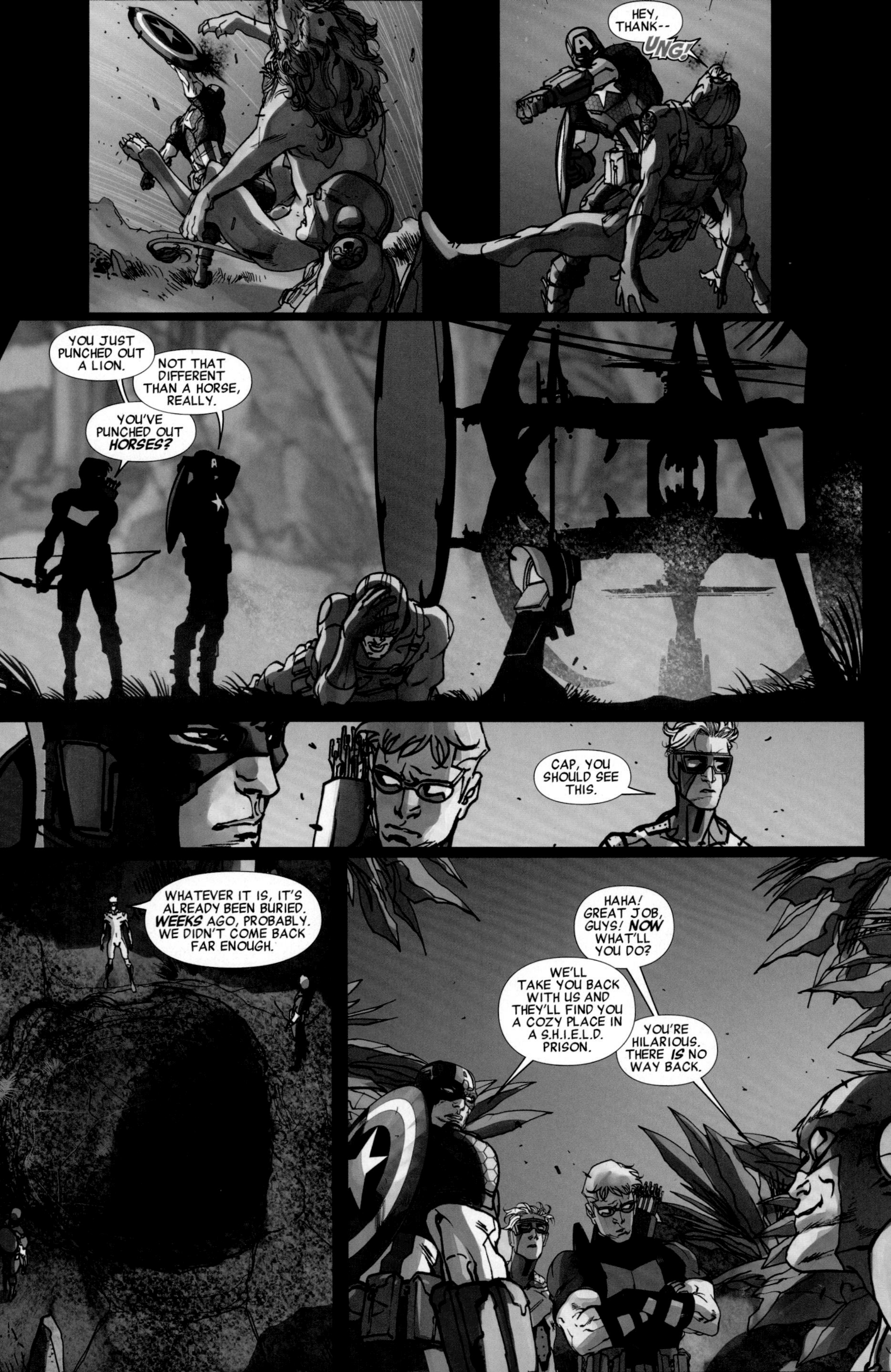
HEY, THANK--
UNG!
YOU JUST PUNCHED OUT A LION.
NOT THAT DIFFERENT THAN A HORSE, REALLY.
YOU'VE PUNCHED OUT HORSES?
CAP, YOU SHOULD SEE THIS.
WHATEVER IT IS, IT'S ALREADY BEEN BURIED. WEEKS AGO, PROBABLY. WE DIDN'T COME BACK FAR ENOUGH.
HAHA! GREAT JOB, GUYS! NOW WHAT'LL YOU DO?
WE'LL TAKE YOU BACK WITH US AND THEY'LL FIND YOU A COZY PLACE IN A S.H.I.E.L.D. PRISON.
YOU'RE HILARIOUS. THERE IS NO WAY BACK.

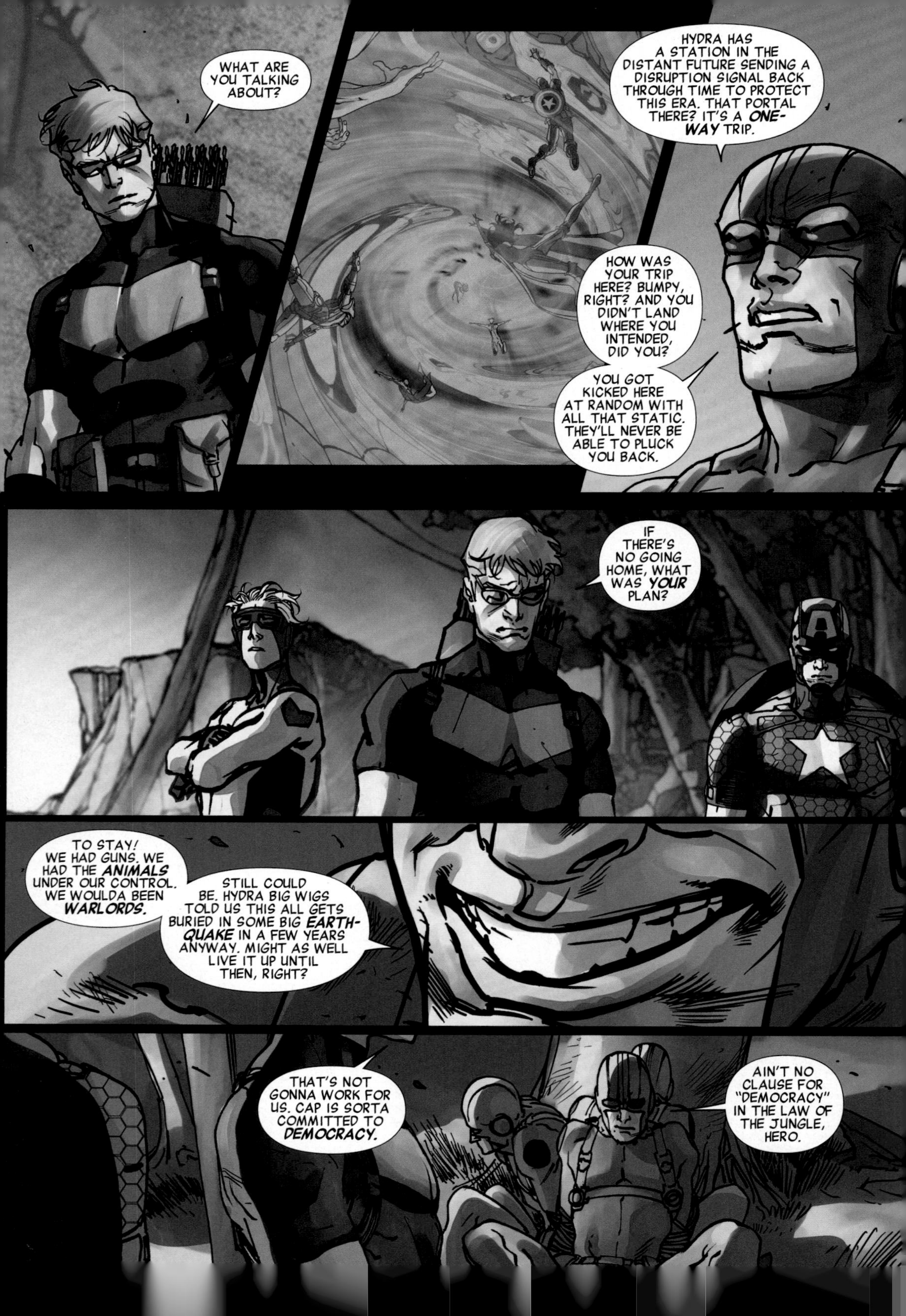
WHAT ARE YOU TALKING ABOUT?
HYDRA HAS A STATION IN THE DISTANT FUTURE SENDING A DISRUPTION SIGNAL BACK THROUGH TIME TO PROTECT THIS ERA. THAT PORTAL THERE? IT'S A ONE-WAY TRIP.
HOW WAS YOUR TRIP HERE? BUMPY, RIGHT? AND YOU DIDN'T LAND WHERE YOU INTENDED, DID YOU?
YOU GOT KICKED HERE AT RANDOM WITH ALL THAT STATIC. THEY'LL NEVER BE ABLE TO PLUCK YOU BACK.
IF THERE'S NO GOING HOME, WHAT WAS YOUR PLAN?
TO STAY! WE HAD GUNS. WE HAD THE ANIMALS UNDER OUR CONTROL. WE WOULDA BEEN WARLORDS.
STILL COULD BE. HYDRA BIG WIGS TOLD US THIS ALL GETS BURIED IN SOME BIG EARTHQUAKE IN A FEW YEARS ANYWAY. MIGHT AS WELL LIVE IT UP UNTIL THEN, RIGHT?
THAT'S NOT GONNA WORK FOR US. CAP IS SORTA COMMITTED TO DEMOCRACY.
AIN'T NO CLAUSE FOR "DEMOCRACY" IN THE LAW OF THE JUNGLE, HERO.

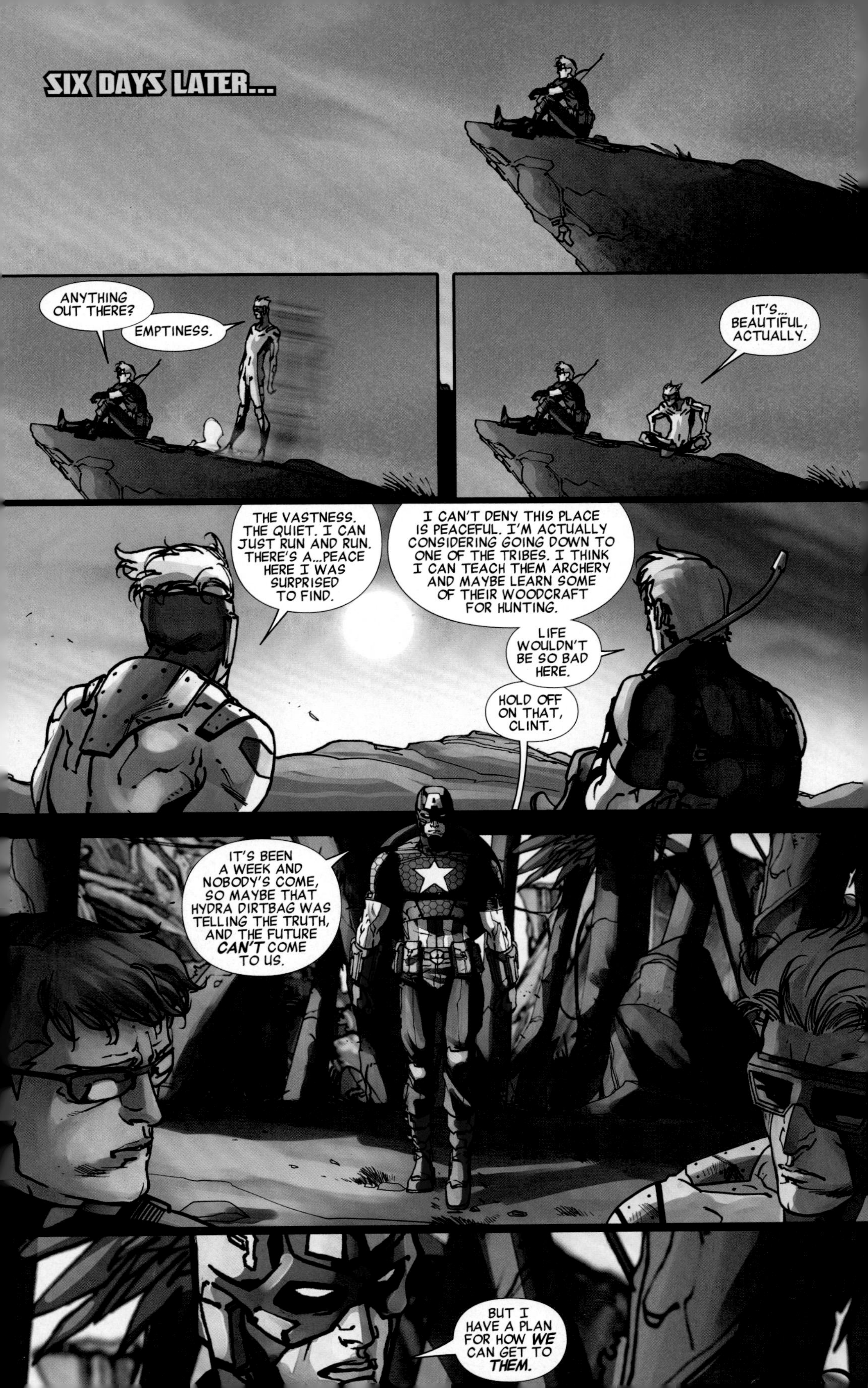
SIX DAYS LATER...
ANYTHING OUT THERE?
EMPTINESS.
IT'S... BEAUTIFUL, ACTUALLY.
THE VASTNESS. THE QUIET. I CAN JUST RUN AND RUN. THERE'S A...PEACE HERE I WAS SURPRISED TO FIND.
I CAN'T DENY THIS PLACE IS PEACEFUL. I'M ACTUALLY CONSIDERING GOING DOWN TO ONE OF THE TRIBES. I THINK I CAN TEACH THEM ARCHERY AND MAYBE LEARN SOME OF THEIR WOODCRAFT FOR HUNTING.
LIFE WOULDN'T BE SO BAD HERE.
HOLD OFF ON THAT, CLINT.
IT'S BEEN A WEEK AND NOBODY'S COME, SO MAYBE THAT HYDRA DIRTBAG WAS TELLING THE TRUTH, AND THE FUTURE CAN'T COME TO US.
BUT I HAVE A PLAN FOR HOW WE CAN GET TO THEM.

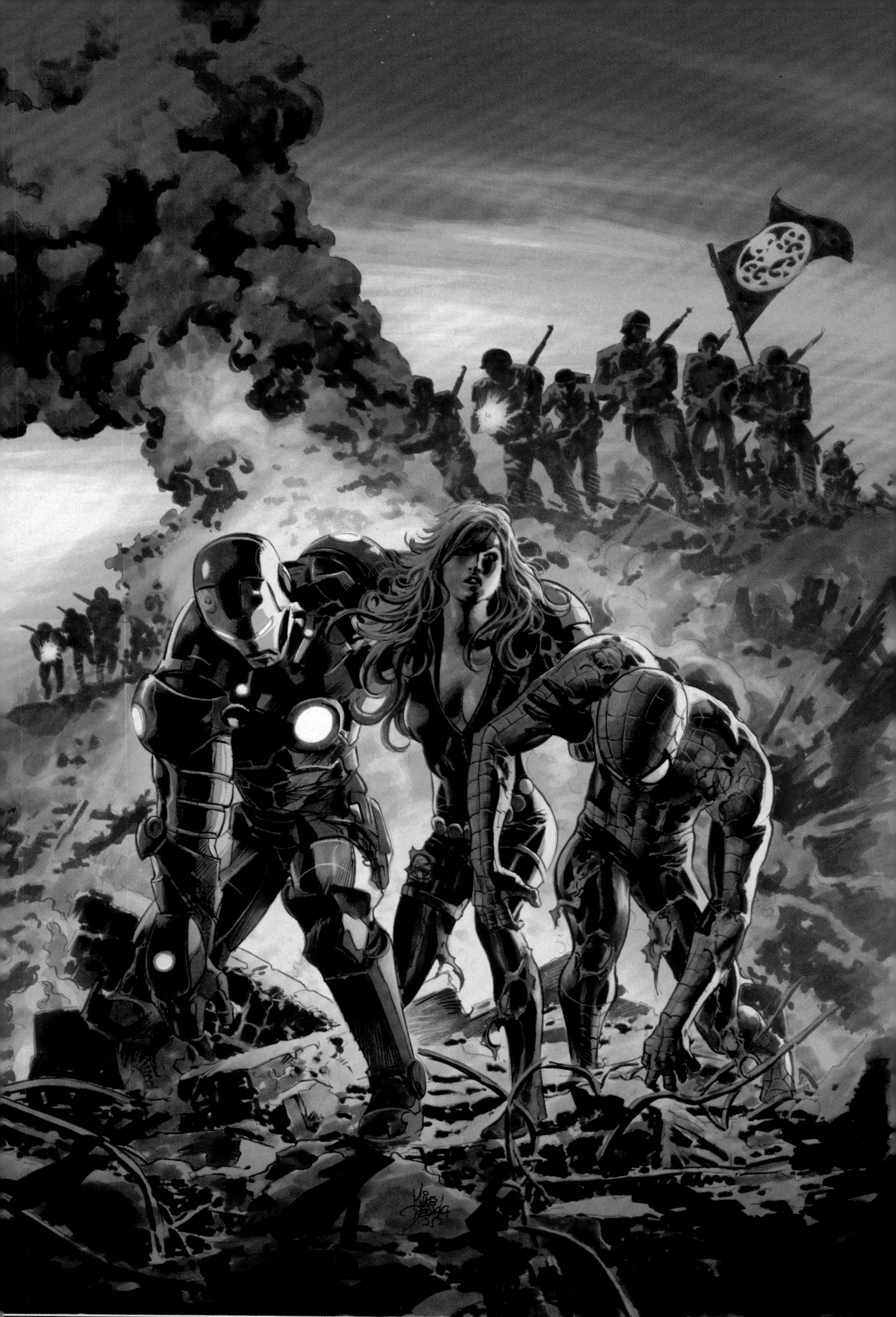

CHAPTER 3

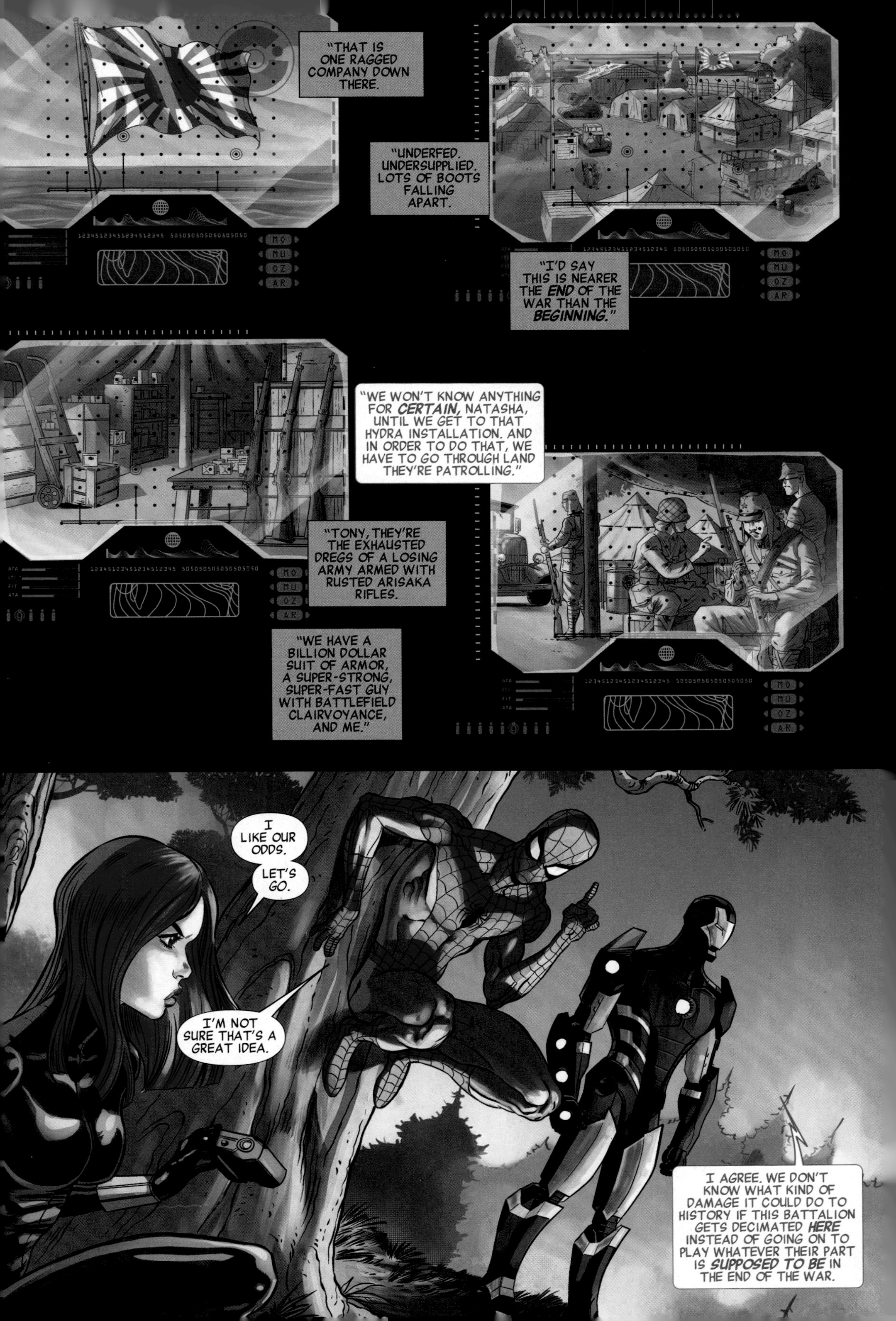

"THAT IS ONE RAGGED COMPANY DOWN THERE.
"UNDERFED. UNDERSUPPLIED. LOTS OF BOOTS FALLING APART.
"I'D SAY THIS IS NEARER THE **END** OF THE WAR THAN THE **BEGINNING**."
"WE WON'T KNOW ANYTHING FOR **CERTAIN**, NATASHA, UNTIL WE GET TO THAT HYDRA INSTALLATION. AND IN ORDER TO DO THAT, WE HAVE TO GO THROUGH LAND THEY'RE PATROLLING."
"TONY, THEY'RE THE EXHAUSTED DREGS OF A LOSING ARMY ARMED WITH RUSTED ARISAKA RIFLES.
"WE HAVE A BILLION DOLLAR SUIT OF ARMOR, A SUPER-STRONG, SUPER-FAST GUY WITH BATTLEFIELD CLAIRVOYANCE, AND ME."
I LIKE OUR ODDS.
LET'S GO.
I'M NOT SURE THAT'S A GREAT IDEA.
I AGREE. WE DON'T KNOW WHAT KIND OF DAMAGE IT COULD DO TO HISTORY IF THIS BATTALION GETS DECIMATED **HERE** INSTEAD OF GOING ON TO PLAY WHATEVER THEIR PART IS **SUPPOSED TO BE** IN THE END OF THE WAR.

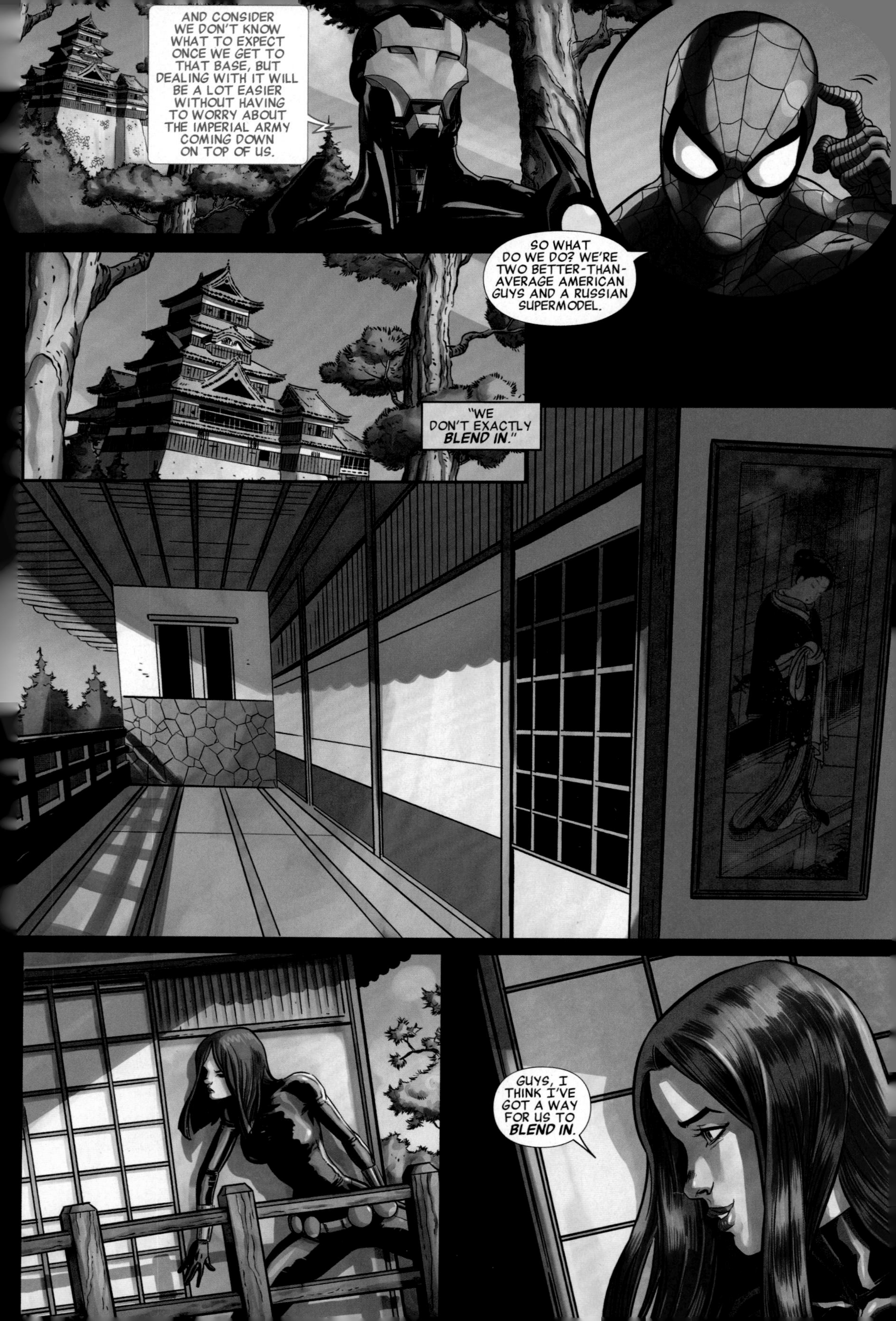
AND CONSIDER WE DON'T KNOW WHAT TO EXPECT ONCE WE GET TO THAT BASE, BUT DEALING WITH IT WILL BE A LOT EASIER WITHOUT HAVING TO WORRY ABOUT THE IMPERIAL ARMY COMING DOWN ON TOP OF US.
SO WHAT DO WE DO? WE'RE TWO BETTER-THAN-AVERAGE AMERICAN GUYS AND A RUSSIAN SUPERMODEL.
"WE DON'T EXACTLY *BLEND IN*."
GUYS, I THINK I'VE GOT A WAY FOR US TO *BLEND IN*.

AVENGERS MILLENNIUM
CHAPTER THREE

BLACK WIDOW | CAPTAIN AMERICA | HAWKEYE | HULK | IRON MAN | QUICKSILVER | SCARLET WITCH | SPIDER-MAN

WANDA MAXIMOFF, THE SCARLET WITCH, SENSED A DISTURBANCE DEEP IN THE EARTH, DIRECTLY BELOW A HYDRA BASE IN JAPAN. WHEN THE AVENGERS WENT TO INVESTIGATE, THEY FOUND A TIME PORTAL--SEEMINGLY ONLY USED TO VISIT THE PREHISTORIC PAST AND THE MID-20TH CENTURY. THE TEAM ENTERED THE TIME PORTAL, HOPING TO FIND AND STOP HYDRA, BUT THEY ENDED UP SCATTERED THROUGH TIME, WITH IRON MAN, BLACK WIDOW, AND SPIDER-MAN ENDING UP IN WORLD WAR II-ERA JAPAN...

YES, THIS WILL WORK.

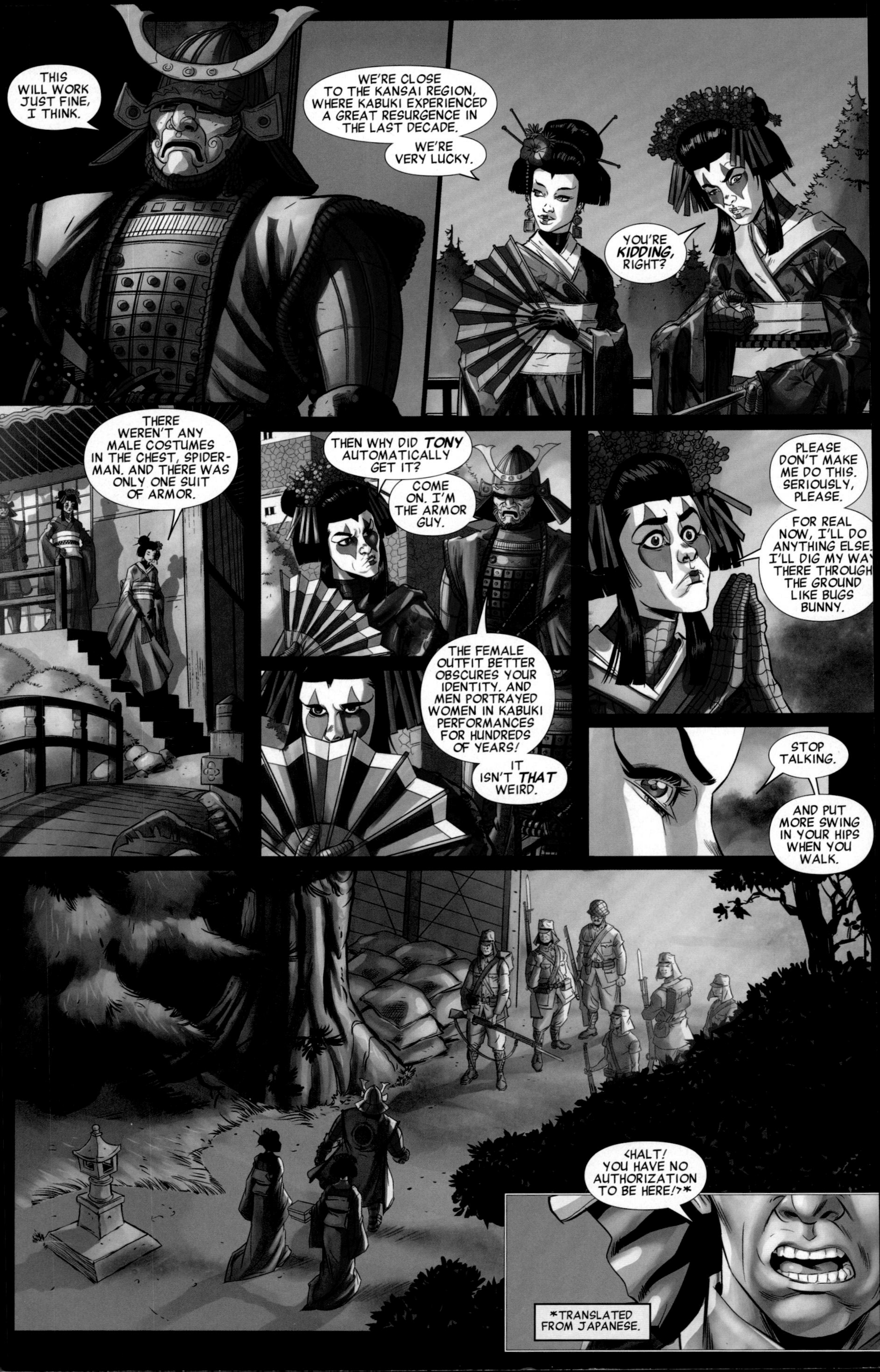
THIS WILL WORK JUST FINE, I THINK.
WE'RE CLOSE TO THE KANSAI REGION, WHERE KABUKI EXPERIENCED A GREAT RESURGENCE IN THE LAST DECADE.
WE'RE VERY LUCKY.
YOU'RE KIDDING, RIGHT?
THERE WEREN'T ANY MALE COSTUMES IN THE CHEST, SPIDER-MAN. AND THERE WAS ONLY ONE SUIT OF ARMOR.
THEN WHY DID TONY AUTOMATICALLY GET IT?
COME ON. I'M THE ARMOR GUY.
THE FEMALE OUTFIT BETTER OBSCURES YOUR IDENTITY. AND MEN PORTRAYED WOMEN IN KABUKI PERFORMANCES FOR HUNDREDS OF YEARS!
IT ISN'T THAT WEIRD.
PLEASE DON'T MAKE ME DO THIS. SERIOUSLY, PLEASE.
FOR REAL NOW, I'LL DO ANYTHING ELSE. I'LL DIG MY WAY THERE THROUGH THE GROUND LIKE BUGS BUNNY.
STOP TALKING.
AND PUT MORE SWING IN YOUR HIPS WHEN YOU WALK.
<HALT! YOU HAVE NO AUTHORIZATION TO BE HERE!>*
*TRANSLATED FROM JAPANESE.

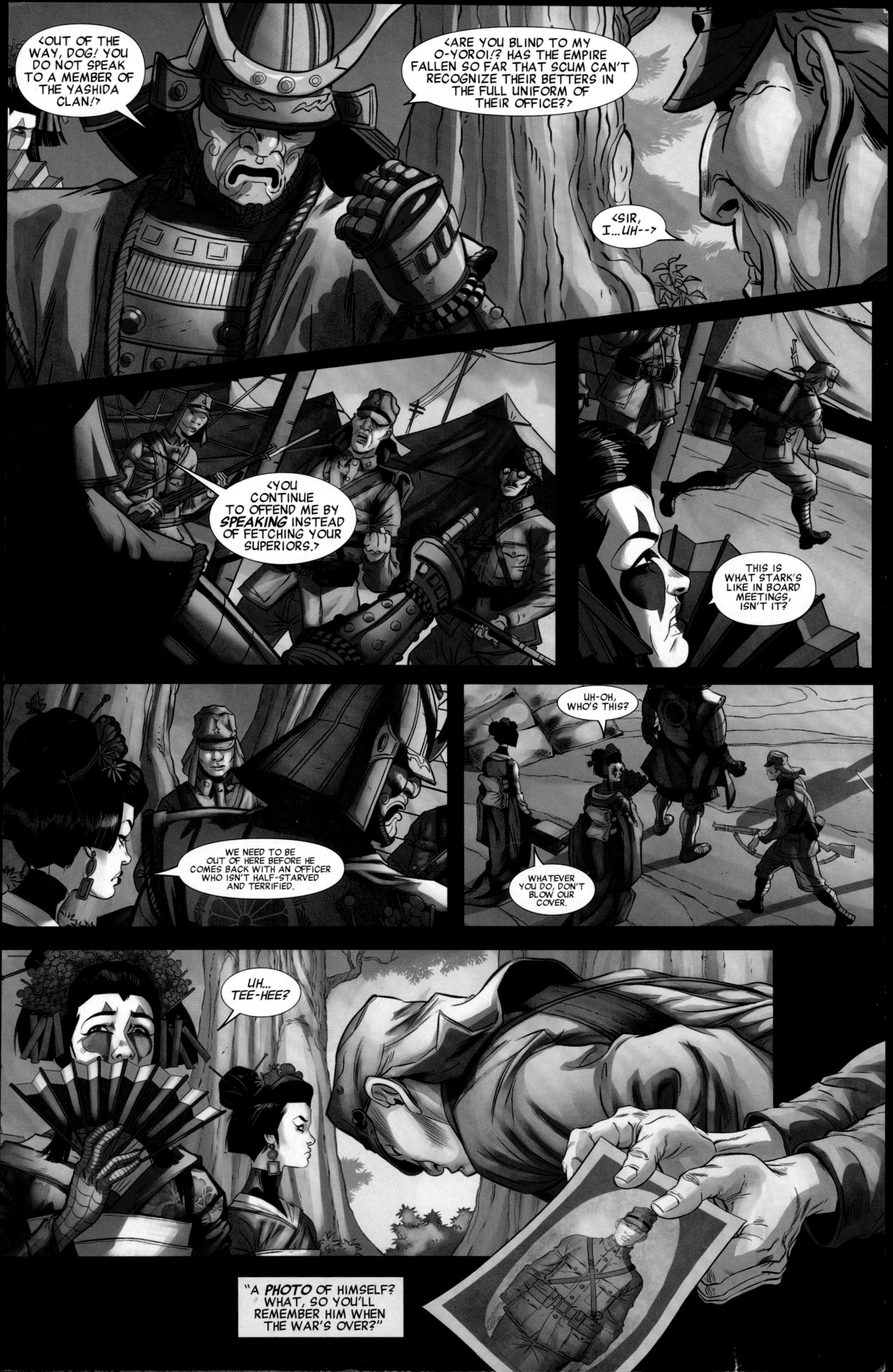
<OUT OF THE WAY, DOG! YOU DO NOT SPEAK TO A MEMBER OF THE YASHIDA CLAN!>
<ARE YOU BLIND TO MY O-YOROI!? HAS THE EMPIRE FALLEN SO FAR THAT SCUM CAN'T RECOGNIZE THEIR BETTERS IN THE FULL UNIFORM OF THEIR OFFICE?>
<SIR, I...UH-->
<YOU CONTINUE TO OFFEND ME BY SPEAKING INSTEAD OF FETCHING YOUR SUPERIORS.>
THIS IS WHAT STARK'S LIKE IN BOARD MEETINGS, ISN'T IT?
WE NEED TO BE OUT OF HERE BEFORE HE COMES BACK WITH AN OFFICER WHO ISN'T HALF-STARVED AND TERRIFIED.
UH-OH, WHO'S THIS?
WHATEVER YOU DO, DON'T BLOW OUR COVER.
UH... TEE-HEE?
"A PHOTO OF HIMSELF? WHAT, SO YOU'LL REMEMBER HIM WHEN THE WAR'S OVER?"

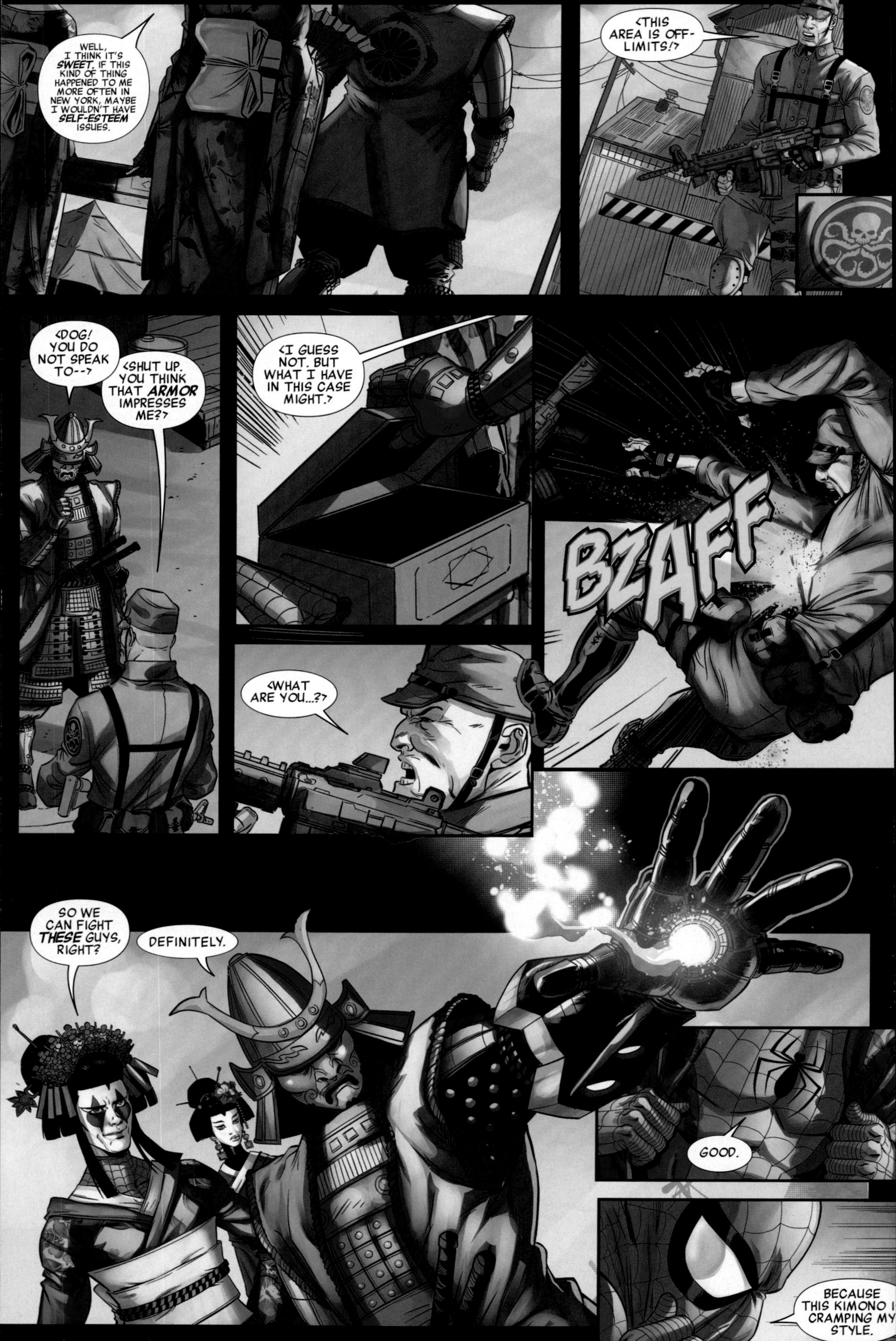
WELL, I THINK IT'S SWEET. IF THIS KIND OF THING HAPPENED TO ME MORE OFTEN IN NEW YORK, MAYBE I WOULDN'T HAVE SELF-ESTEEM ISSUES.
<THIS AREA IS OFF-LIMITS!>
<DOG! YOU DO NOT SPEAK TO-->
<SHUT UP. YOU THINK THAT ARMOR IMPRESSES ME?>
<I GUESS NOT. BUT WHAT I HAVE IN THIS CASE MIGHT.>
<WHAT ARE YOU...?>
BZAFF
SO WE CAN FIGHT THESE GUYS, RIGHT?
DEFINITELY.
GOOD.
BECAUSE THIS KIMONO I CRAMPING MY STYLE.

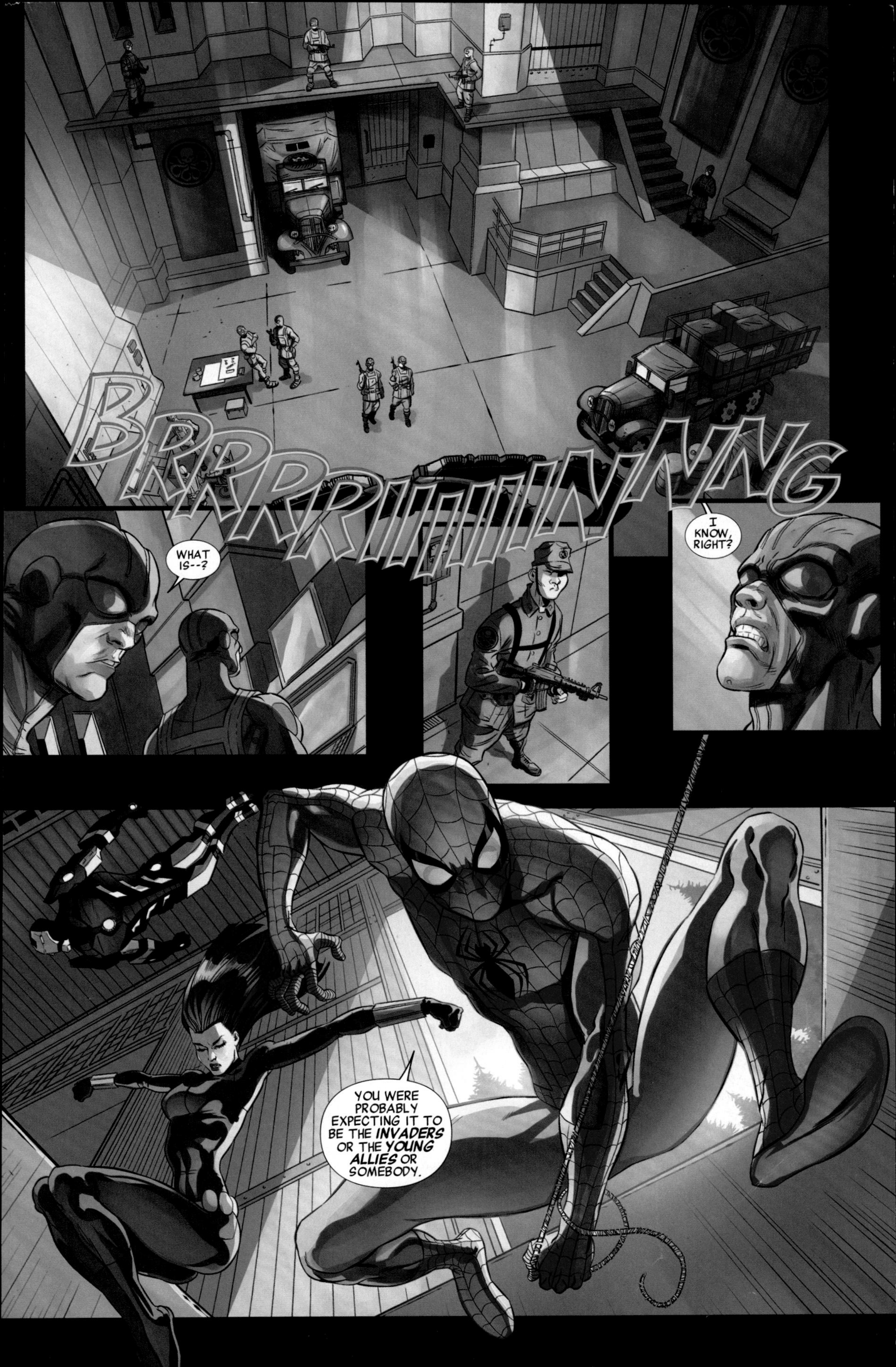
BRRRRIIIIIINNNG
WHAT IS--?
I KNOW, RIGHT?
YOU WERE PROBABLY EXPECTING IT TO BE THE INVADERS OR THE YOUNG ALLIES OR SOMEBODY.

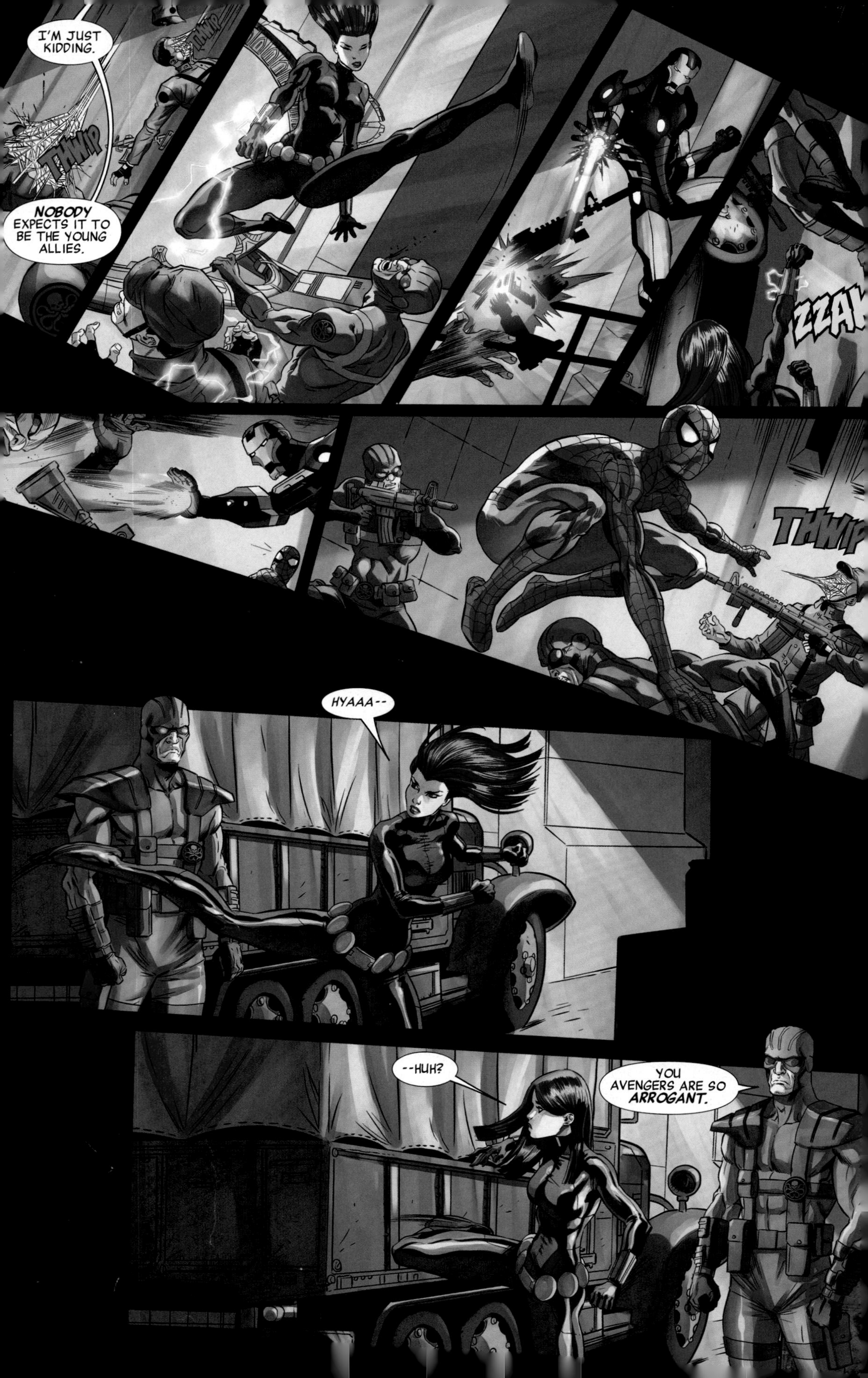
I'M JUST KIDDING.
THWIP
THWIP
NOBODY EXPECTS IT TO BE THE YOUNG ALLIES.
ZZAK
THWIP
HYAAA--
--HUH?
YOU AVENGERS ARE SO ARROGANT.

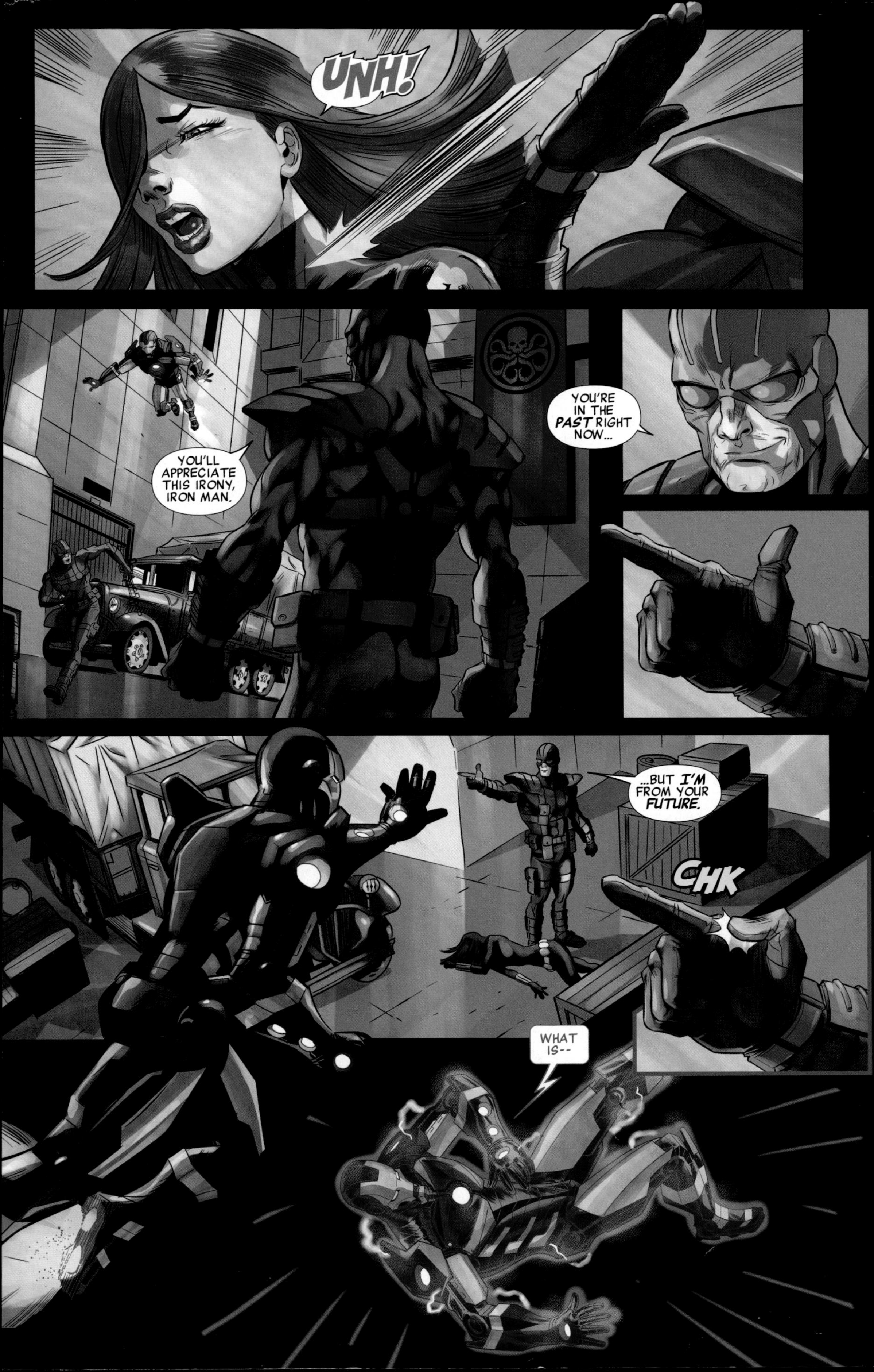
UNH!
YOU'LL APPRECIATE THIS IRONY, IRON MAN.
YOU'RE IN THE PAST RIGHT NOW...
...BUT I'M FROM YOUR FUTURE.
CHK
WHAT IS--

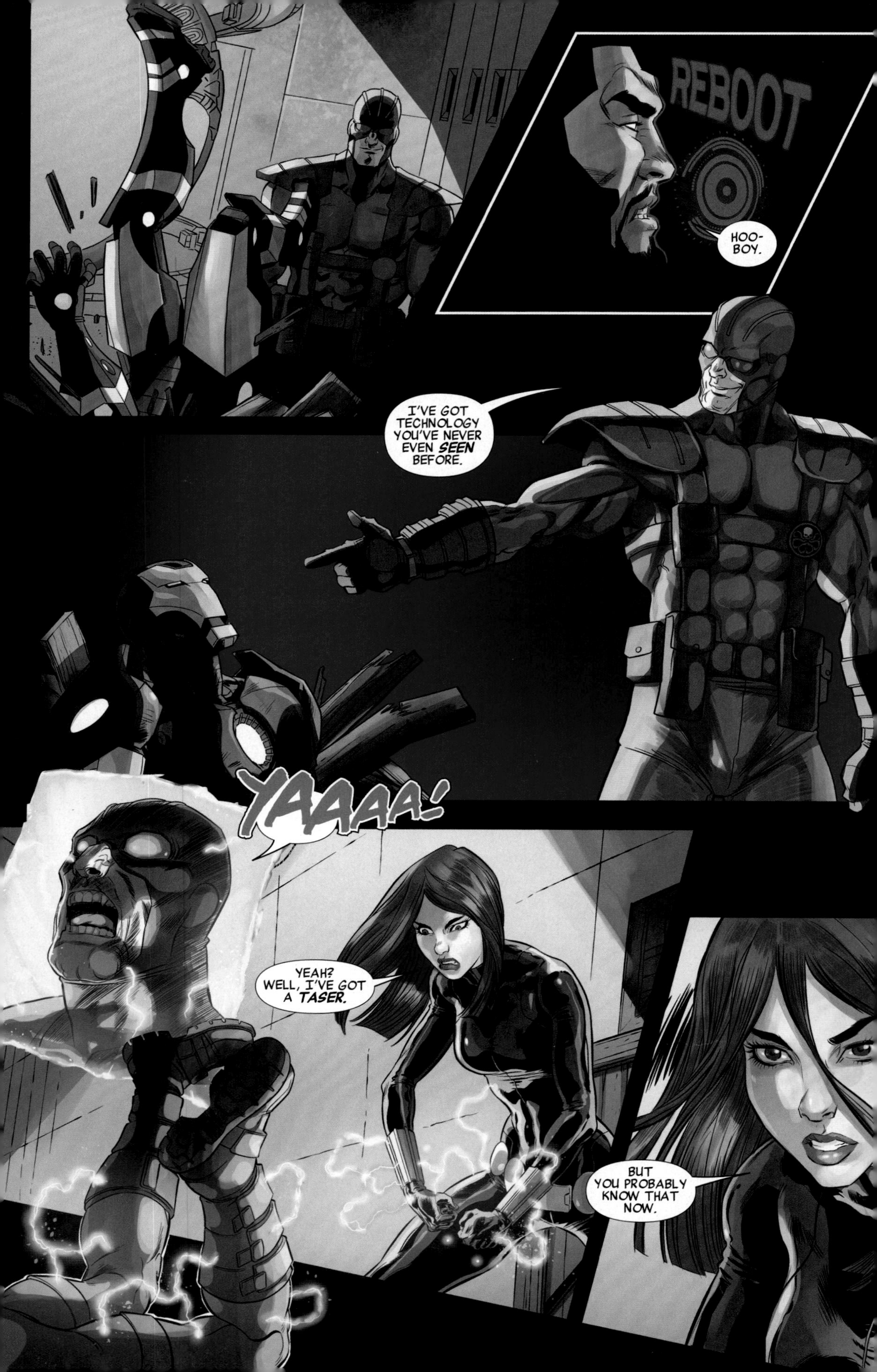
REBOOT
HOO-BOY.
I'VE GOT TECHNOLOGY YOU'VE NEVER EVEN SEEN BEFORE.
YAAAA!
YEAH? WELL, I'VE GOT A TASER.
BUT YOU PROBABLY KNOW THAT NOW.

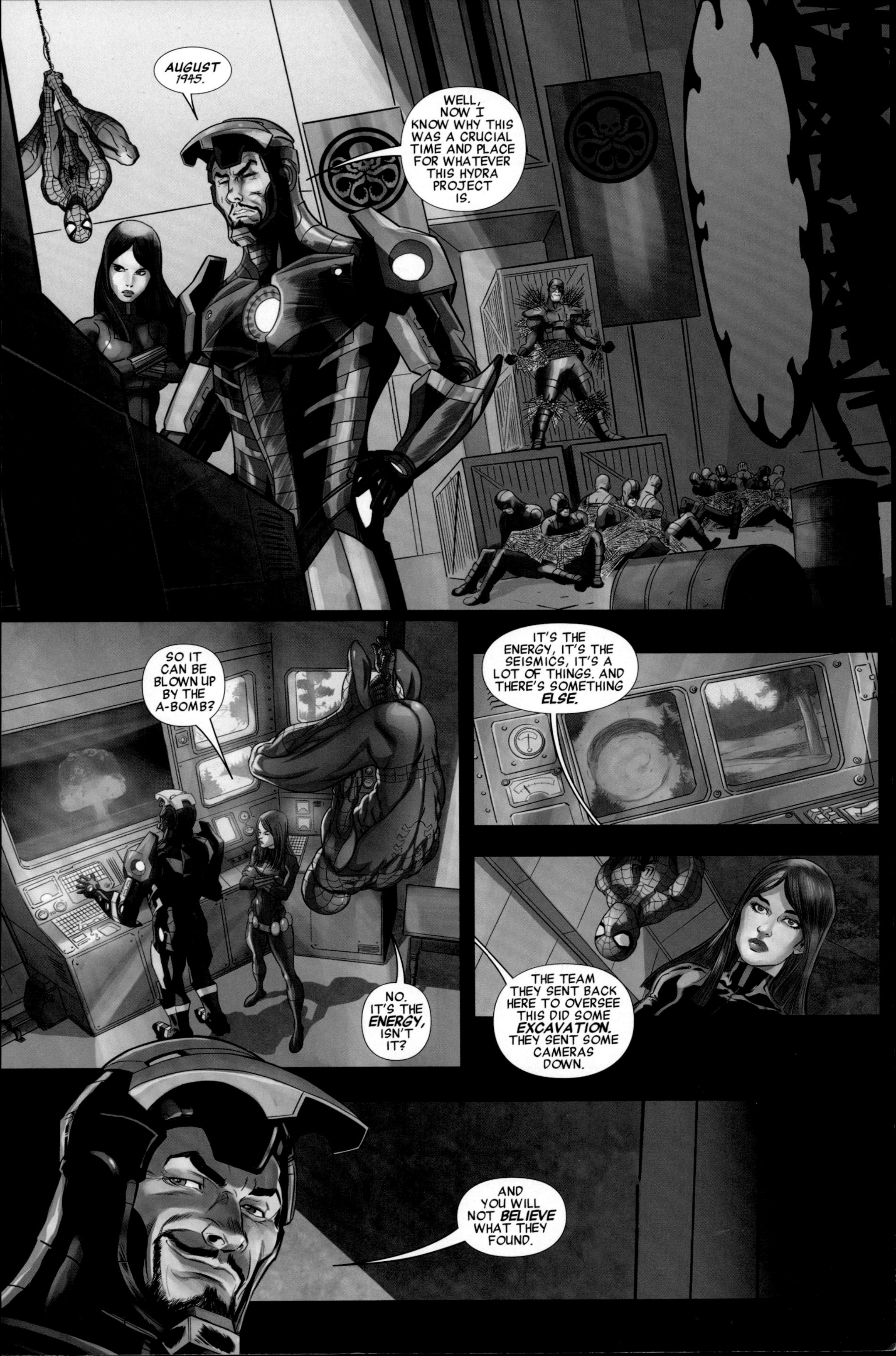
AUGUST 1945.
WELL, NOW I KNOW WHY THIS WAS A CRUCIAL TIME AND PLACE FOR WHATEVER THIS HYDRA PROJECT IS.
SO IT CAN BE BLOWN UP BY THE A-BOMB?
NO. IT'S THE ENERGY, ISN'T IT?
IT'S THE ENERGY, IT'S THE SEISMICS, IT'S A LOT OF THINGS. AND THERE'S SOMETHING ELSE.
THE TEAM THEY SENT BACK HERE TO OVERSEE THIS DID SOME EXCAVATION. THEY SENT SOME CAMERAS DOWN.
AND YOU WILL NOT BELIEVE WHAT THEY FOUND.

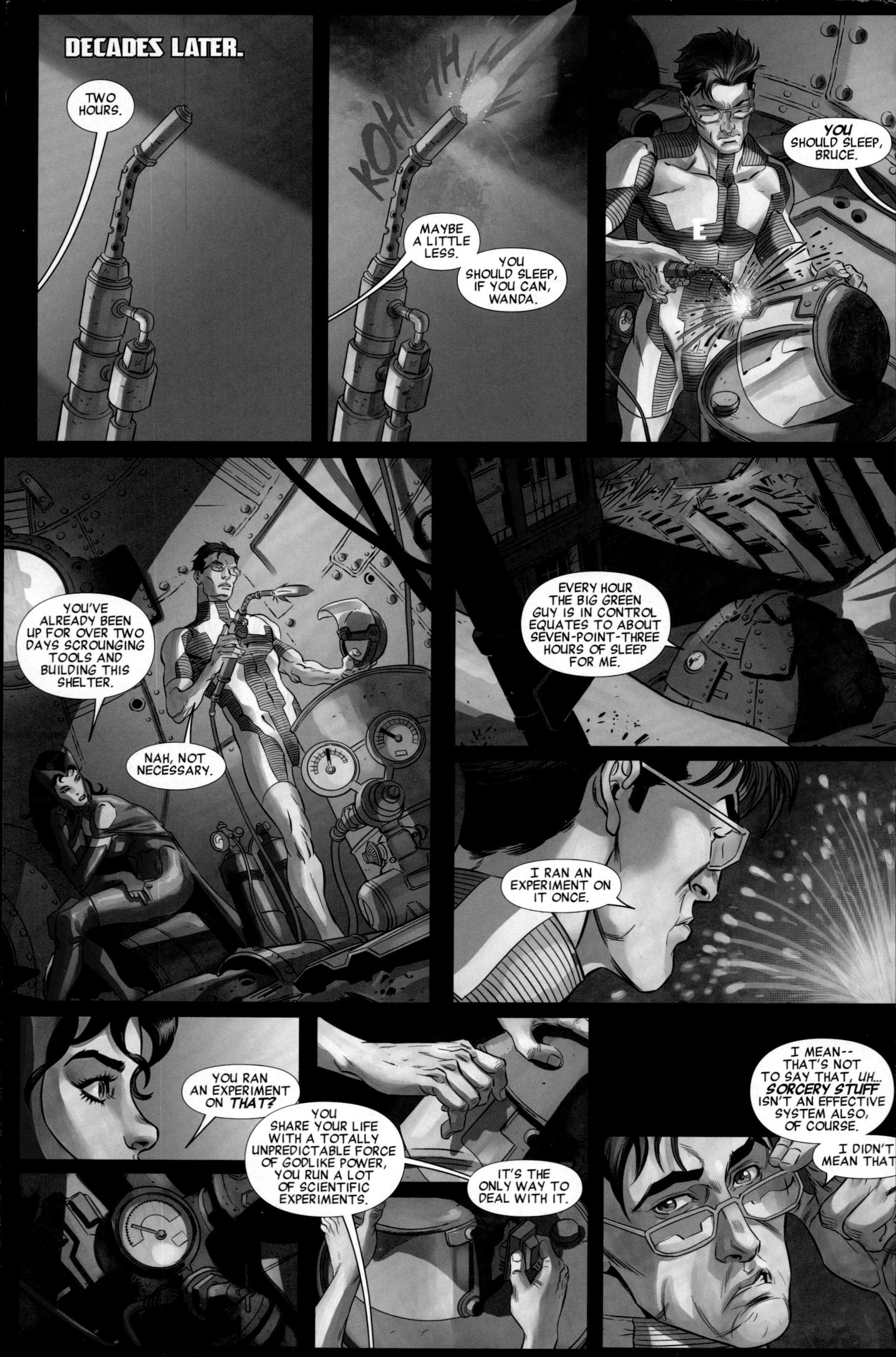
DECADES LATER.
TWO HOURS.
KOHHHH
MAYBE A LITTLE LESS.
YOU SHOULD SLEEP, IF YOU CAN, WANDA.
YOU SHOULD SLEEP, BRUCE.
YOU'VE ALREADY BEEN UP FOR OVER TWO DAYS SCROUNGING TOOLS AND BUILDING THIS SHELTER.
NAH, NOT NECESSARY.
EVERY HOUR THE BIG GREEN GUY IS IN CONTROL EQUATES TO ABOUT SEVEN-POINT-THREE HOURS OF SLEEP FOR ME.
I RAN AN EXPERIMENT ON IT ONCE.
YOU RAN AN EXPERIMENT ON THAT?
YOU SHARE YOUR LIFE WITH A TOTALLY UNPREDICTABLE FORCE OF GODLIKE POWER, YOU RUN A LOT OF SCIENTIFIC EXPERIMENTS.
IT'S THE ONLY WAY TO DEAL WITH IT.
I MEAN-- THAT'S NOT TO SAY THAT, UH... SORCERY STUFF ISN'T AN EFFECTIVE SYSTEM ALSO, OF COURSE.
I DIDN'T MEAN THAT

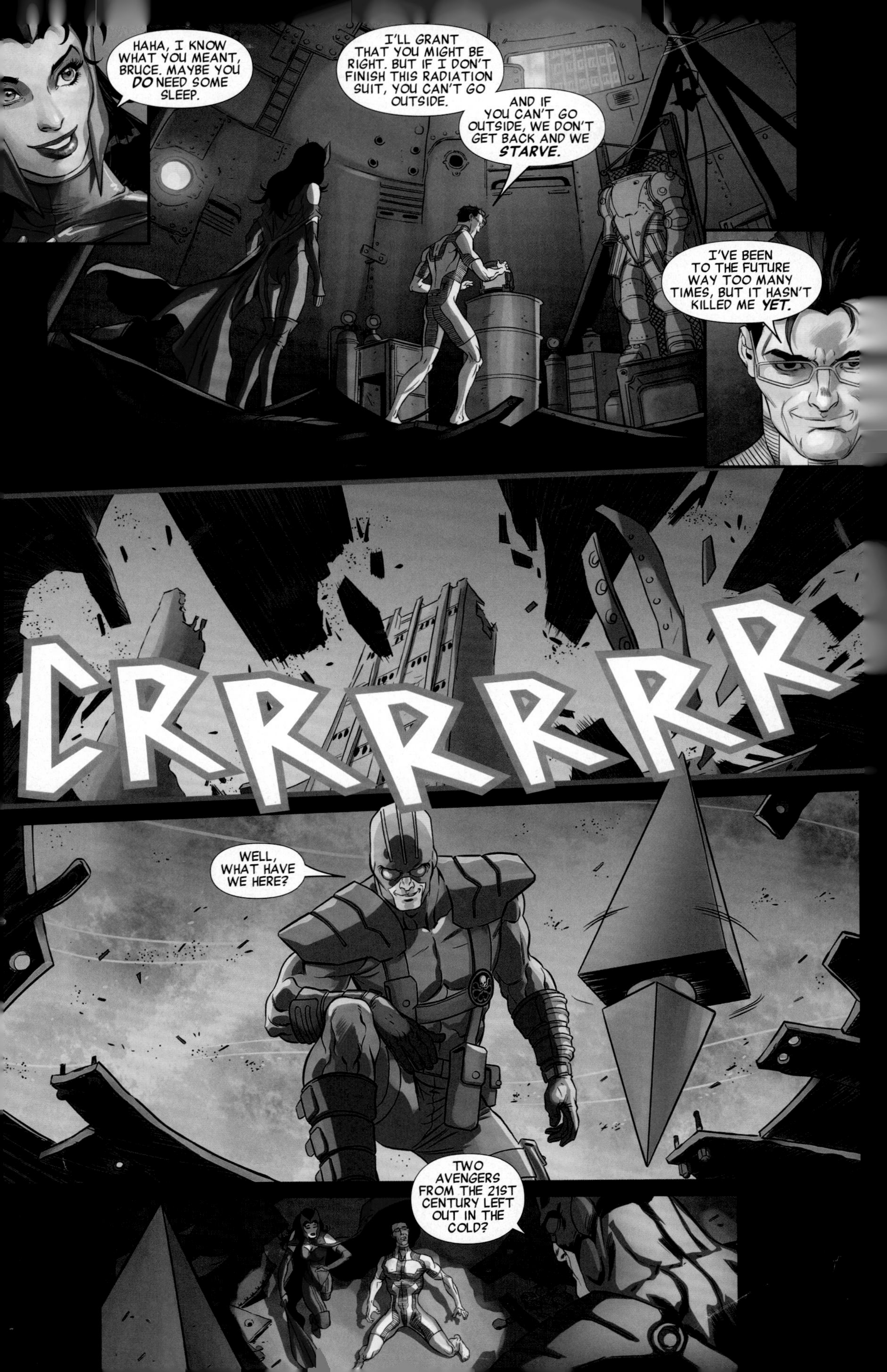
HAHA, I KNOW WHAT YOU MEANT, BRUCE. MAYBE YOU DO NEED SOME SLEEP.
I'LL GRANT THAT YOU MIGHT BE RIGHT. BUT IF I DON'T FINISH THIS RADIATION SUIT, YOU CAN'T GO OUTSIDE.
AND IF YOU CAN'T GO OUTSIDE, WE DON'T GET BACK AND WE STARVE.
I'VE BEEN TO THE FUTURE WAY TOO MANY TIMES, BUT IT HASN'T KILLED ME YET.
CRRRRR
WELL, WHAT HAVE WE HERE?
TWO AVENGERS FROM THE 21ST CENTURY LEFT OUT IN THE COLD?

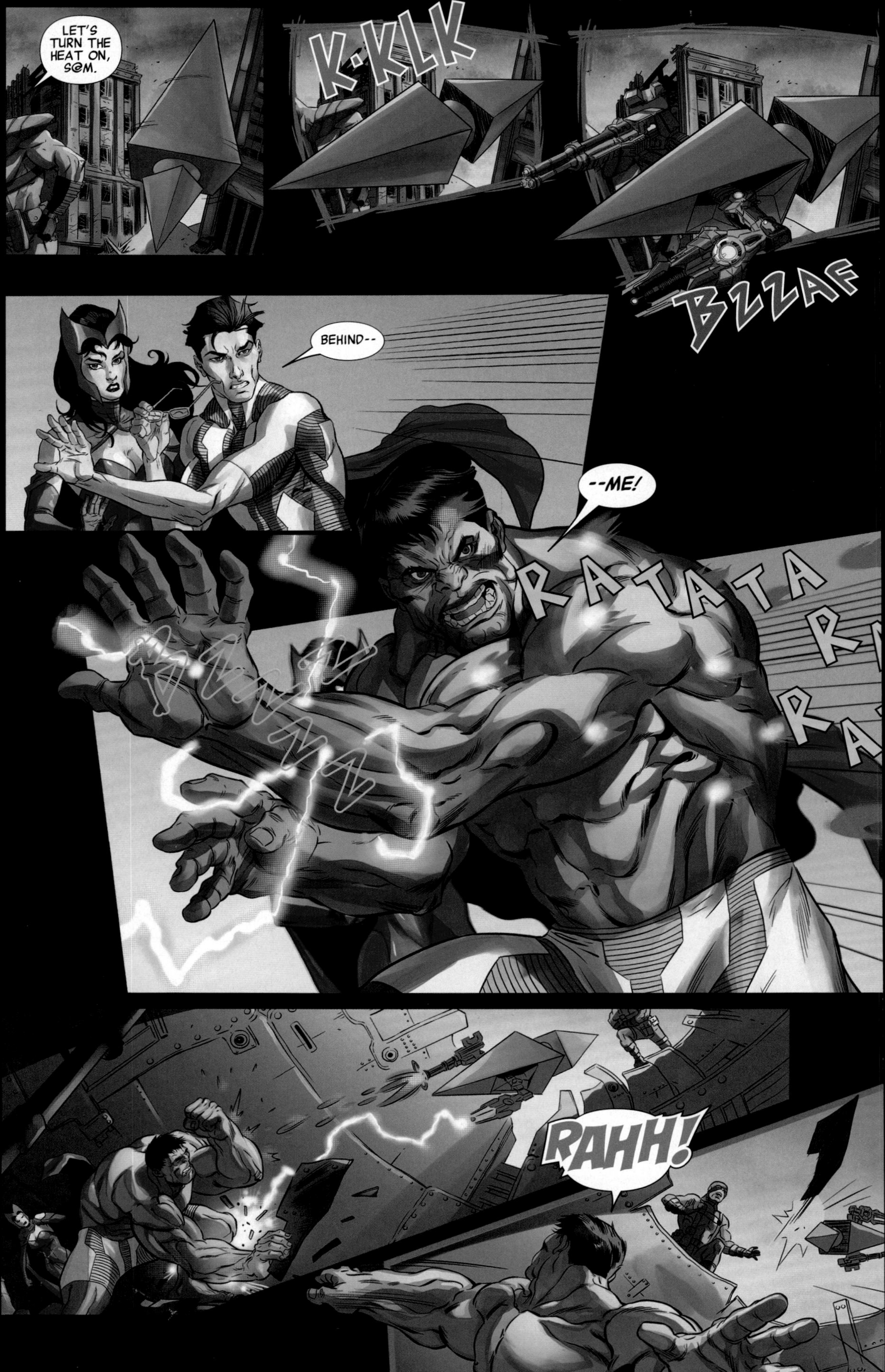

LET'S TURN THE HEAT ON, S@M.
K-KLK
BZZAF
BEHIND--
--ME!
RATATA
RAHH!

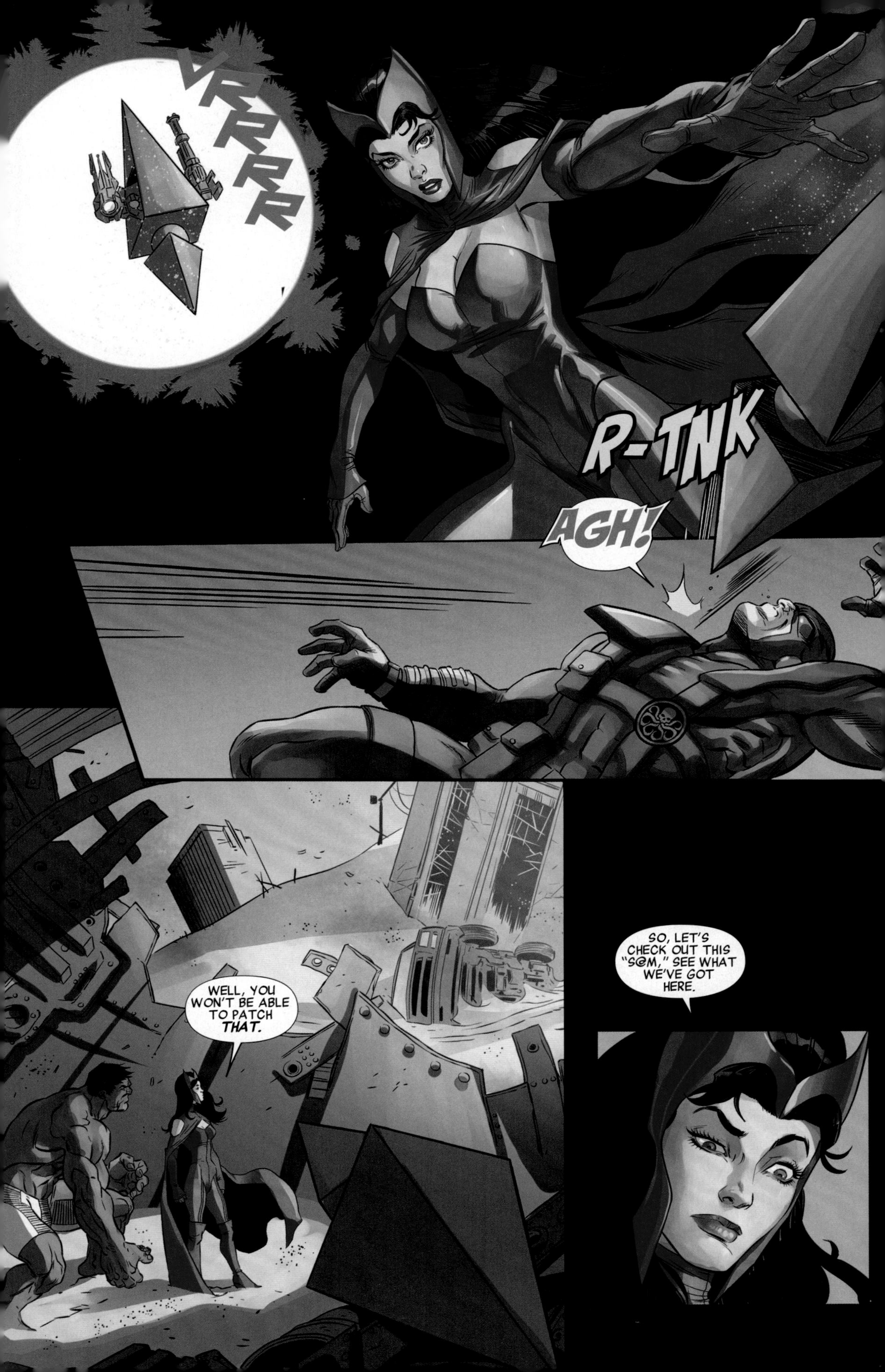
VRRRR
R-TNK
AGH!
WELL, YOU WON'T BE ABLE TO PATCH THAT.
SO, LET'S CHECK OUT THIS "S@M," SEE WHAT WE'VE GOT HERE.

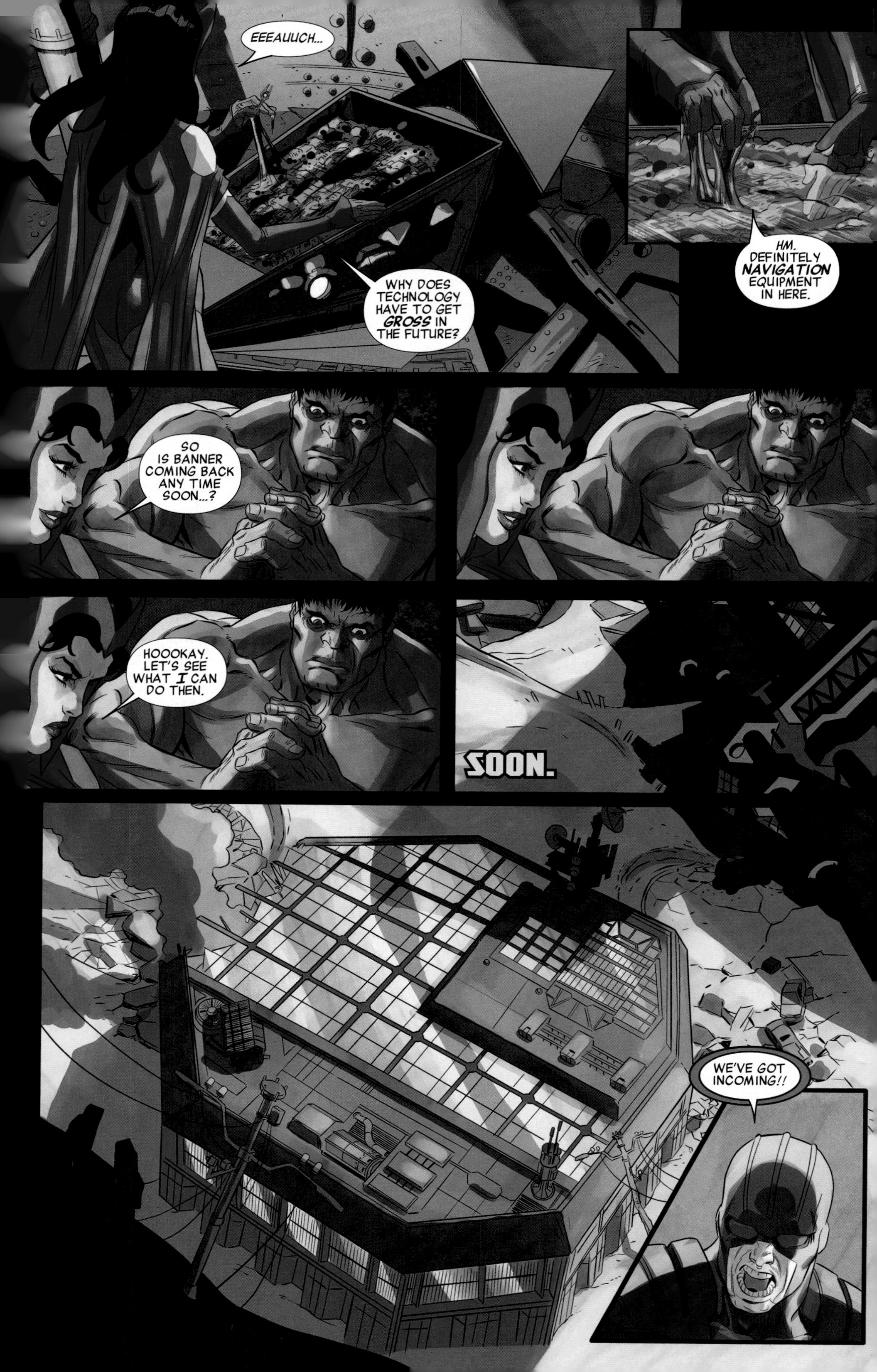
EEEAUUCH...
WHY DOES TECHNOLOGY HAVE TO GET GROSS IN THE FUTURE?
HM. DEFINITELY NAVIGATION EQUIPMENT IN HERE.
SO IS BANNER COMING BACK ANY TIME SOON...?
HOOOKAY. LET'S SEE WHAT I CAN DO THEN.
SOON.
WE'VE GOT INCOMING!!

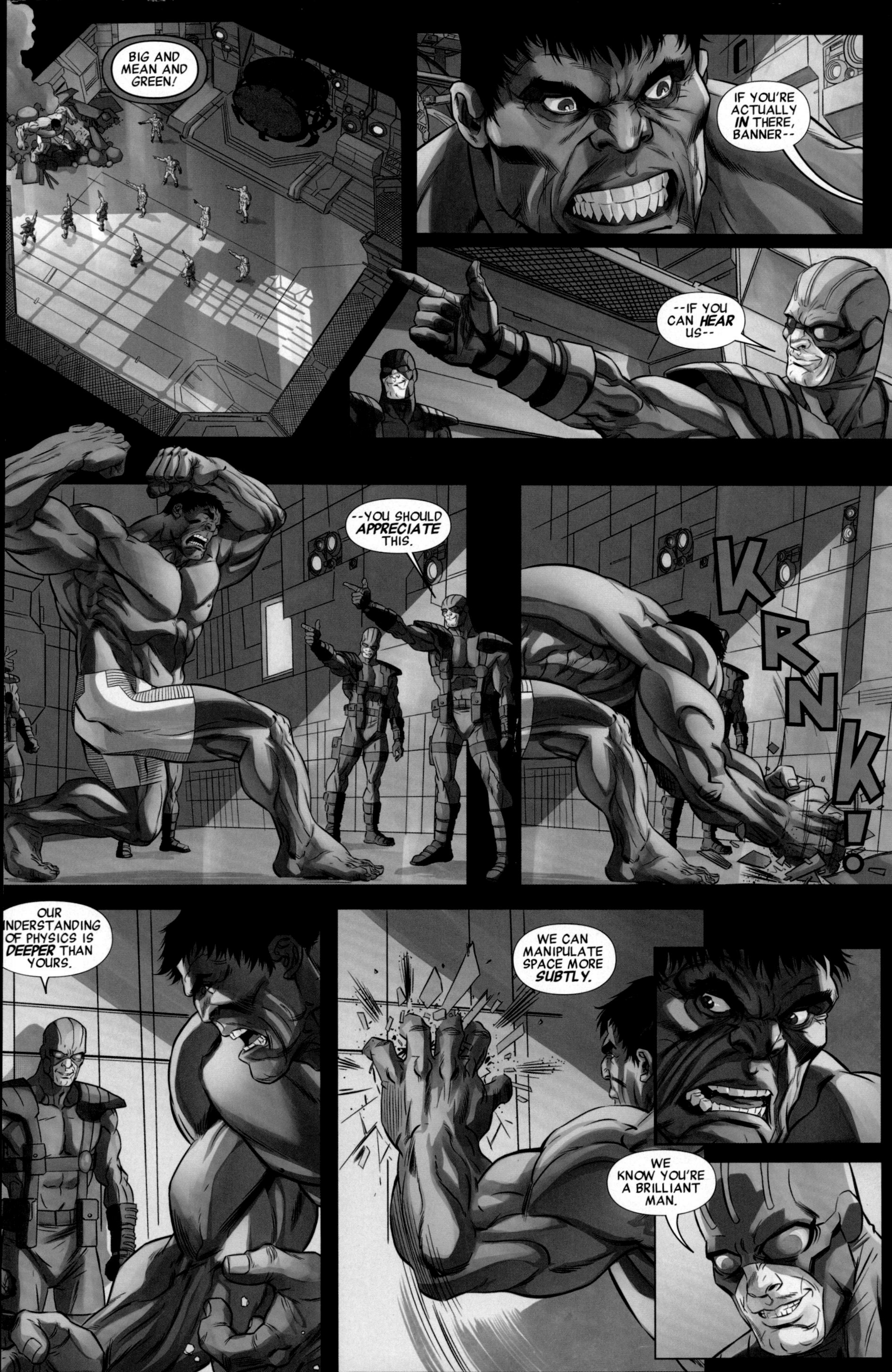
BIG AND MEAN AND GREEN!
IF YOU'RE ACTUALLY IN THERE, BANNER--
--IF YOU CAN HEAR US--
--YOU SHOULD APPRECIATE THIS.
KRNK!
OUR UNDERSTANDING OF PHYSICS IS DEEPER THAN YOURS.
WE CAN MANIPULATE SPACE MORE SUBTLY.
WE KNOW YOU'RE A BRILLIANT MAN.

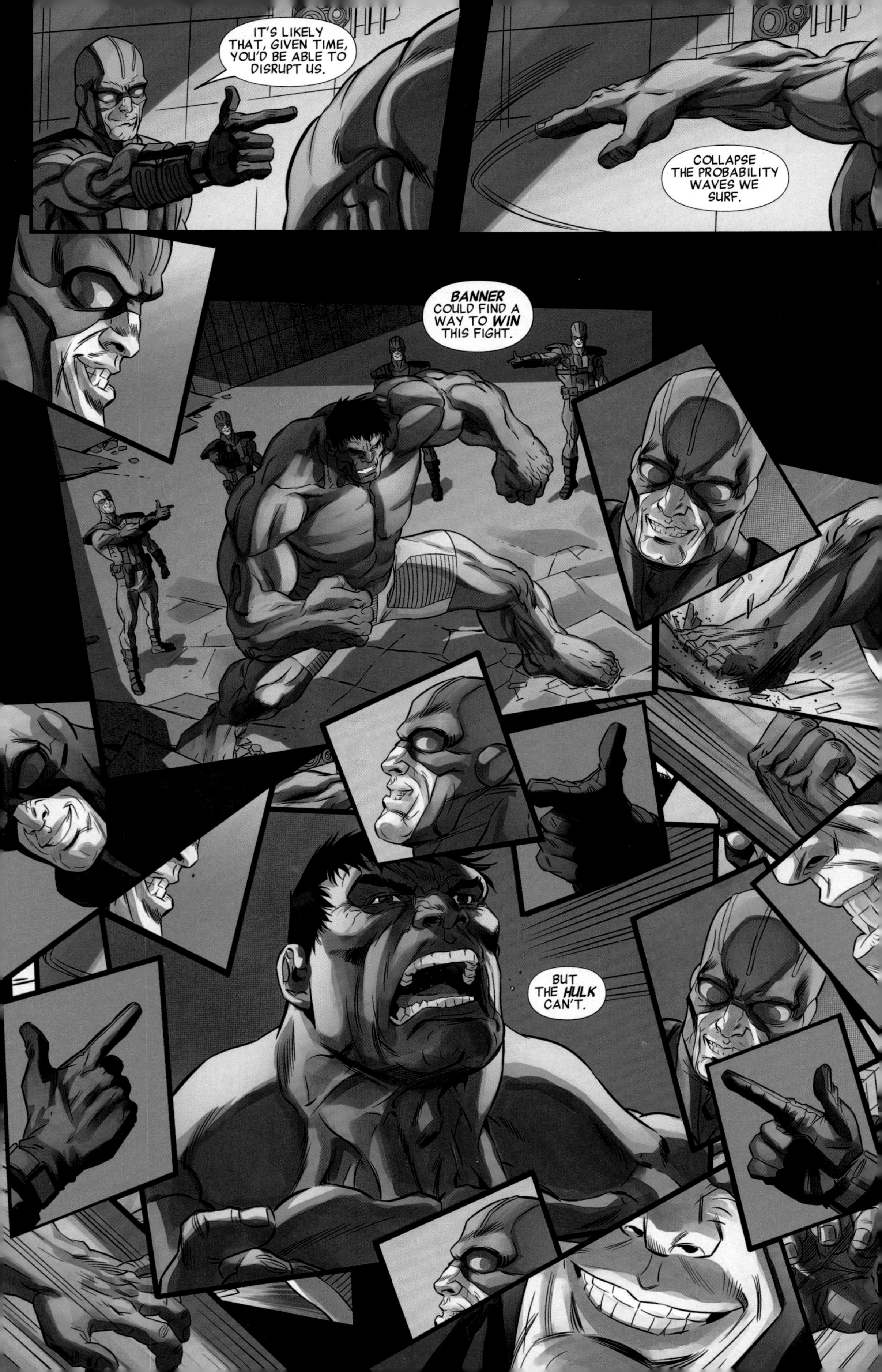
IT'S LIKELY THAT, GIVEN TIME, YOU'D BE ABLE TO DISRUPT US.
COLLAPSE THE PROBABILITY WAVES WE SURF.
BANNER COULD FIND A WAY TO WIN THIS FIGHT.
BUT THE HULK CAN'T.

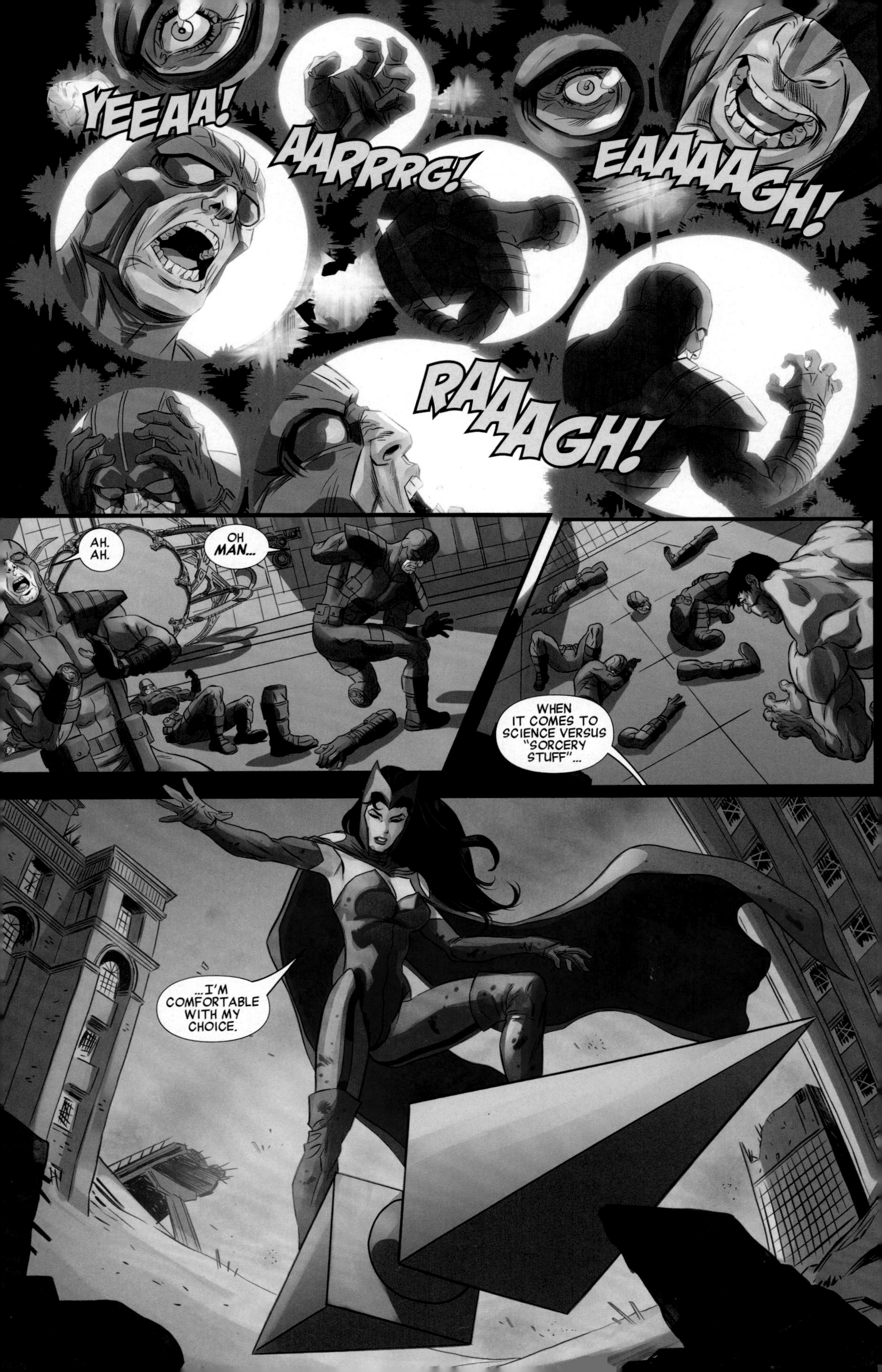
YEEAA!
AARRRG!
EAAAAAGH!
RAAAAGH!
AH. AH.
OH MAN...
WHEN IT COMES TO SCIENCE VERSUS "SORCERY STUFF"...
...I'M COMFORTABLE WITH MY CHOICE.

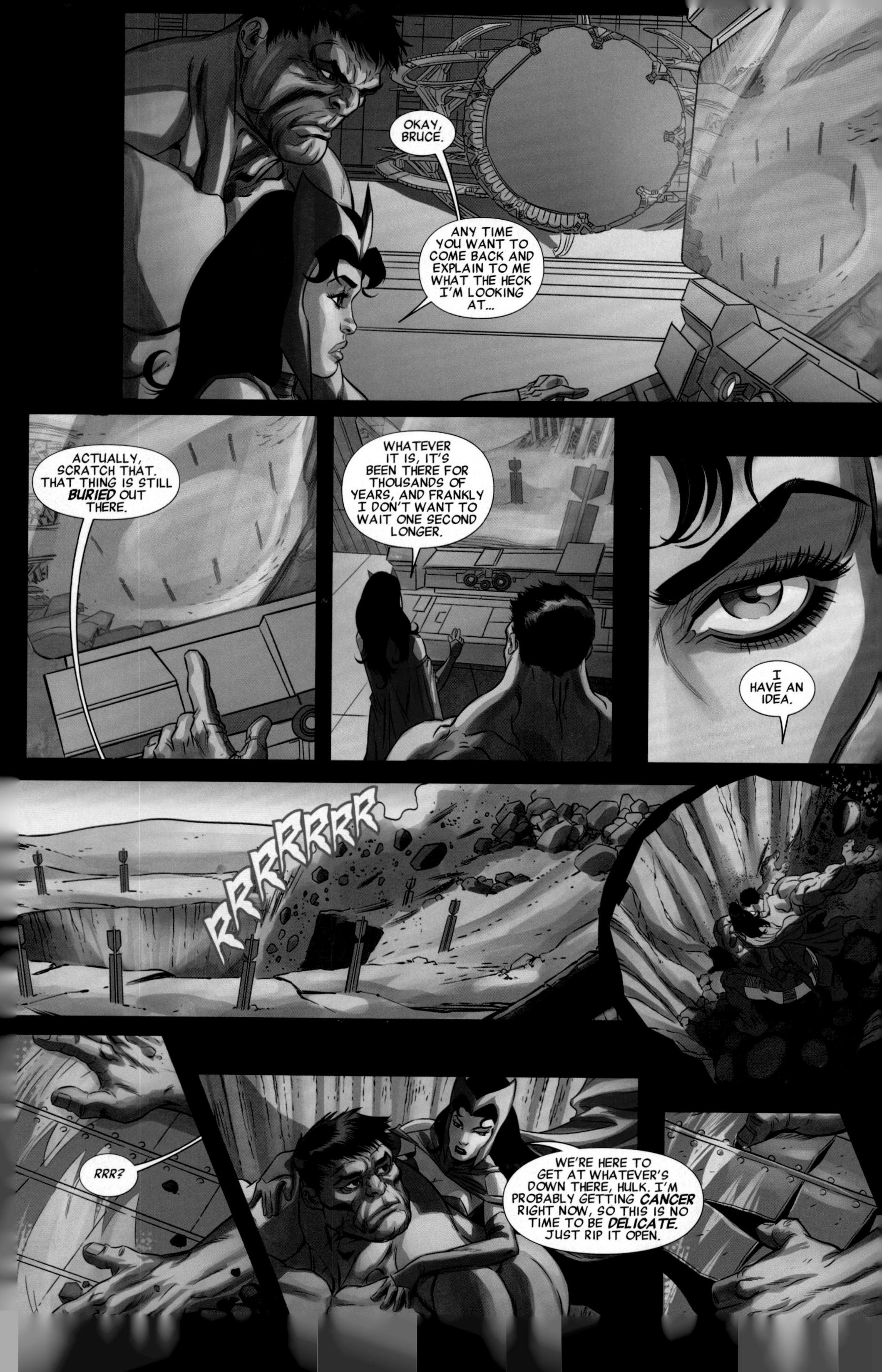
OKAY, BRUCE.
ANY TIME YOU WANT TO COME BACK AND EXPLAIN TO ME WHAT THE HECK I'M LOOKING AT...
ACTUALLY, SCRATCH THAT. THAT THING IS STILL *BURIED* OUT THERE.
WHATEVER IT IS, IT'S BEEN THERE FOR THOUSANDS OF YEARS, AND FRANKLY I DON'T WANT TO WAIT ONE SECOND LONGER.
I HAVE AN IDEA.
RRRRRRRR
RRR?
WE'RE HERE TO GET AT WHATEVER'S DOWN THERE, HULK. I'M PROBABLY GETTING *CANCER* RIGHT NOW, SO THIS IS NO TIME TO BE *DELICATE*. JUST RIP IT OPEN.

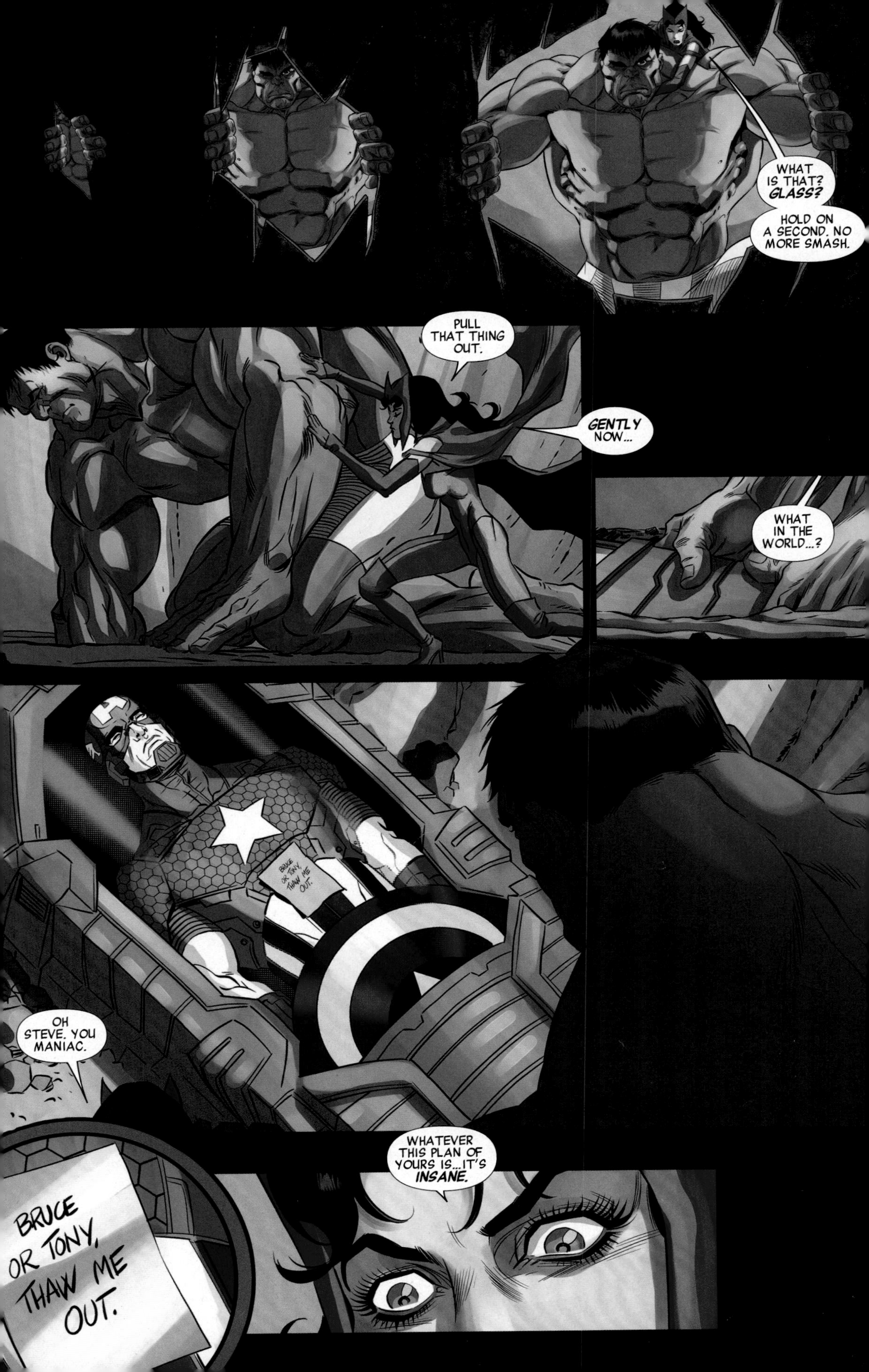

WHAT IS THAT? GLASS?
HOLD ON A SECOND. NO MORE SMASH.
PULL THAT THING OUT.
GENTLY NOW...
WHAT IN THE WORLD...?
BRUCE OR TONY, THAW ME OUT.
OH STEVE. YOU MANIAC.
WHATEVER THIS PLAN OF YOURS IS...IT'S INSANE.
BRUCE OR TONY, THAW ME OUT.

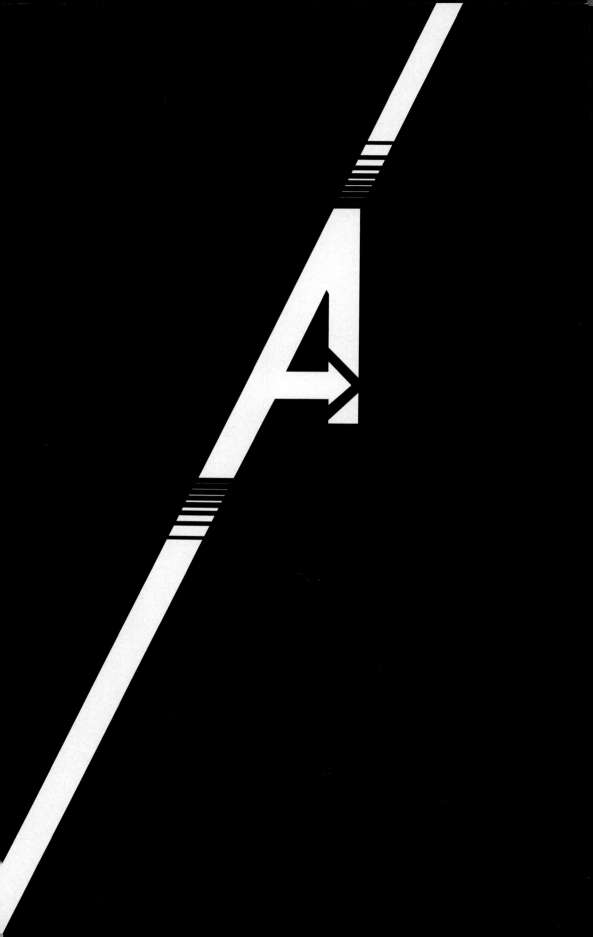

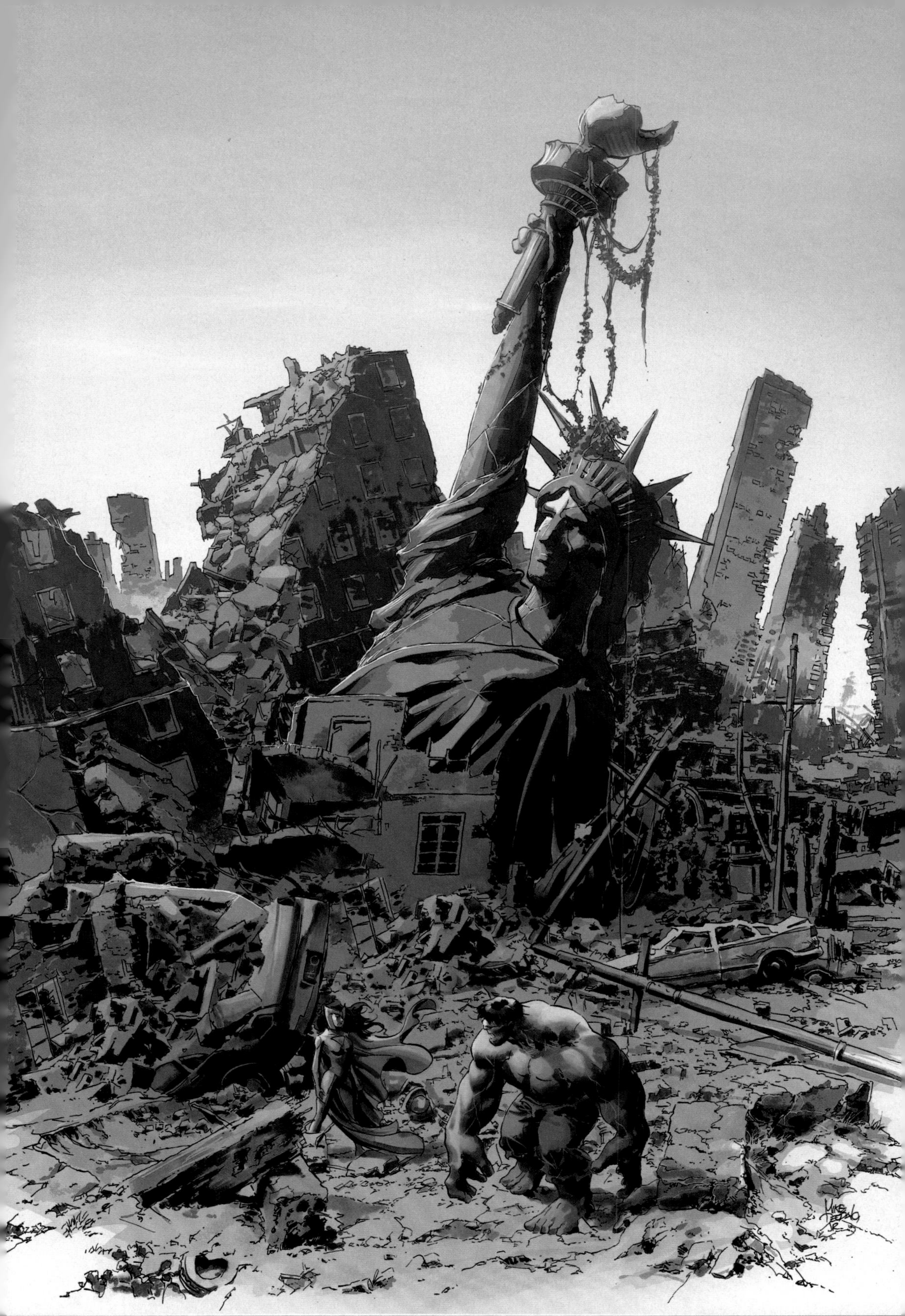

CHAPTER 4

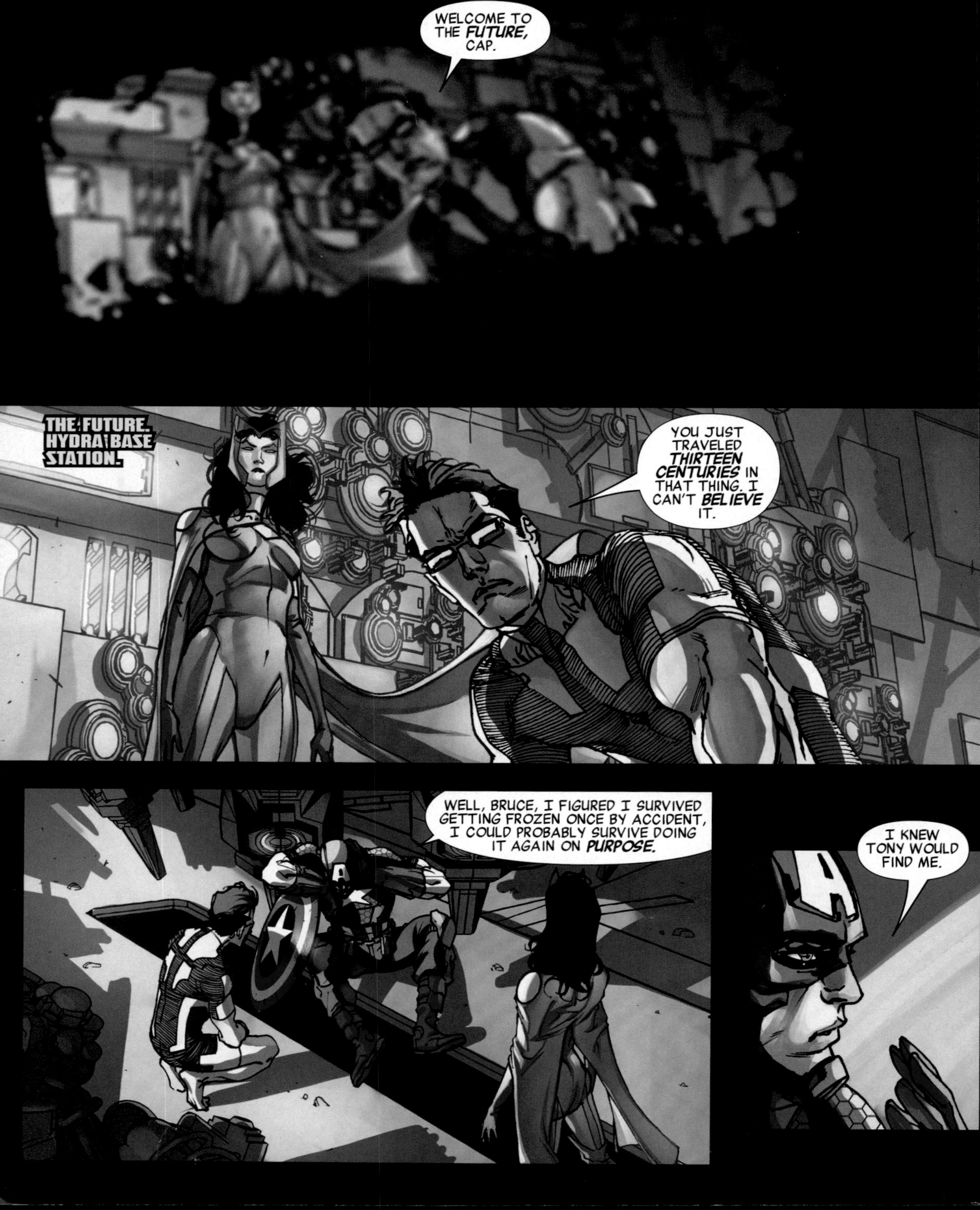
WELCOME TO THE FUTURE, CAP.
THE FUTURE. HYDRA BASE STATION.
YOU JUST TRAVELED THIRTEEN CENTURIES IN THAT THING. I CAN'T BELIEVE IT.
WELL, BRUCE, I FIGURED I SURVIVED GETTING FROZEN ONCE BY ACCIDENT, I COULD PROBABLY SURVIVE DOING IT AGAIN ON PURPOSE.
I KNEW TONY WOULD FIND ME.

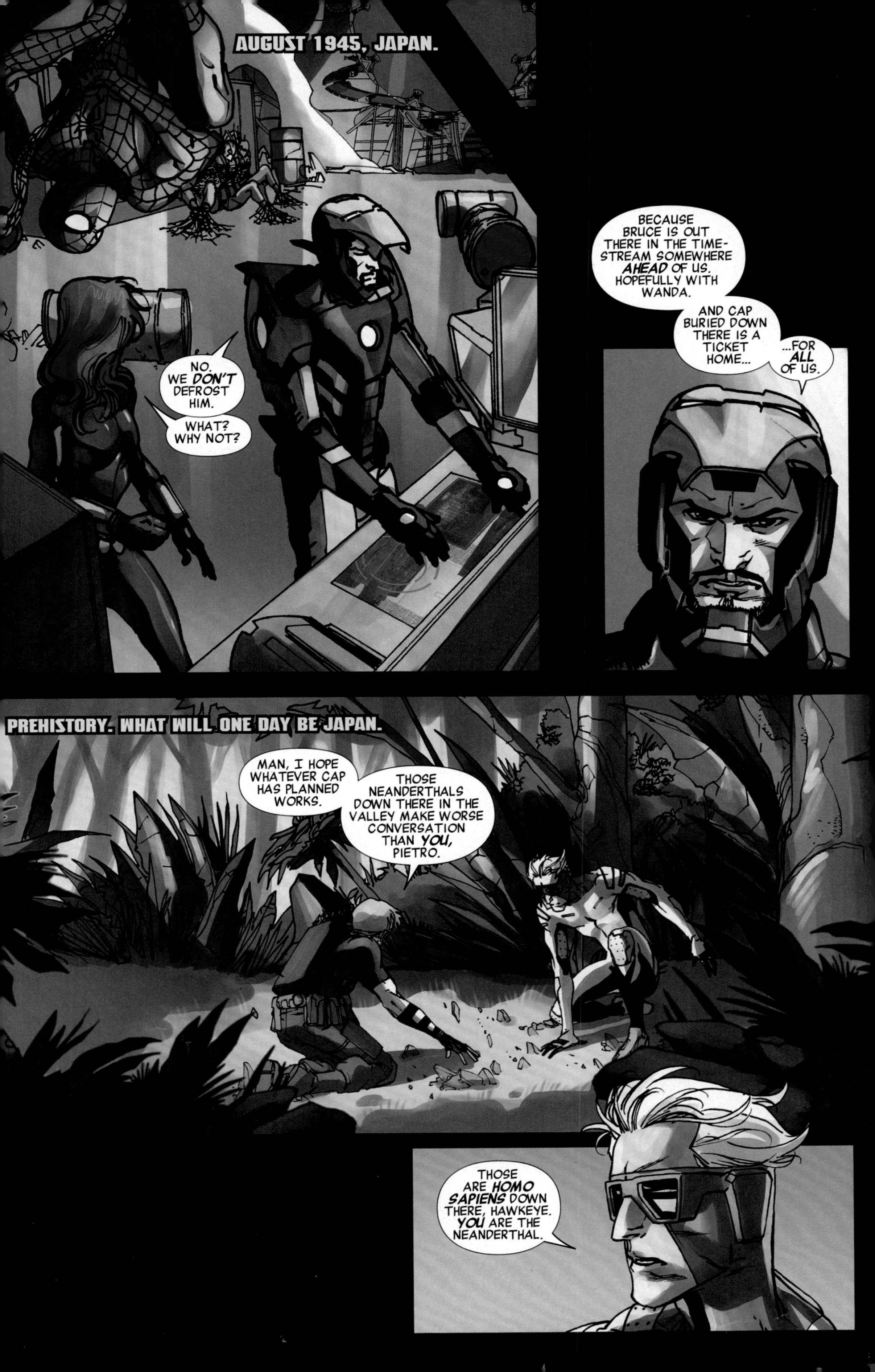
AUGUST 1945, JAPAN.
NO. WE DON'T DEFROST HIM.
WHAT? WHY NOT?
BECAUSE BRUCE IS OUT THERE IN THE TIME-STREAM SOMEWHERE AHEAD OF US. HOPEFULLY WITH WANDA.
AND CAP BURIED DOWN THERE IS A TICKET HOME...
...FOR ALL OF US.
PREHISTORY. WHAT WILL ONE DAY BE JAPAN.
MAN, I HOPE WHATEVER CAP HAS PLANNED WORKS.
THOSE NEANDERTHALS DOWN THERE IN THE VALLEY MAKE WORSE CONVERSATION THAN YOU, PIETRO.
THOSE ARE HOMO SAPIENS DOWN THERE, HAWKEYE. YOU ARE THE NEANDERTHAL.

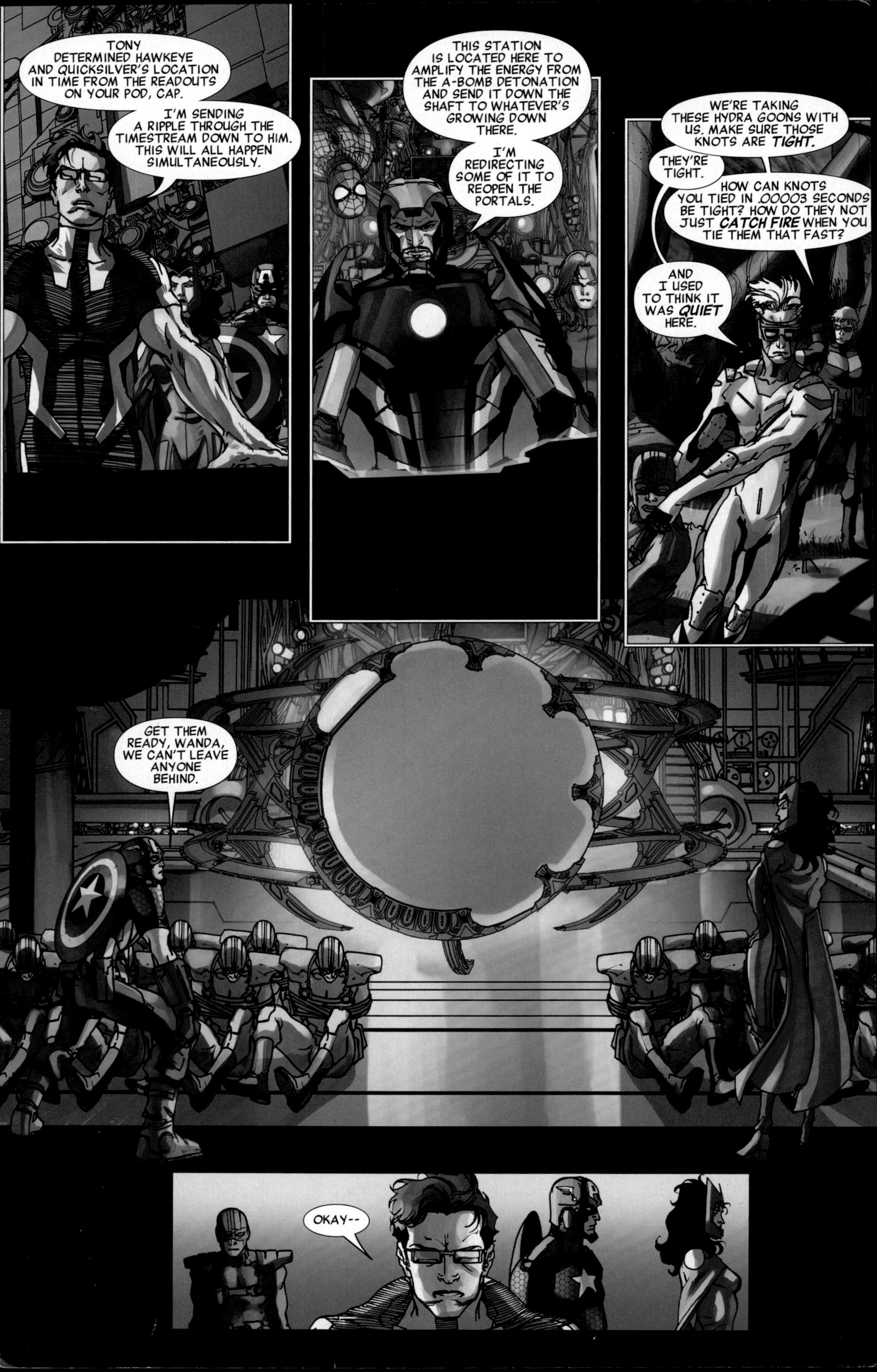
TONY DETERMINED HAWKEYE AND QUICKSILVER'S LOCATION IN TIME FROM THE READOUTS ON YOUR POD, CAP.
I'M SENDING A RIPPLE THROUGH THE TIMESTREAM DOWN TO HIM. THIS WILL ALL HAPPEN SIMULTANEOUSLY.
THIS STATION IS LOCATED HERE TO AMPLIFY THE ENERGY FROM THE A-BOMB DETONATION AND SEND IT DOWN THE SHAFT TO WHATEVER'S GROWING DOWN THERE.
I'M REDIRECTING SOME OF IT TO REOPEN THE PORTALS.
WE'RE TAKING THESE HYDRA GOONS WITH US. MAKE SURE THOSE KNOTS ARE TIGHT.
THEY'RE TIGHT.
HOW CAN KNOTS YOU TIED IN .00003 SECONDS BE TIGHT? HOW DO THEY NOT JUST CATCH FIRE WHEN YOU TIE THEM THAT FAST?
AND I USED TO THINK IT WAS QUIET HERE.
GET THEM READY, WANDA, WE CAN'T LEAVE ANYONE BEHIND.
OKAY--

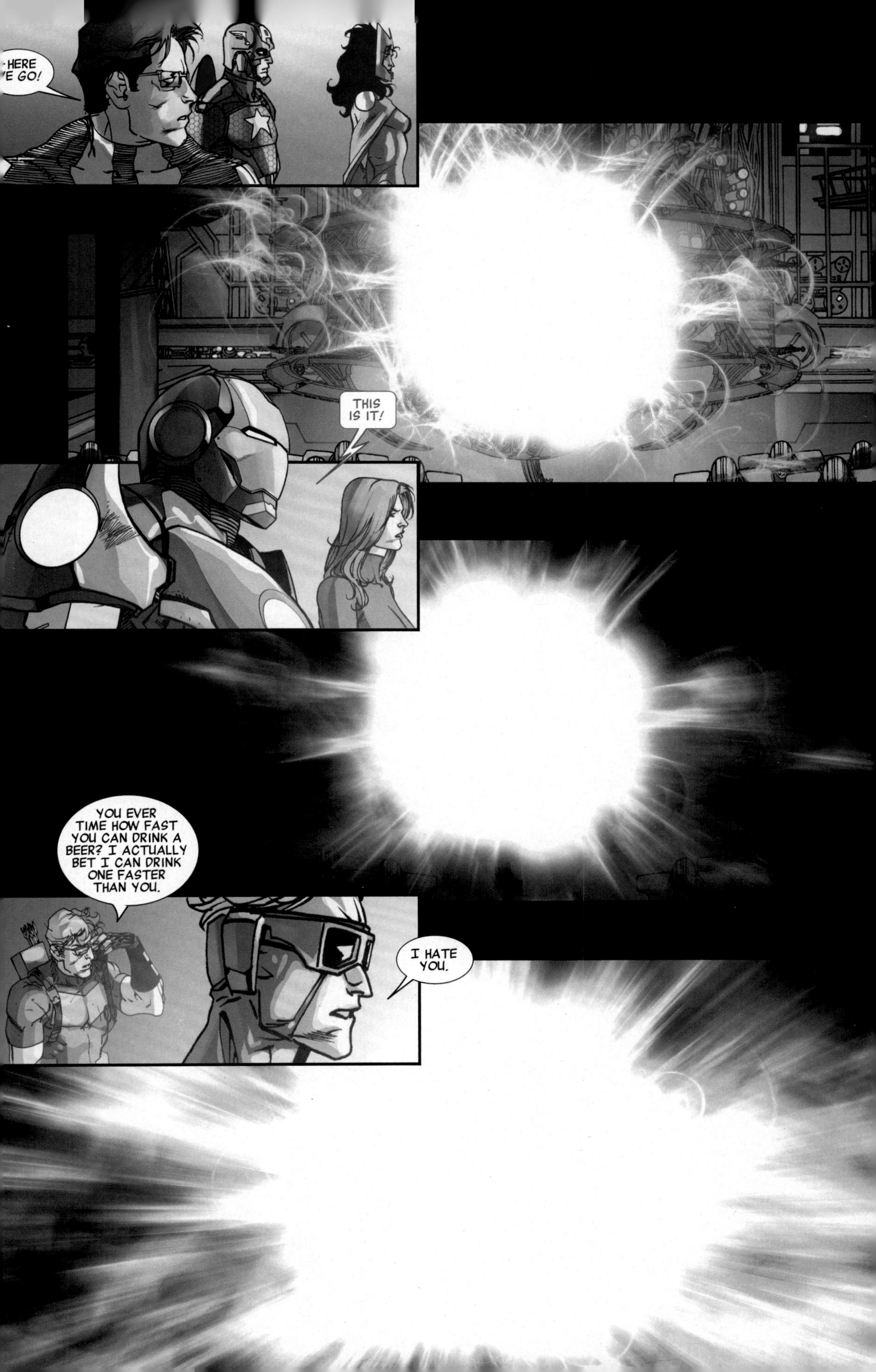
HERE WE GO!
THIS IS IT!
YOU EVER TIME HOW FAST YOU CAN DRINK A BEER? I ACTUALLY BET I CAN DRINK ONE FASTER THAN YOU.
I HATE YOU.

AVENGERS MILLENNIUM
CHAPTER FOUR

BLACK WIDOW | CAPTAIN AMERICA | HAWKEYE | HULK | IRON MAN | QUICKSILVER | SCARLET WITCH | SPIDER-MAN

WANDA MAXIMOFF, THE SCARLET WITCH, SENSED A DISTURBANCE DEEP IN THE EARTH, DIRECTLY BELOW A HYDRA BASE IN JAPAN. WHEN THE AVENGERS WENT TO INVESTIGATE, THEY FOUND A TIME PORTAL--SEEMINGLY UNUSED--TO CHANGE THE TIMESTREAM. THE TEAM ENTERED THE TIME PORTAL, HOPING TO FIND AND STOP HYDRA, BUT THEY ENDED UP SCATTERED THROUGH TIME, TRAPPED IN PREHISTORY, WORLD WAR II-ERA JAPAN, AND THE DISTANT FUTURE. WHEN THE SCARLET WITCH AND THE HULK ATTEMPTED TO DIG UP WHAT HYDRA BURIED THOUSANDS OF YEARS IN THE PAST, THEY FOUND SOMETHING UNEXPECTED: THE CRYOGENICALLY FROZEN FORM OF CAPTAIN AMERICA!

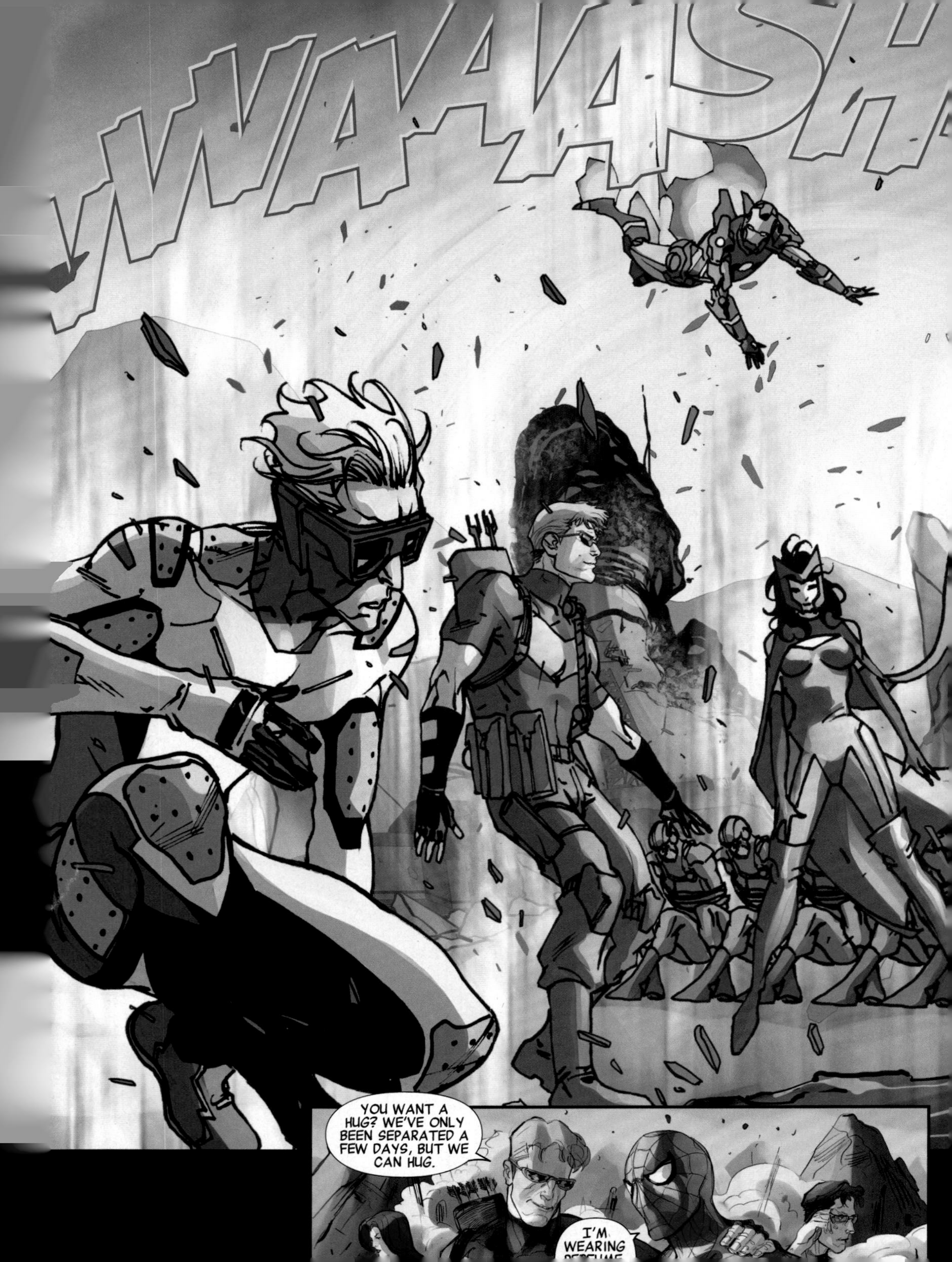

SHWAAASH
YOU WANT A HUG? WE'VE ONLY BEEN SEPARATED A FEW DAYS, BUT WE CAN HUG.
I'M WEARING

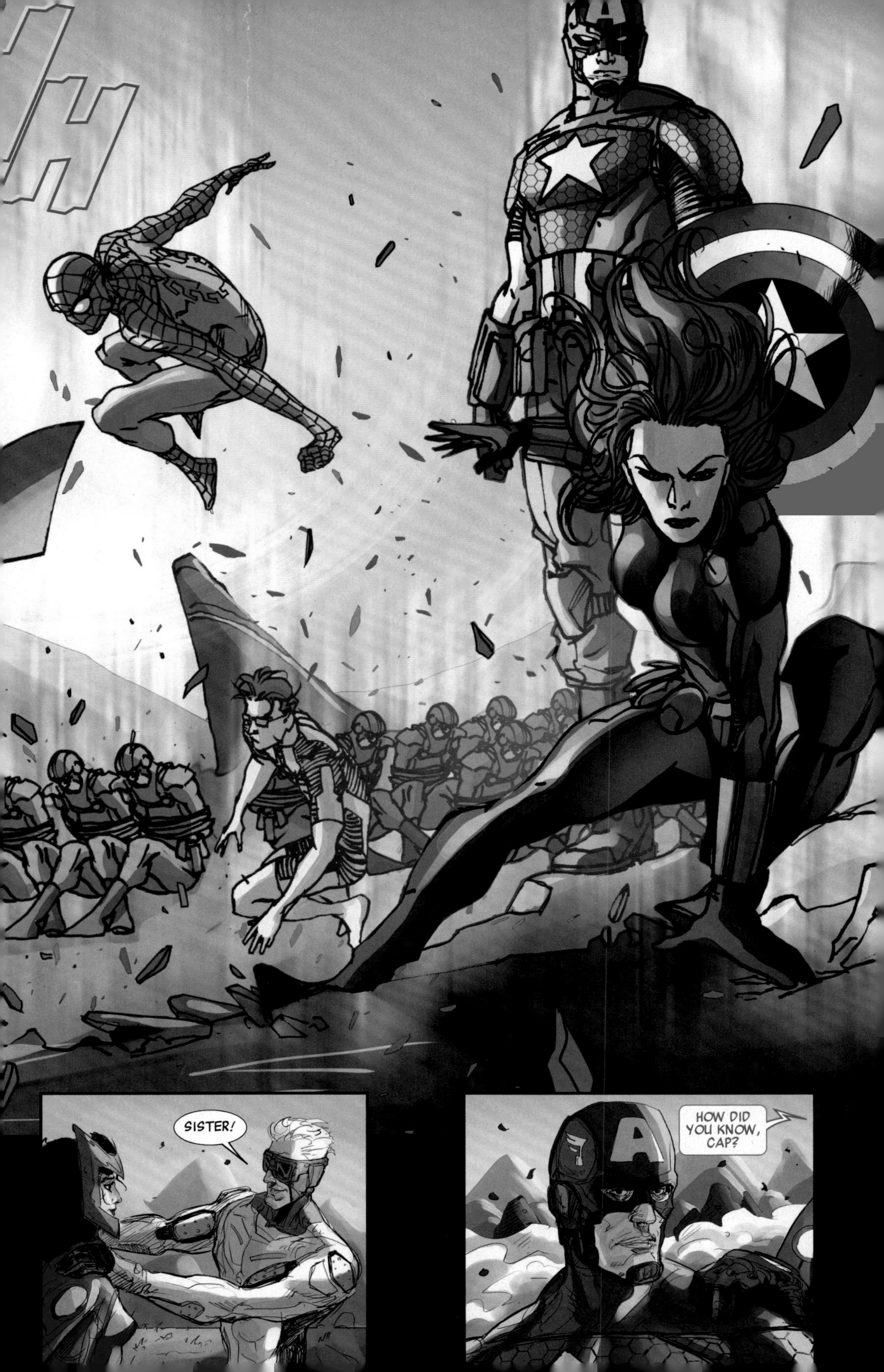
SISTER!
HOW DID YOU KNOW, CAP?

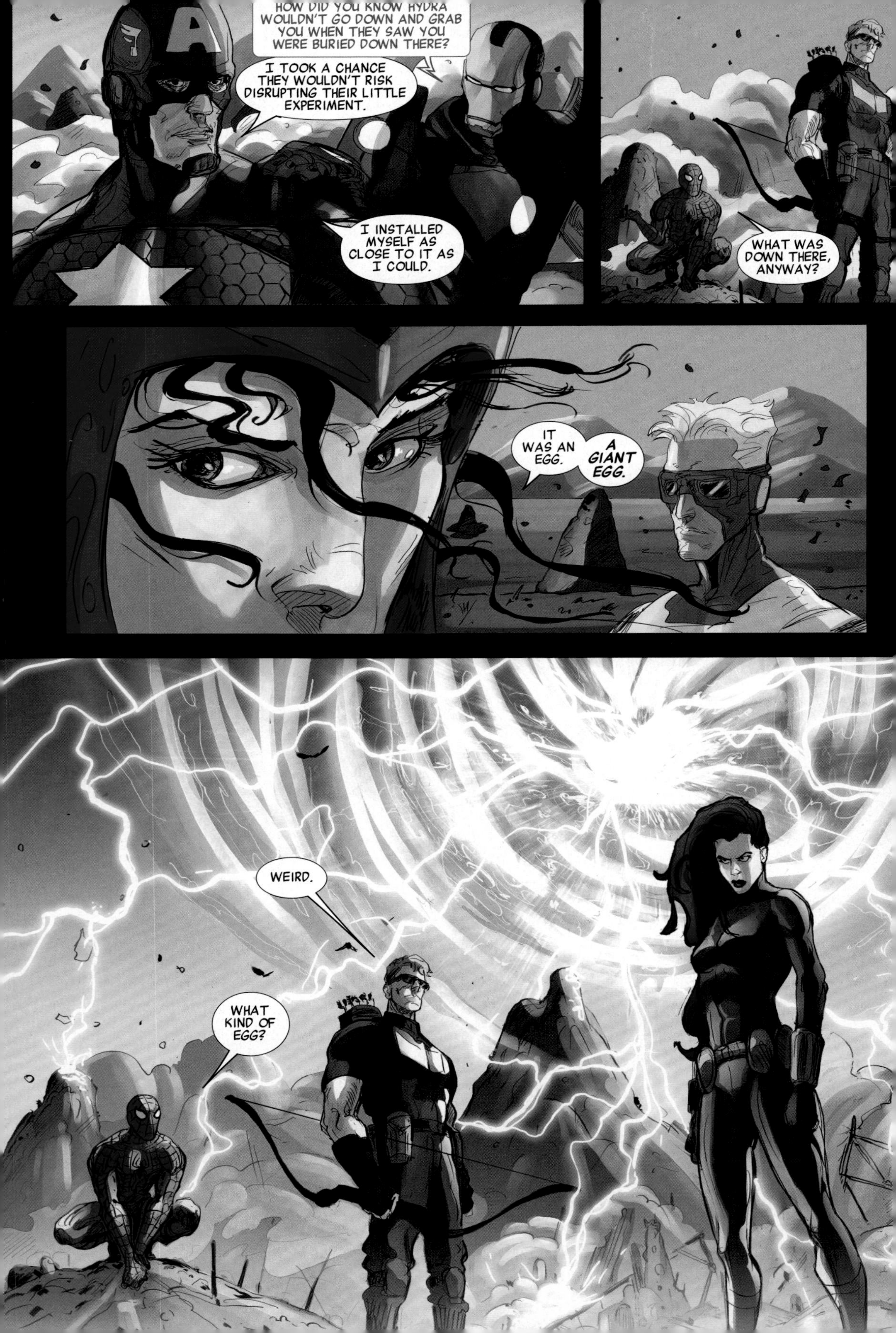
HOW DID YOU KNOW HYDRA WOULDN'T GO DOWN AND GRAB YOU WHEN THEY SAW YOU WERE BURIED DOWN THERE?
I TOOK A CHANCE THEY WOULDN'T RISK DISRUPTING THEIR LITTLE EXPERIMENT.
I INSTALLED MYSELF AS CLOSE TO IT AS I COULD.
WHAT WAS DOWN THERE, ANYWAY?
IT WAS AN EGG.
A GIANT EGG.
WEIRD.
WHAT KIND OF EGG?

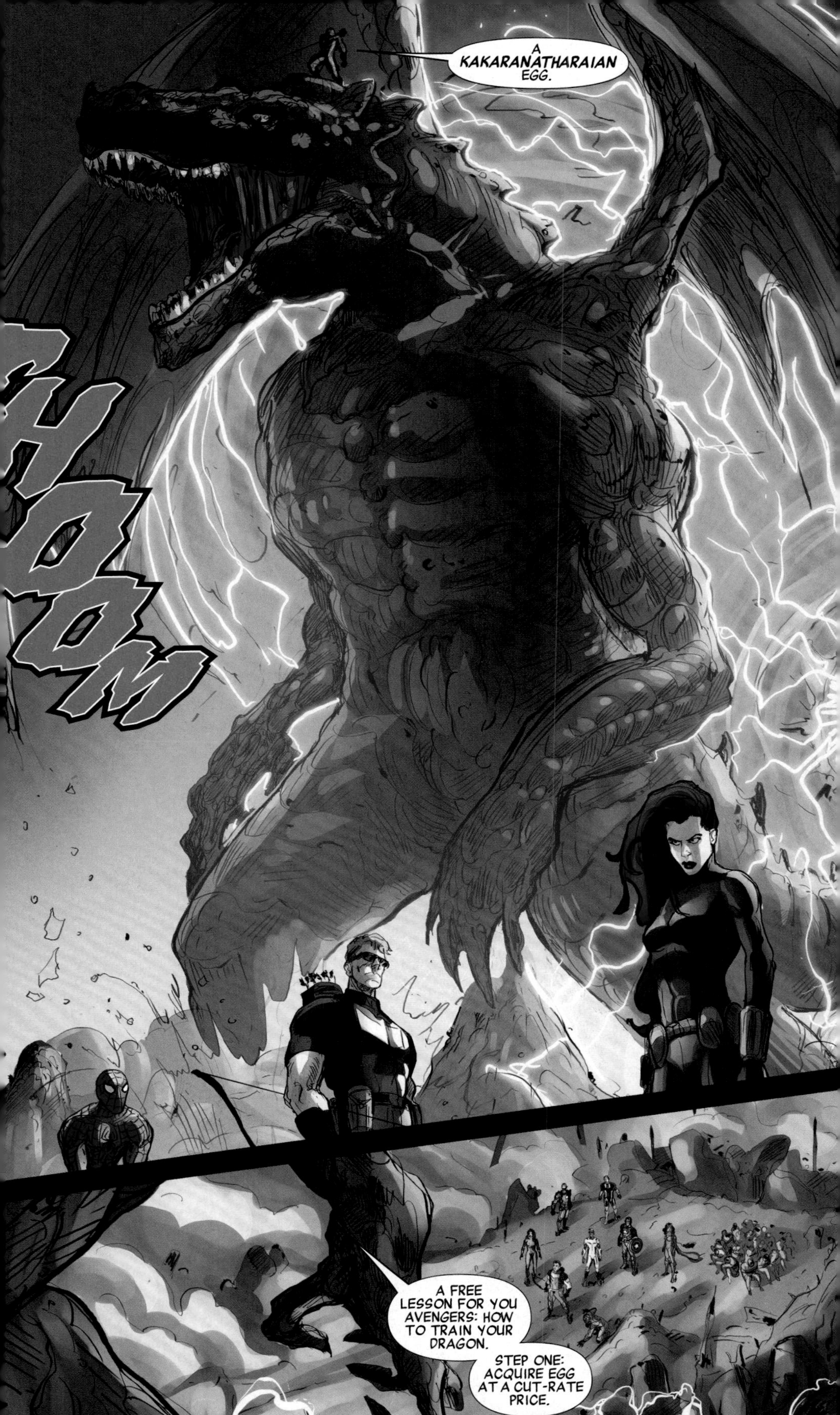

A KAKARANATHARAIAN EGG.
THOOM
A FREE LESSON FOR YOU AVENGERS: HOW TO TRAIN YOUR DRAGON.
STEP ONE: ACQUIRE EGG AT A CUT-RATE PRICE.

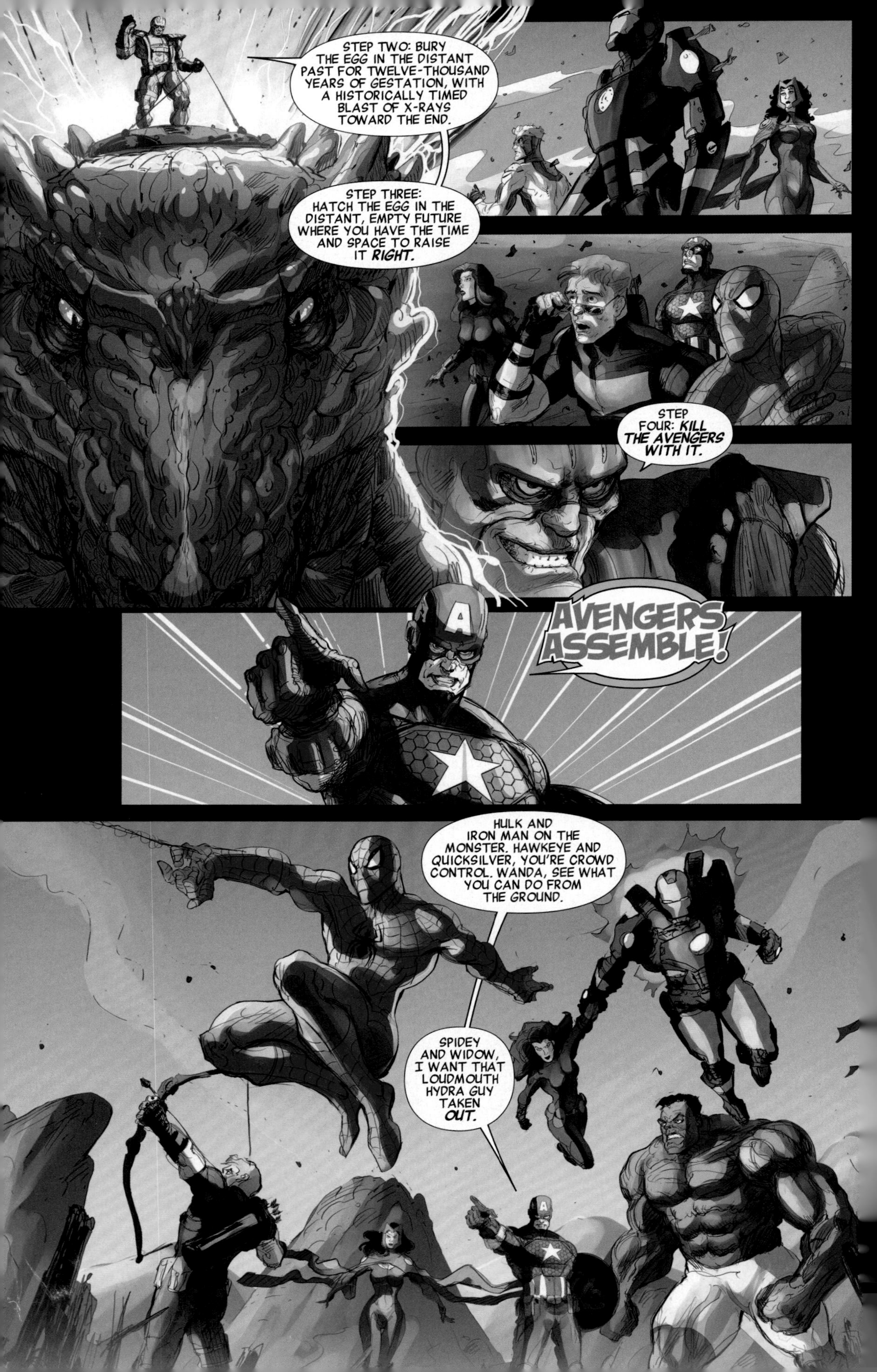
STEP TWO: BURY THE EGG IN THE DISTANT PAST FOR TWELVE-THOUSAND YEARS OF GESTATION, WITH A HISTORICALLY TIMED BLAST OF X-RAYS TOWARD THE END.
STEP THREE: HATCH THE EGG IN THE DISTANT, EMPTY FUTURE WHERE YOU HAVE THE TIME AND SPACE TO RAISE IT RIGHT.
STEP FOUR: KILL THE AVENGERS WITH IT.
AVENGERS ASSEMBLE!
HULK AND IRON MAN ON THE MONSTER. HAWKEYE AND QUICKSILVER, YOU'RE CROWD CONTROL. WANDA, SEE WHAT YOU CAN DO FROM THE GROUND.
SPIDEY AND WIDOW, I WANT THAT LOUDMOUTH HYDRA GUY TAKEN OUT.

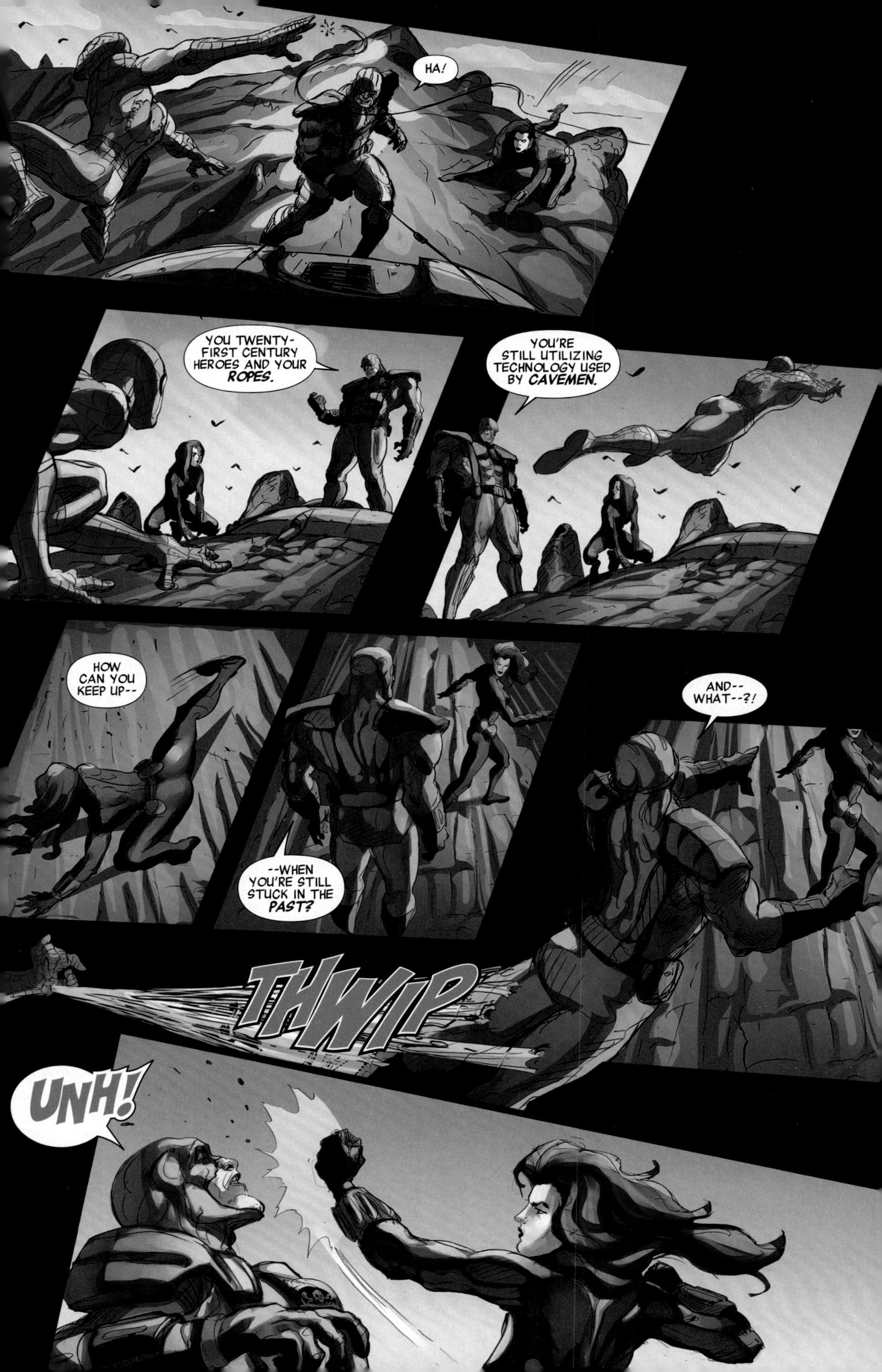
HA!
YOU TWENTY-FIRST CENTURY HEROES AND YOUR ROPES.
YOU'RE STILL UTILIZING TECHNOLOGY USED BY CAVEMEN.
HOW CAN YOU KEEP UP--
--WHEN YOU'RE STILL STUCK IN THE PAST?
AND-- WHAT--?!
THWIP
UNH!

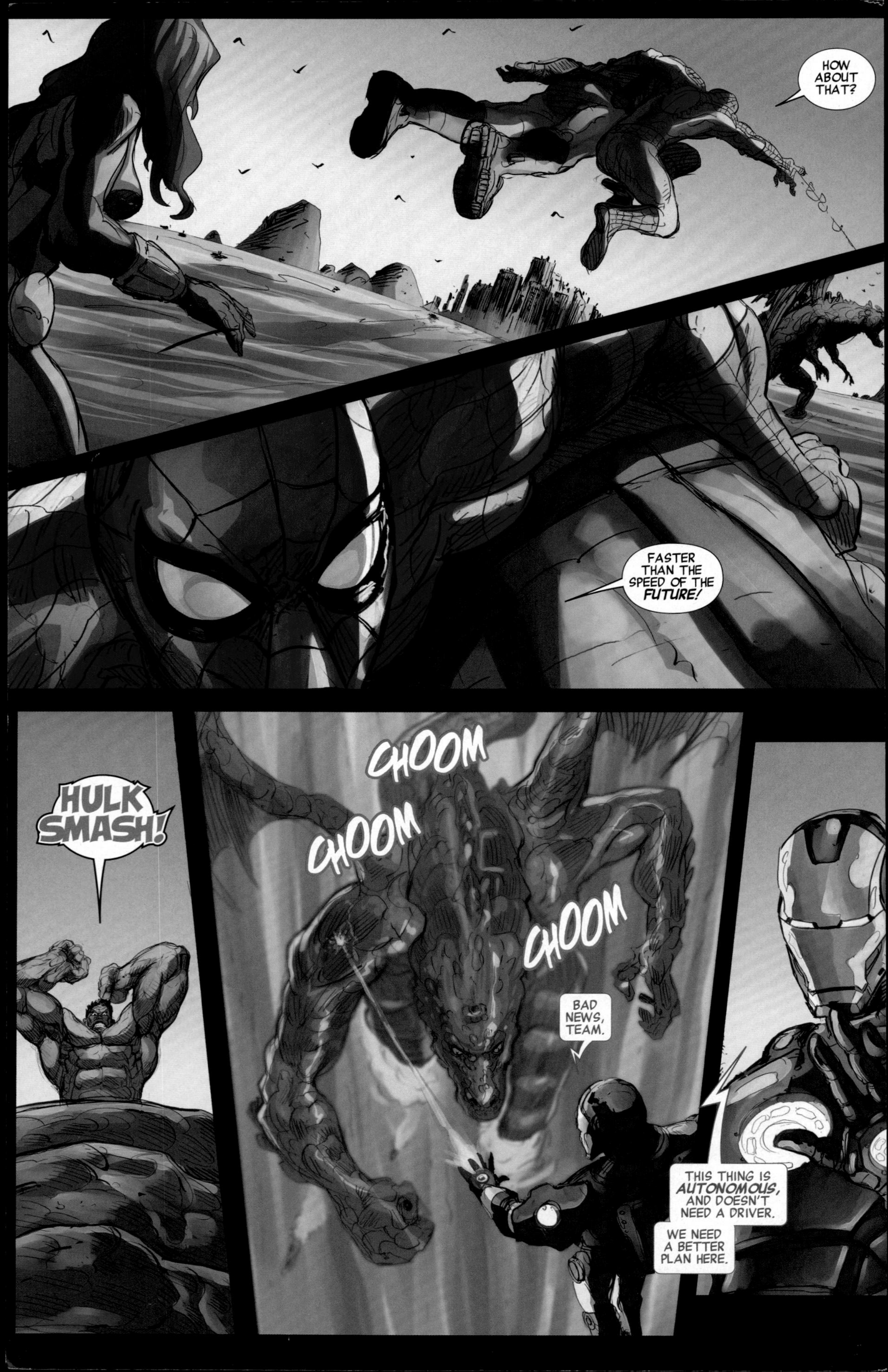

HOW ABOUT THAT?
FASTER THAN THE SPEED OF THE FUTURE!
HULK SMASH!
CHOOM
CHOOM
CHOOM
BAD NEWS, TEAM.
THIS THING IS AUTONOMOUS, AND DOESN'T NEED A DRIVER.
WE NEED A BETTER PLAN HERE.

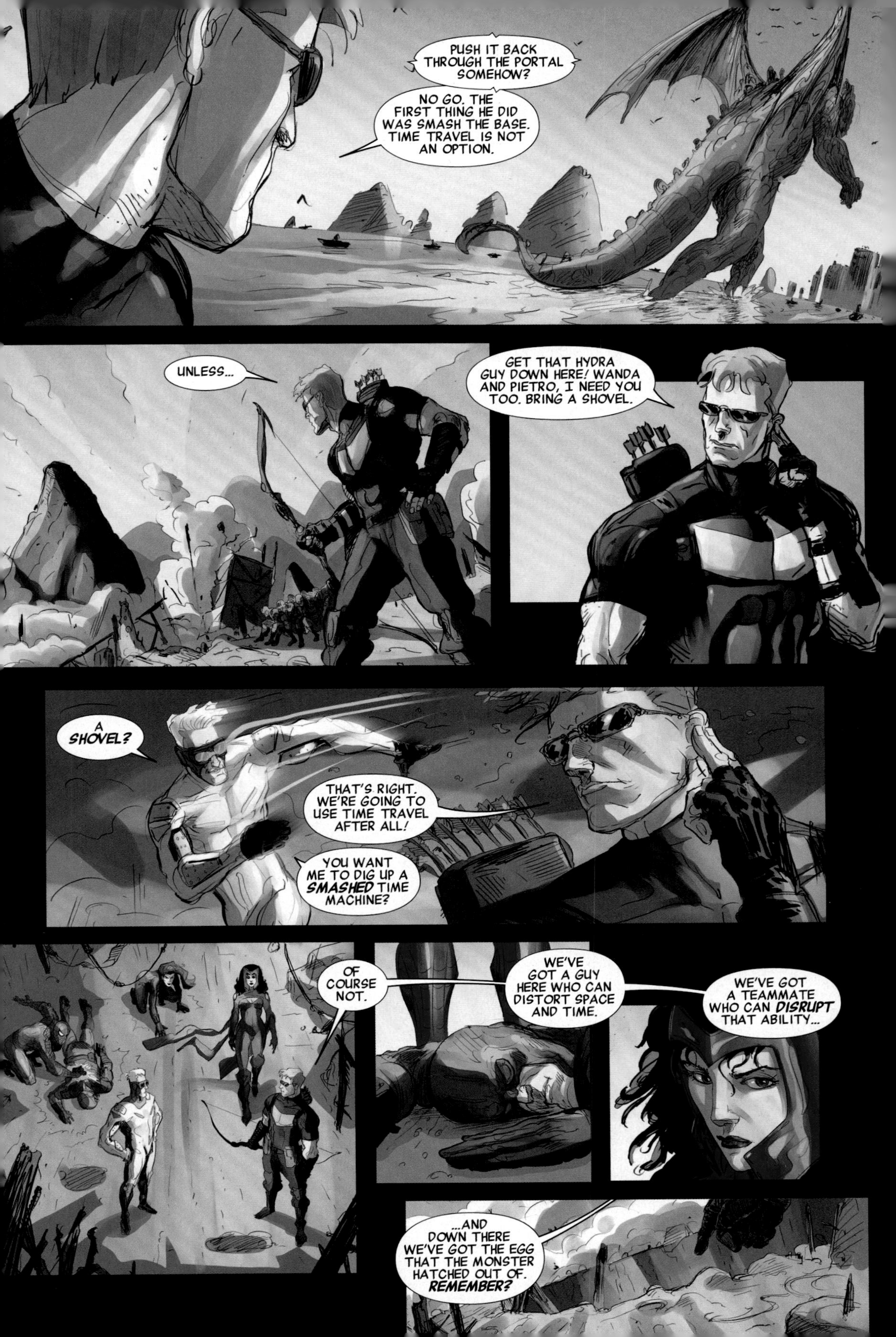
PUSH IT BACK THROUGH THE PORTAL SOMEHOW?
NO GO. THE FIRST THING HE DID WAS SMASH THE BASE. TIME TRAVEL IS NOT AN OPTION.
UNLESS...
GET THAT HYDRA GUY DOWN HERE! WANDA AND PIETRO, I NEED YOU TOO. BRING A SHOVEL.
A *SHOVEL?*
THAT'S RIGHT. WE'RE GOING TO USE TIME TRAVEL AFTER ALL!
YOU WANT ME TO DIG UP A *SMASHED* TIME MACHINE?
OF COURSE NOT.
WE'VE GOT A GUY HERE WHO CAN DISTORT SPACE AND TIME.
WE'VE GOT A TEAMMATE WHO CAN *DISRUPT* THAT ABILITY...
...AND DOWN THERE WE'VE GOT THE EGG THAT THE MONSTER HATCHED OUT OF. *REMEMBER?*

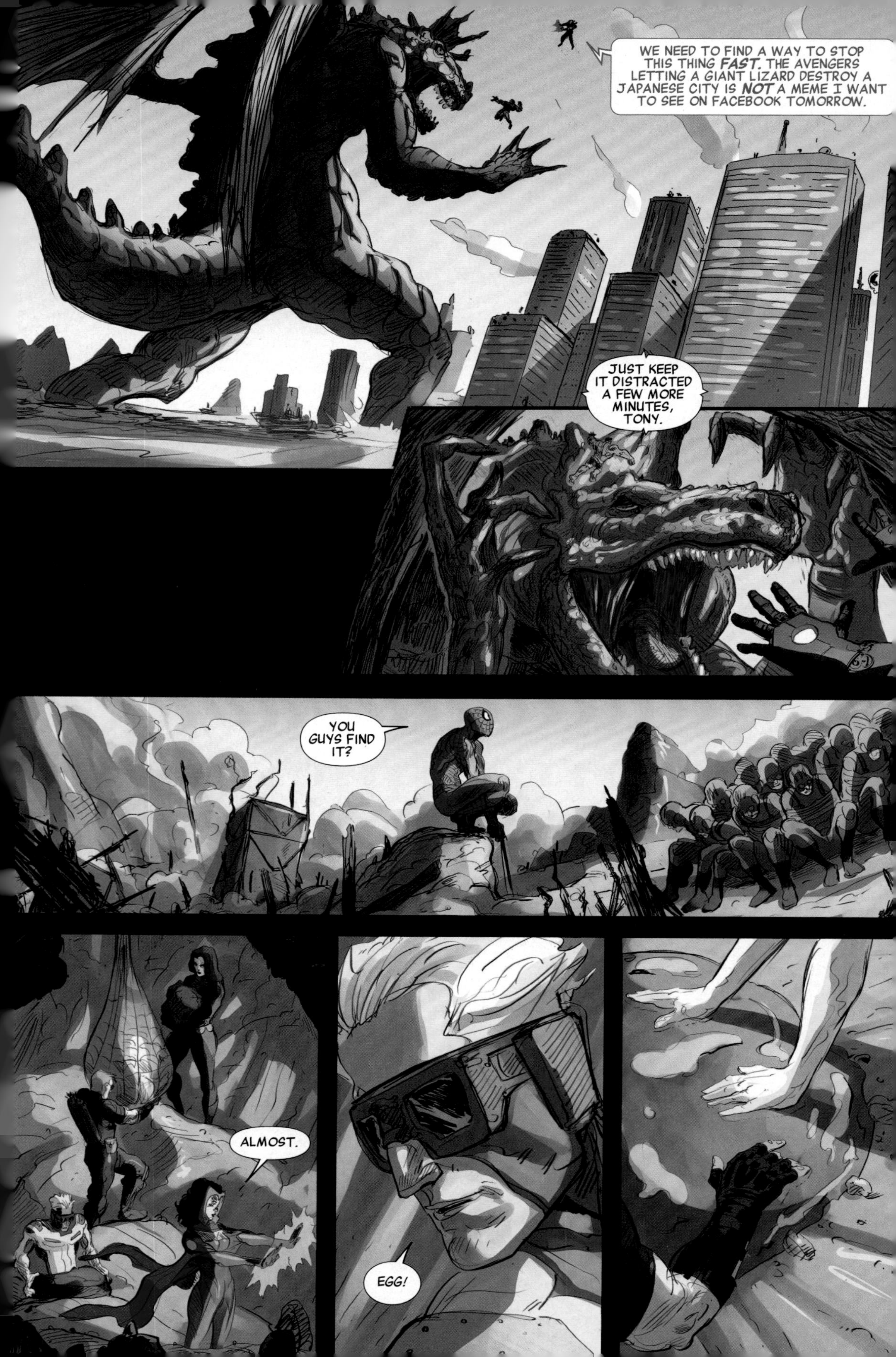

WE NEED TO FIND A WAY TO STOP THIS THING FAST. THE AVENGERS LETTING A GIANT LIZARD DESTROY A JAPANESE CITY IS NOT A MEME I WANT TO SEE ON FACEBOOK TOMORROW.
JUST KEEP IT DISTRACTED A FEW MORE MINUTES, TONY.
YOU GUYS FIND IT?
ALMOST.
EGG!

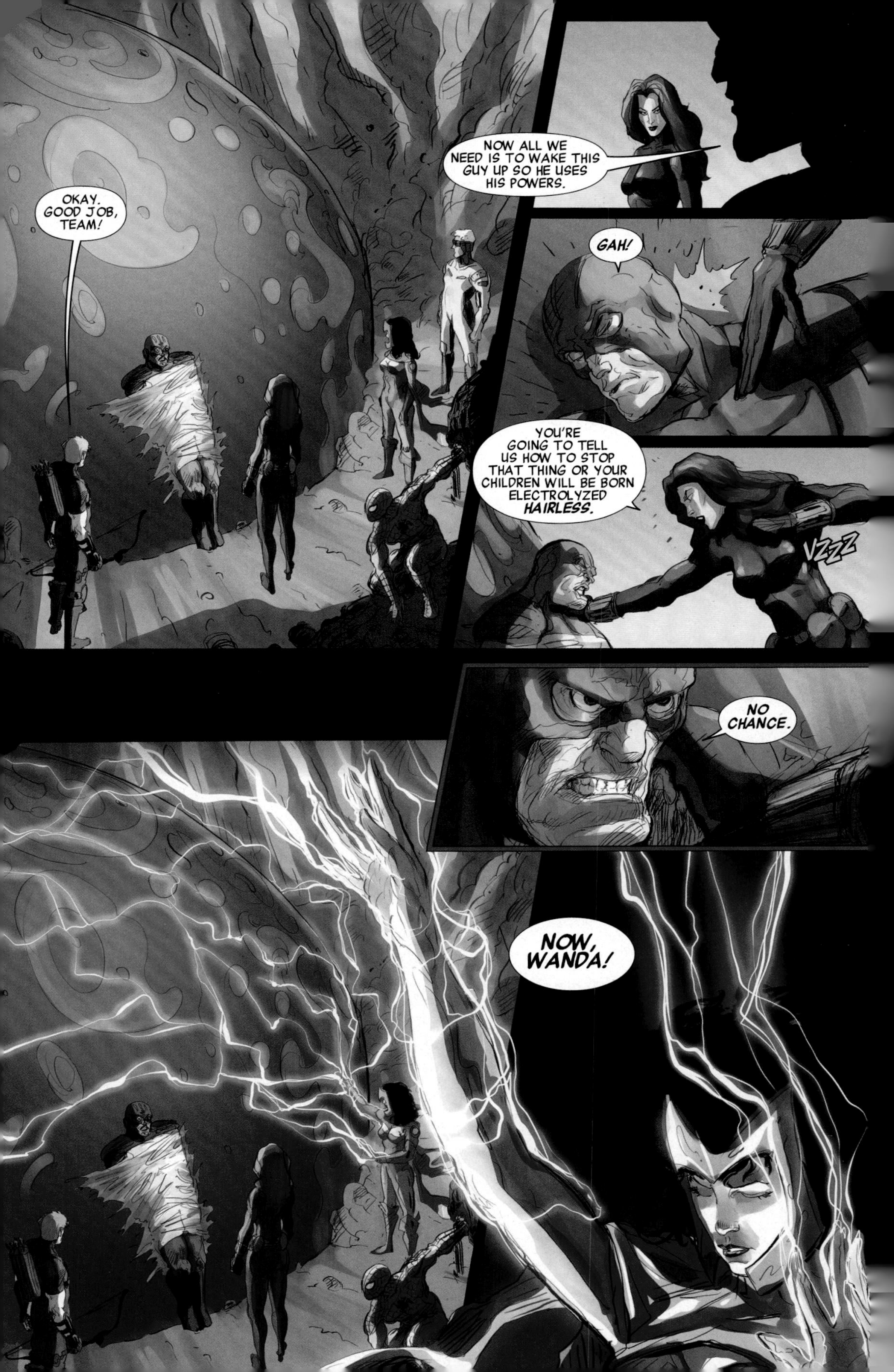
OKAY. GOOD JOB, TEAM!
NOW ALL WE NEED IS TO WAKE THIS GUY UP SO HE USES HIS POWERS.
GAH!
YOU'RE GOING TO TELL US HOW TO STOP THAT THING OR YOUR CHILDREN WILL BE BORN ELECTROLYZED HAIRLESS.
VZZZ
NO CHANCE.
NOW, WANDA!

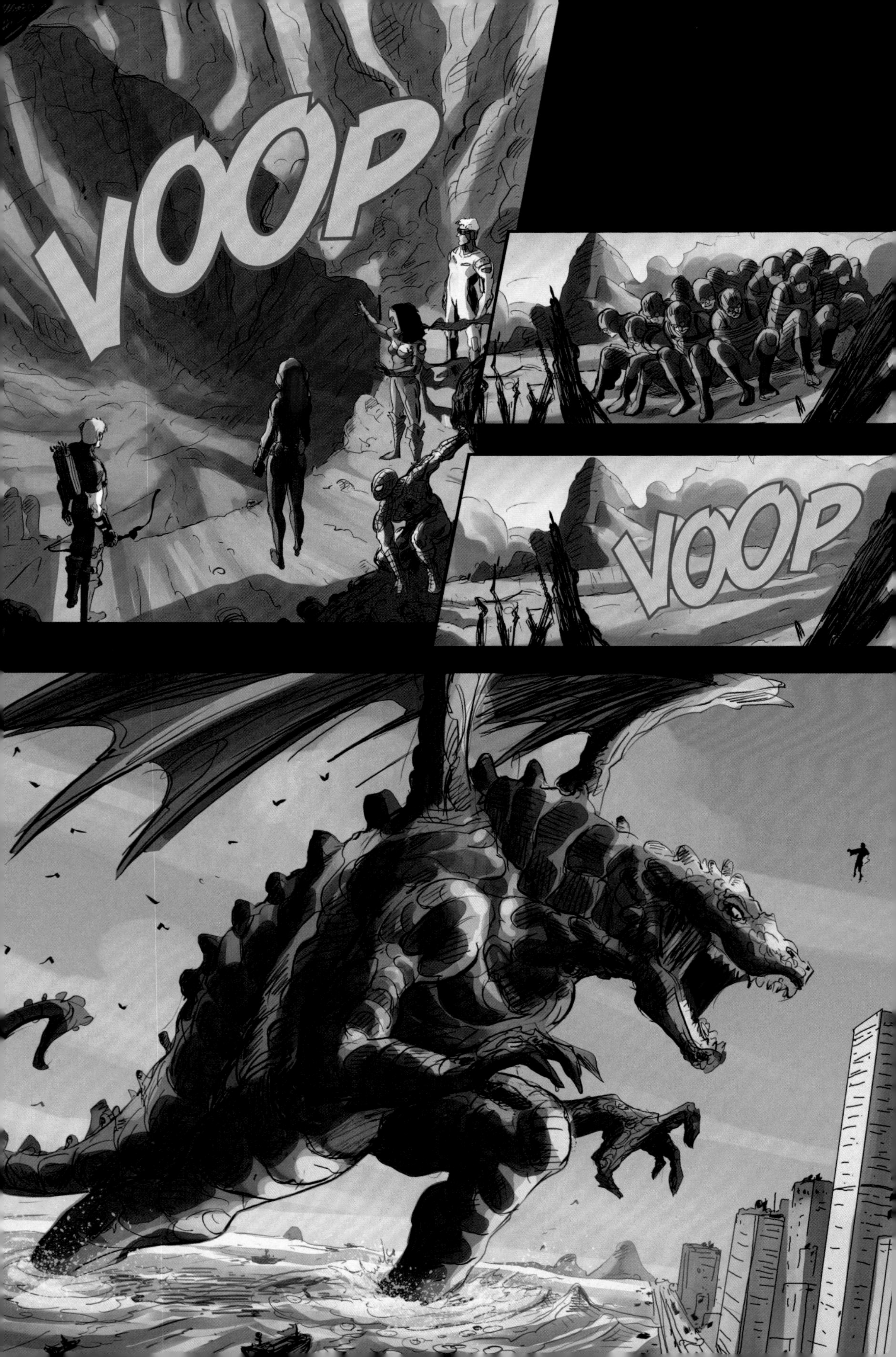
VOOP
VOOP

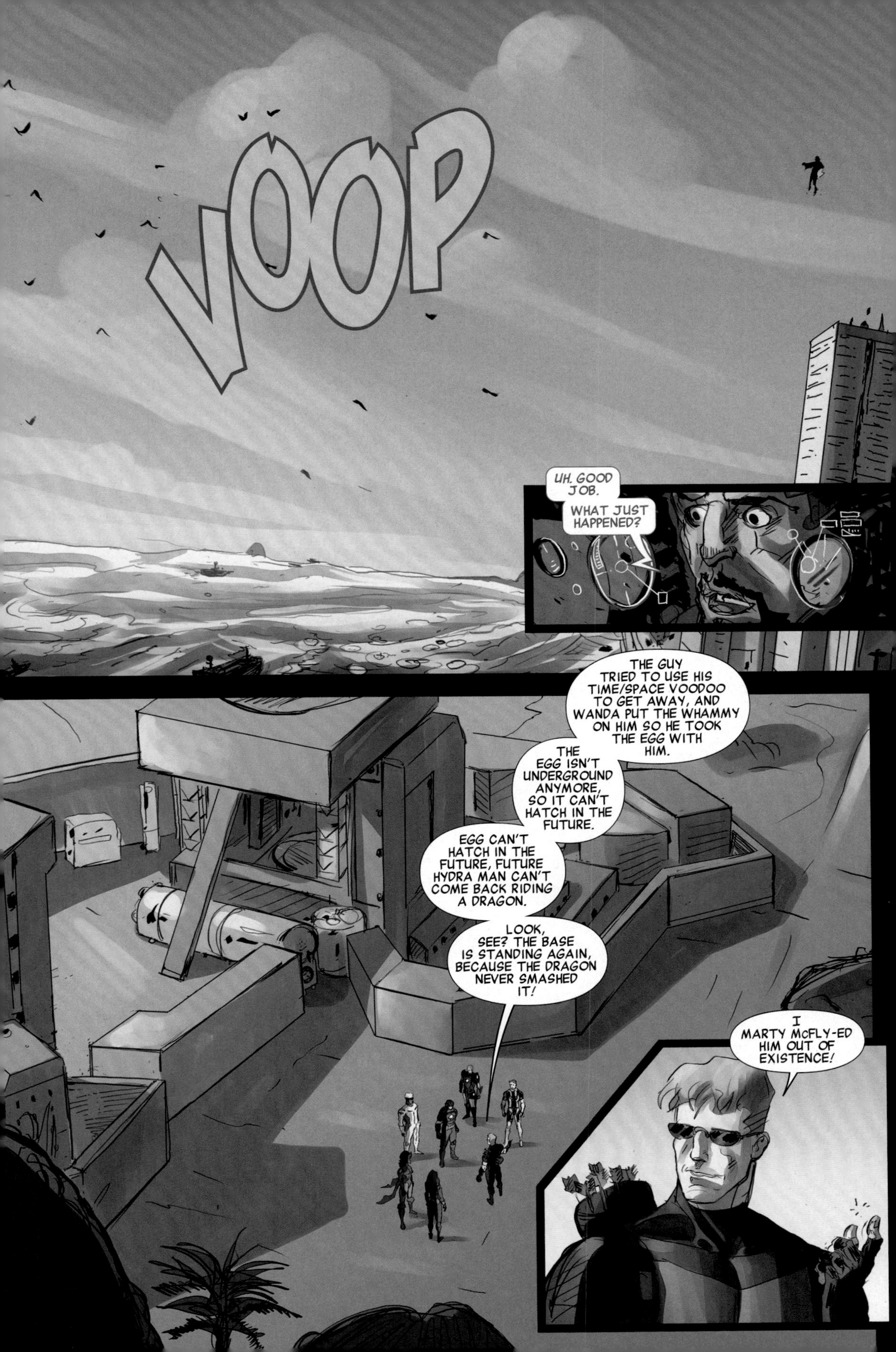
VOOP
UH. GOOD JOB.
WHAT JUST HAPPENED?
THE GUY TRIED TO USE HIS TIME/SPACE VOODOO TO GET AWAY, AND WANDA PUT THE WHAMMY ON HIM SO HE TOOK THE EGG WITH HIM.
THE EGG ISN'T UNDERGROUND ANYMORE, SO IT CAN'T HATCH IN THE FUTURE.
EGG CAN'T HATCH IN THE FUTURE, FUTURE HYDRA MAN CAN'T COME BACK RIDING A DRAGON.
LOOK, SEE? THE BASE IS STANDING AGAIN, BECAUSE THE DRAGON NEVER SMASHED IT!
I MARTY McFLY-ED HIM OUT OF EXISTENCE!

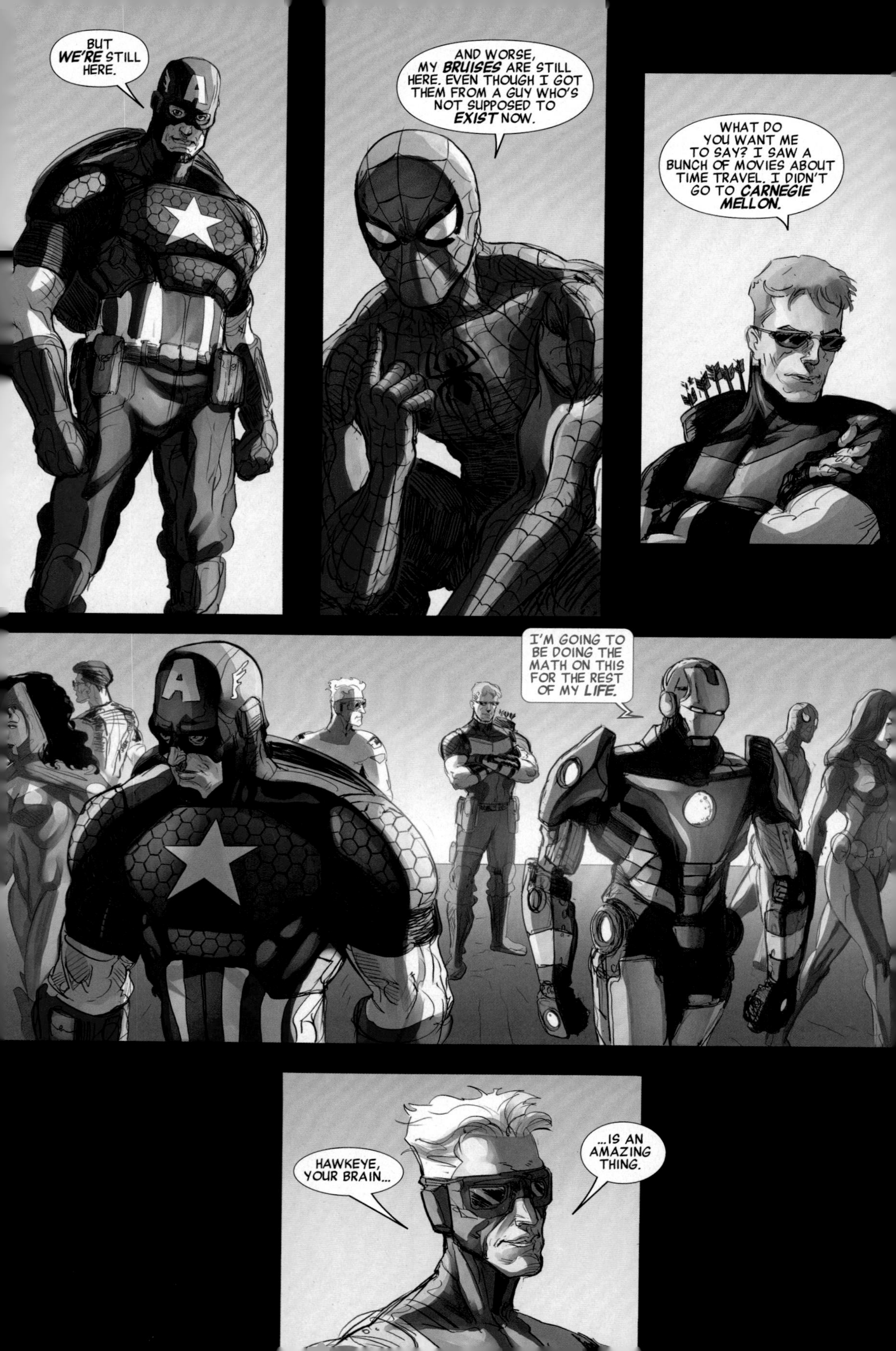
BUT WE'RE STILL HERE.
AND WORSE, MY BRUISES ARE STILL HERE. EVEN THOUGH I GOT THEM FROM A GUY WHO'S NOT SUPPOSED TO EXIST NOW.
WHAT DO YOU WANT ME TO SAY? I SAW A BUNCH OF MOVIES ABOUT TIME TRAVEL. I DIDN'T GO TO CARNEGIE MELLON.
I'M GOING TO BE DOING THE MATH ON THIS FOR THE REST OF MY LIFE.
HAWKEYE, YOUR BRAIN...
...IS AN AMAZING THING.

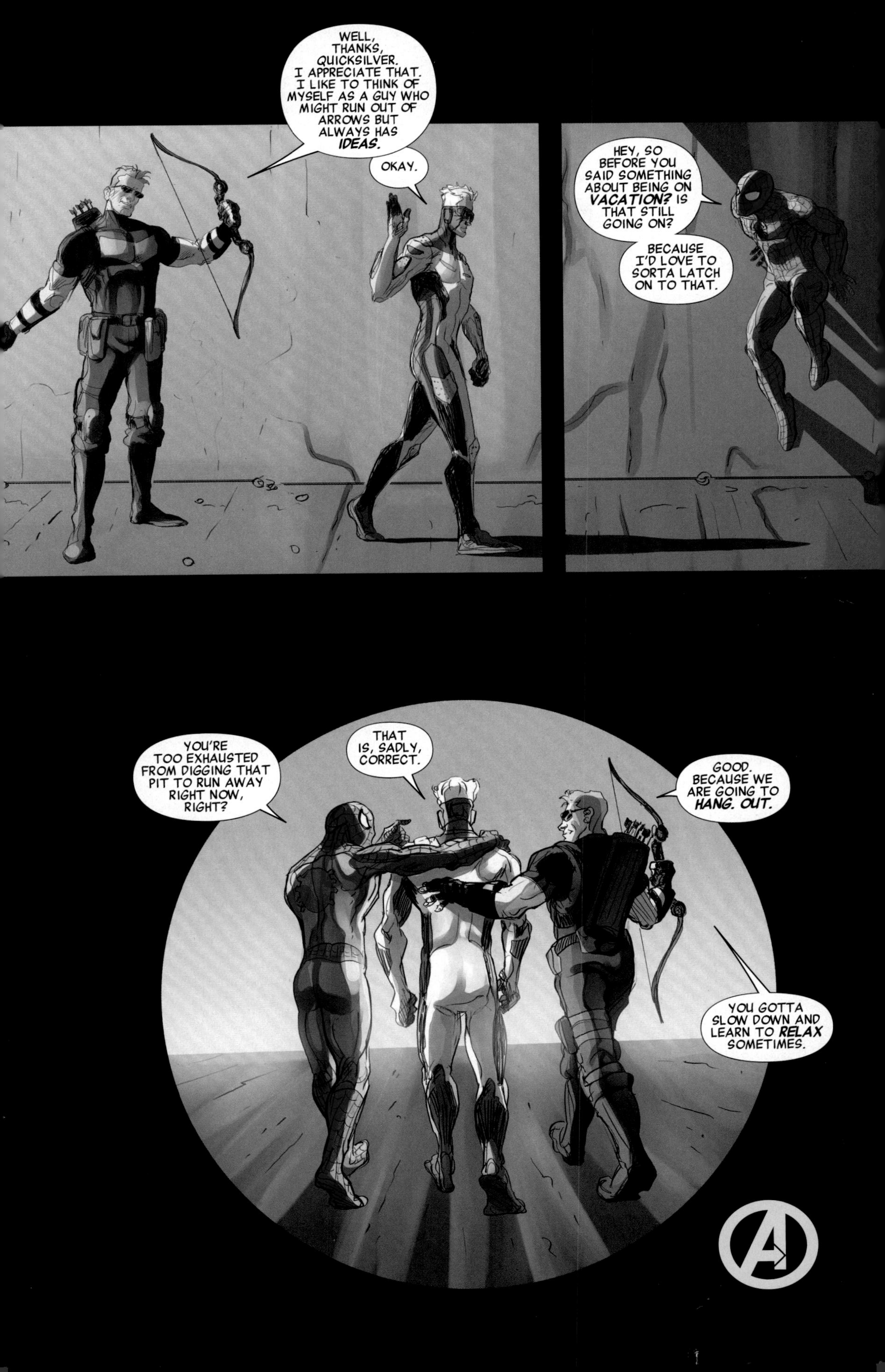
WELL, THANKS, QUICKSILVER. I APPRECIATE THAT. I LIKE TO THINK OF MYSELF AS A GUY WHO MIGHT RUN OUT OF ARROWS BUT ALWAYS HAS IDEAS.
OKAY.
HEY, SO BEFORE YOU SAID SOMETHING ABOUT BEING ON VACATION? IS THAT STILL GOING ON?
BECAUSE I'D LOVE TO SORTA LATCH ON TO THAT.
YOU'RE TOO EXHAUSTED FROM DIGGING THAT PIT TO RUN AWAY RIGHT NOW, RIGHT?
THAT IS, SADLY, CORRECT.
GOOD. BECAUSE WE ARE GOING TO HANG. OUT.
YOU GOTTA SLOW DOWN AND LEARN TO RELAX SOMETIMES.

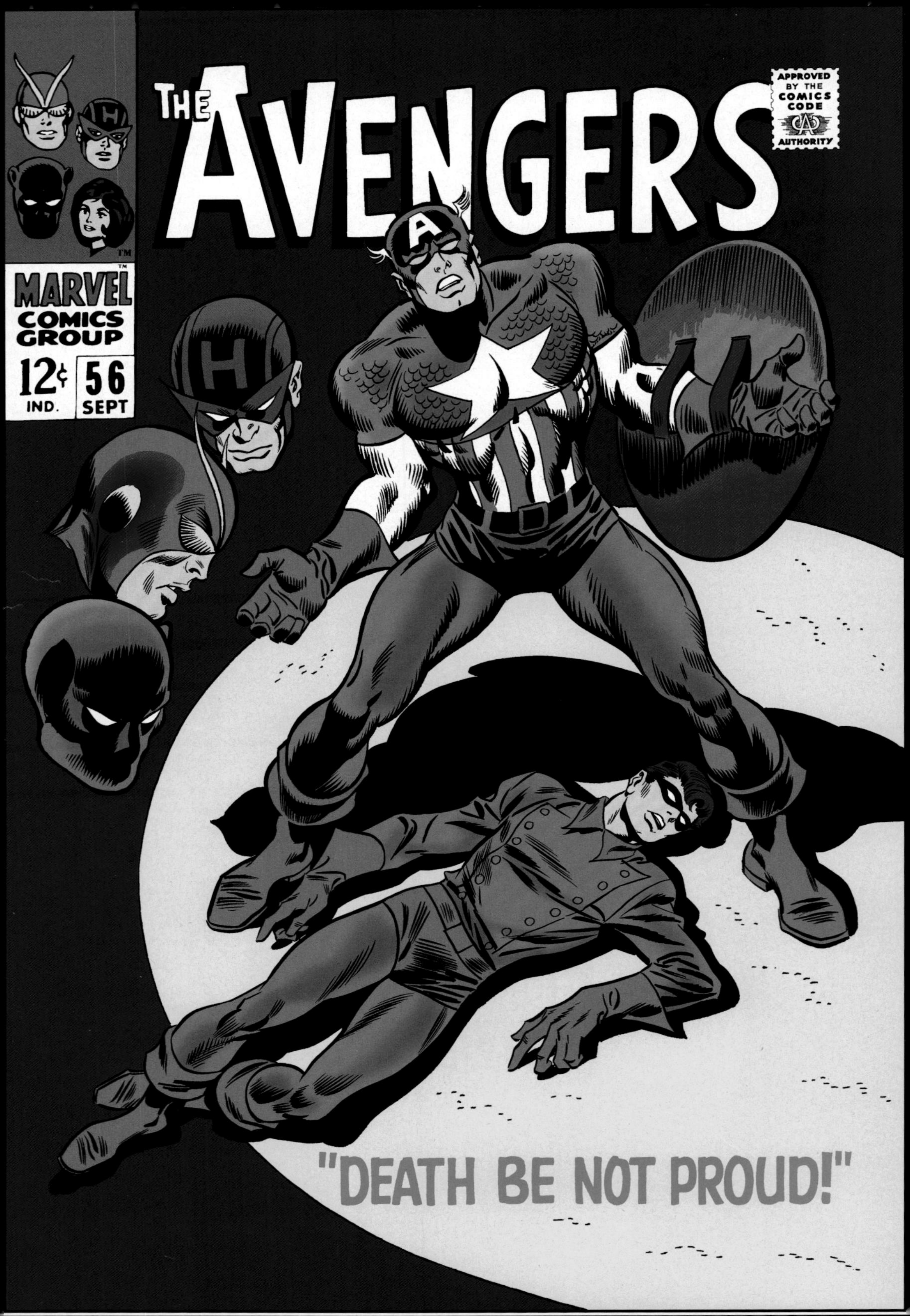

THE AVENGERS
APPROVED BY THE COMICS CODE AUTHORITY
MARVEL COMICS GROUP
12¢ IND.
56 SEPT
"DEATH BE NOT PROUD!"

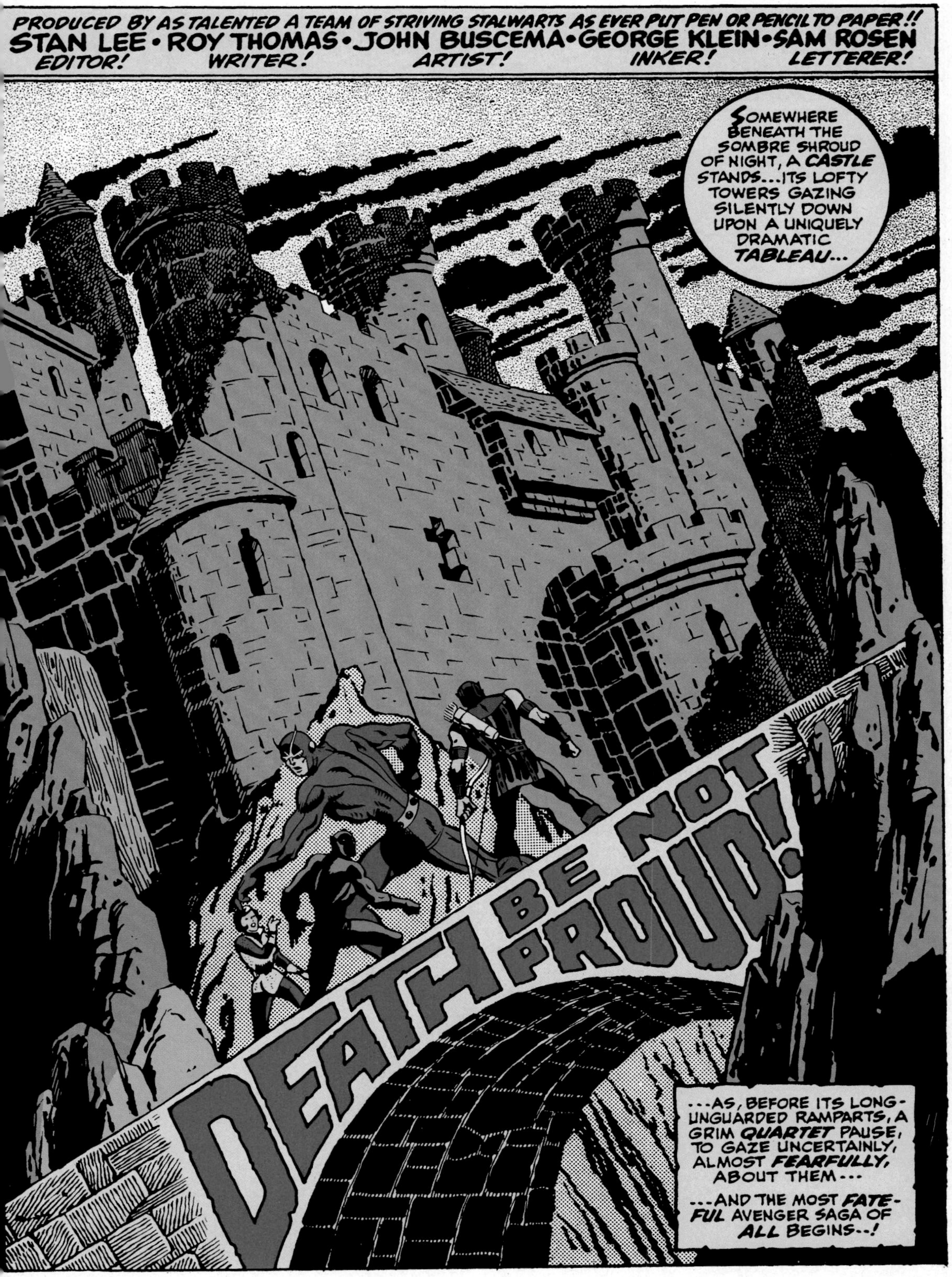
PRODUCED BY AS TALENTED A TEAM OF STRIVING STALWARTS AS EVER PUT PEN OR PENCIL TO PAPER!!
STAN LEE • ROY THOMAS • JOHN BUSCEMA • GEORGE KLEIN • SAM ROSEN
EDITOR! WRITER! ARTIST! INKER! LETTERER!
SOMEWHERE BENEATH THE SOMBRE SHROUD OF NIGHT, A CASTLE STANDS... ITS LOFTY TOWERS GAZING SILENTLY DOWN UPON A UNIQUELY DRAMATIC TABLEAU...
DEATH BE NOT PROUD!
...AS, BEFORE ITS LONG-UNGUARDED RAMPARTS, A GRIM QUARTET PAUSE, TO GAZE UNCERTAINLY, ALMOST FEARFULLY, ABOUT THEM...
...AND THE MOST FATE-FUL AVENGER SAGA OF ALL BEGINS..!

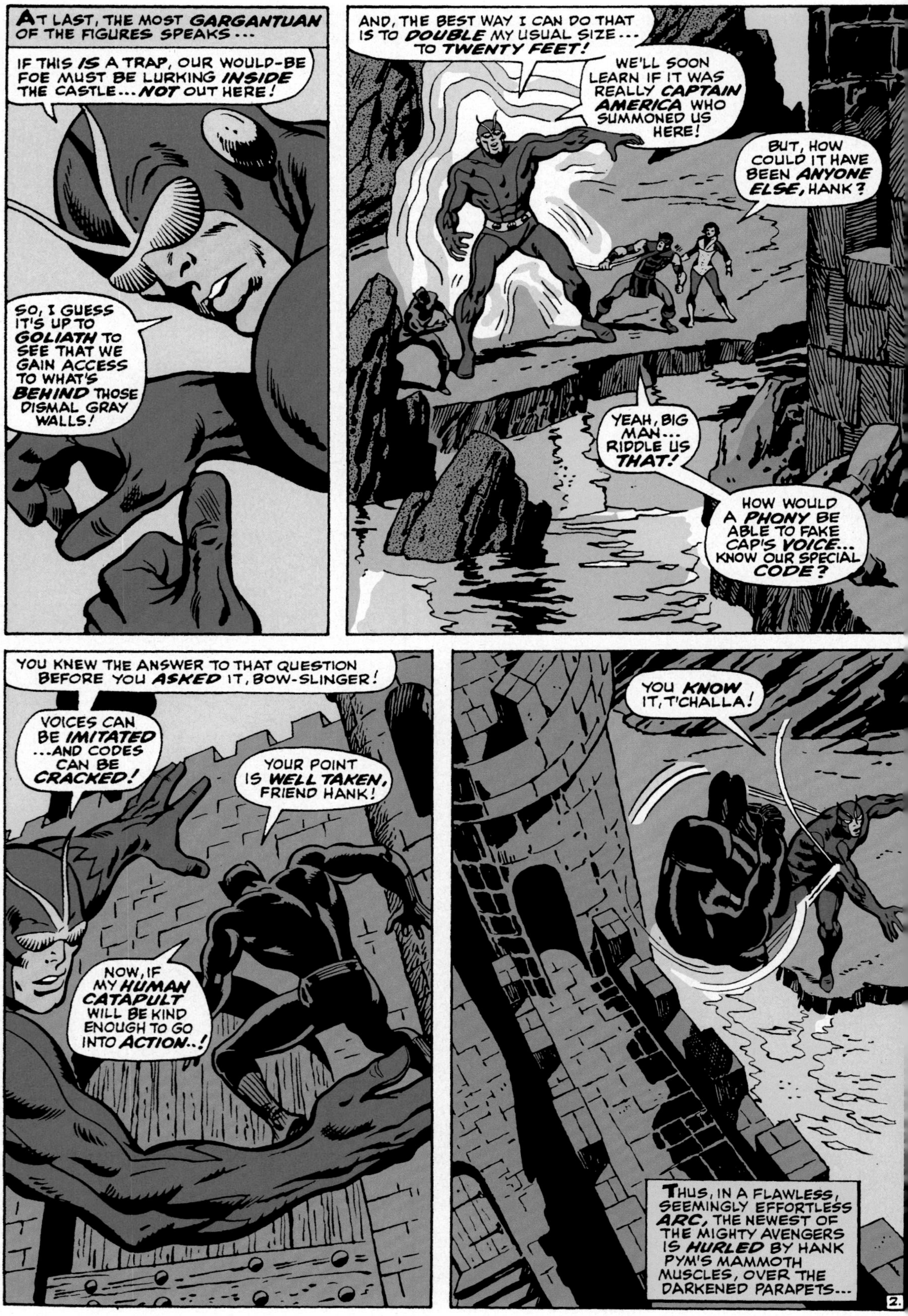

AT LAST, THE MOST GARGANTUAN OF THE FIGURES SPEAKS...
IF THIS IS A TRAP, OUR WOULD-BE FOE MUST BE LURKING INSIDE THE CASTLE... NOT OUT HERE!
SO, I GUESS IT'S UP TO GOLIATH TO SEE THAT WE GAIN ACCESS TO WHAT'S BEHIND THOSE DISMAL GRAY WALLS!
AND, THE BEST WAY I CAN DO THAT IS TO DOUBLE MY USUAL SIZE... TO TWENTY FEET!
WE'LL SOON LEARN IF IT WAS REALLY CAPTAIN AMERICA WHO SUMMONED US HERE!
BUT, HOW COULD IT HAVE BEEN ANYONE ELSE, HANK?
YEAH, BIG MAN... RIDDLE US THAT!
HOW WOULD A PHONY BE ABLE TO FAKE CAP'S VOICE... KNOW OUR SPECIAL CODE?
YOU KNEW THE ANSWER TO THAT QUESTION BEFORE YOU ASKED IT, BOW-SLINGER!
VOICES CAN BE IMITATED ...AND CODES CAN BE CRACKED!
YOUR POINT IS WELL TAKEN, FRIEND HANK!
NOW, IF MY HUMAN CATAPULT WILL BE KIND ENOUGH TO GO INTO ACTION..!
YOU KNOW IT, T'CHALLA!
THUS, IN A FLAWLESS, SEEMINGLY EFFORTLESS ARC, THE NEWEST OF THE MIGHTY AVENGERS IS HURLED BY HANK PYM'S MAMMOTH MUSCLES, OVER THE DARKENED PARAPETS...
2.

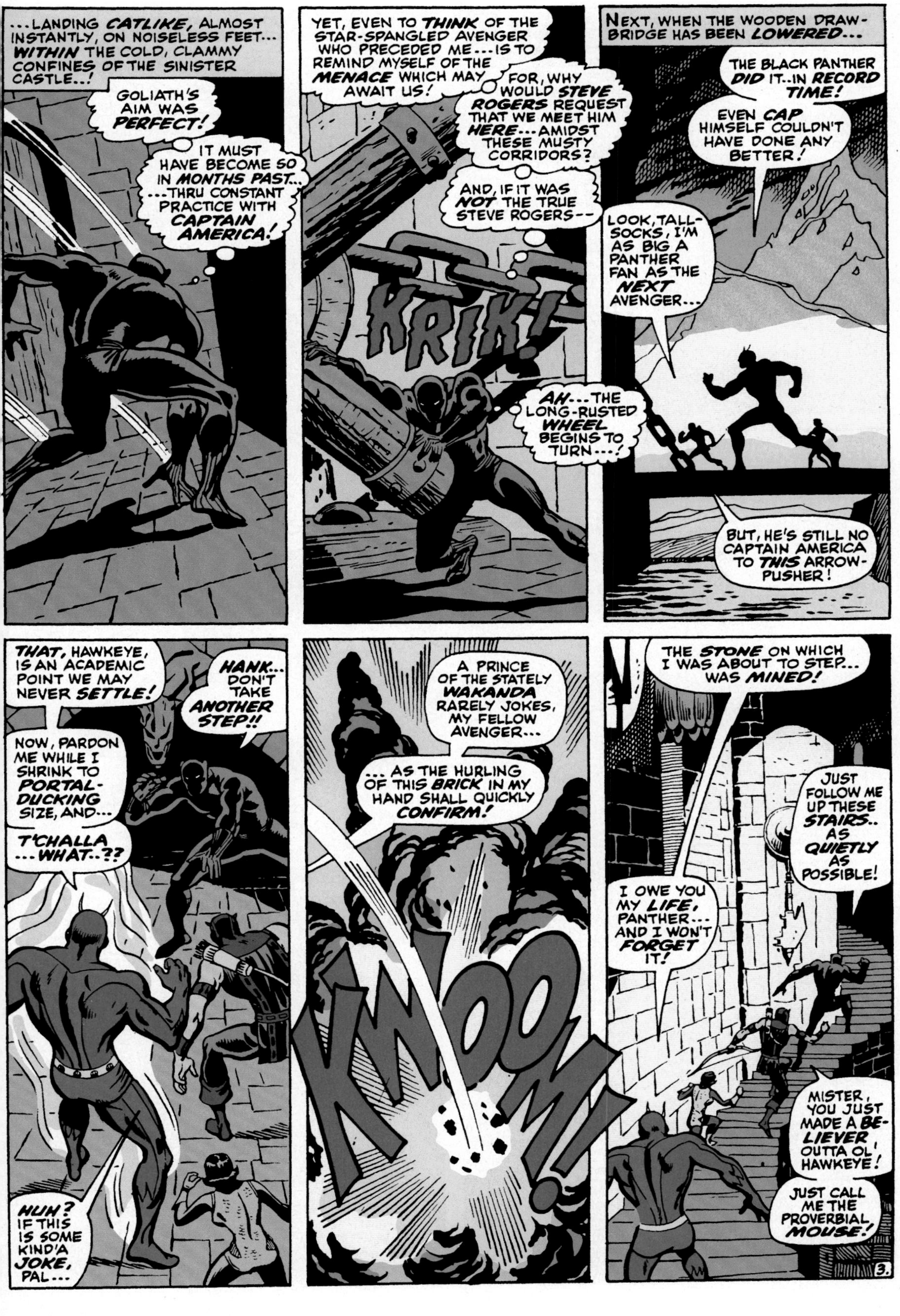
...LANDING CATLIKE, ALMOST INSTANTLY, ON NOISELESS FEET... WITHIN THE COLD, CLAMMY CONFINES OF THE SINISTER CASTLE..!
GOLIATH'S AIM WAS PERFECT!
IT MUST HAVE BECOME SO IN MONTHS PAST... ...THRU CONSTANT PRACTICE WITH CAPTAIN AMERICA!
YET, EVEN TO THINK OF THE STAR-SPANGLED AVENGER WHO PRECEDED ME...IS TO REMIND MYSELF OF THE MENACE WHICH MAY AWAIT US!
FOR, WHY WOULD STEVE ROGERS REQUEST THAT WE MEET HIM HERE...AMIDST THESE MUSTY CORRIDORS?
AND, IF IT WAS NOT THE TRUE STEVE ROGERS--
KRIK!
AH...THE LONG-RUSTED WHEEL BEGINS TO TURN...!
NEXT, WHEN THE WOODEN DRAW-BRIDGE HAS BEEN LOWERED...
THE BLACK PANTHER DID IT..IN RECORD TIME!
EVEN CAP HIMSELF COULDN'T HAVE DONE ANY BETTER!
LOOK, TALL-SOCKS, I'M AS BIG A PANTHER FAN AS THE NEXT AVENGER...
BUT, HE'S STILL NO CAPTAIN AMERICA TO THIS ARROW-PUSHER!
THAT, HAWKEYE, IS AN ACADEMIC POINT WE MAY NEVER SETTLE!
NOW, PARDON ME WHILE I SHRINK TO PORTAL-DUCKING SIZE, AND...
HANK... DON'T TAKE ANOTHER STEP!!
T'CHALLA ...WHAT..??
HUH? IF THIS IS SOME KIND'A JOKE, PAL...
A PRINCE OF THE STATELY WAKANDA RARELY JOKES, MY FELLOW AVENGER...
...AS THE HURLING OF THIS BRICK IN MY HAND SHALL QUICKLY CONFIRM!
KWOOM!
THE STONE ON WHICH I WAS ABOUT TO STEP... WAS MINED!
JUST FOLLOW ME UP THESE STAIRS.. AS QUIETLY AS POSSIBLE!
I OWE YOU MY LIFE, PANTHER... AND I WON'T FORGET IT!
MISTER, YOU JUST MADE A BE-LIEVER OUTTA OL' HAWKEYE!
JUST CALL ME THE PROVERBIAL MOUSE!
3.

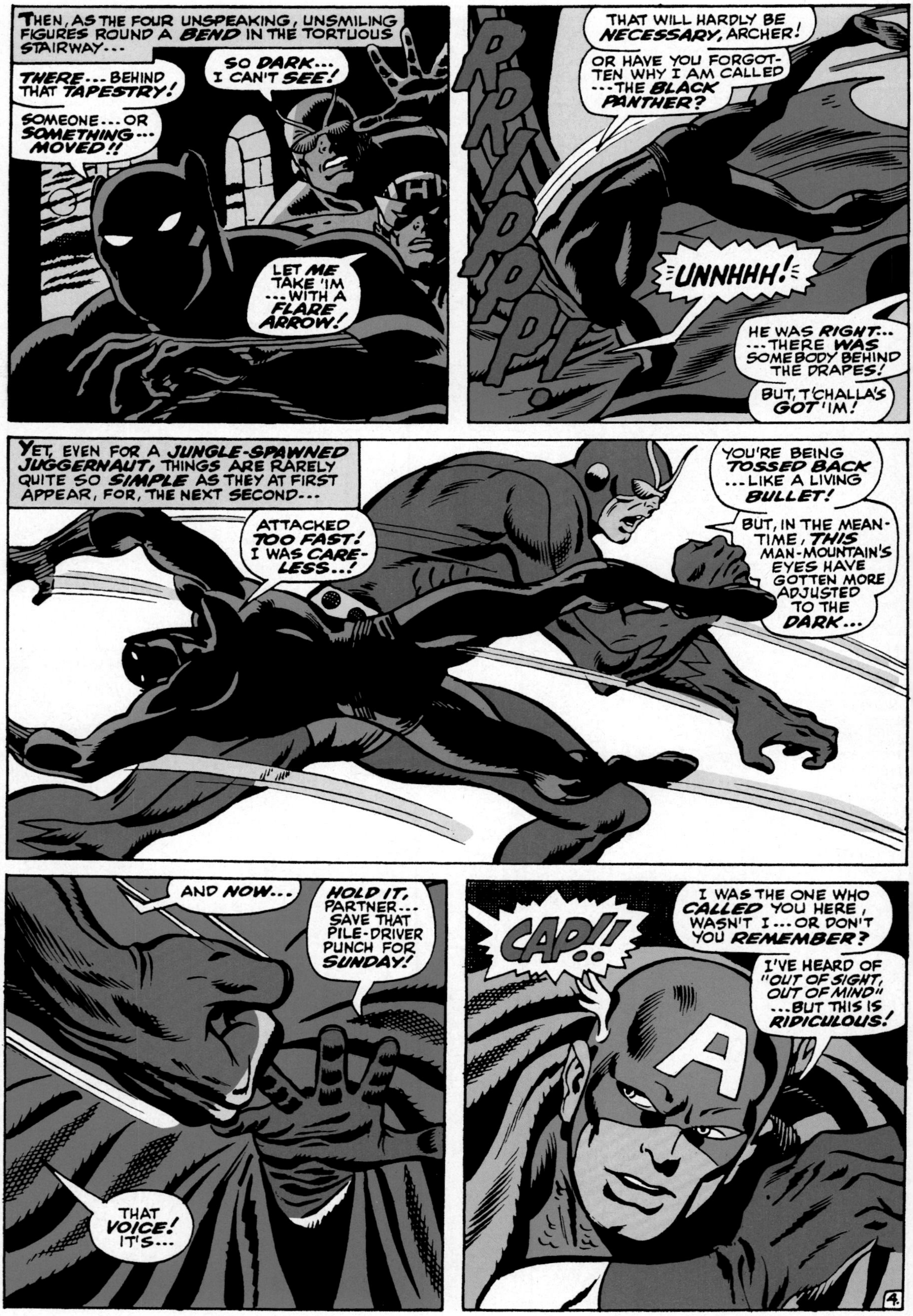
THEN, AS THE FOUR UNSPEAKING, UNSMILING FIGURES ROUND A BEND IN THE TORTUOUS STAIRWAY...
SO DARK... I CAN'T SEE!
THERE... BEHIND THAT TAPESTRY!
SOMEONE... OR SOMETHING... MOVED!!
LET ME TAKE 'IM ...WITH A FLARE ARROW!
THAT WILL HARDLY BE NECESSARY, ARCHER!
OR HAVE YOU FORGOTTEN WHY I AM CALLED ---THE BLACK PANTHER?
RRRIPPP!
UNNHHH!
HE WAS RIGHT... ---THERE WAS SOMEBODY BEHIND THE DRAPES!
BUT, T'CHALLA'S GOT 'IM!
YET, EVEN FOR A JUNGLE-SPAWNED JUGGERNAUT, THINGS ARE RARELY QUITE SO SIMPLE AS THEY AT FIRST APPEAR, FOR, THE NEXT SECOND---
ATTACKED TOO FAST! I WAS CARELESS..!
YOU'RE BEING TOSSED BACK ...LIKE A LIVING BULLET!
BUT, IN THE MEANTIME, THIS MAN-MOUNTAIN'S EYES HAVE GOTTEN MORE ADJUSTED TO THE DARK...
AND NOW...
HOLD IT, PARTNER... SAVE THAT PILE-DRIVER PUNCH FOR SUNDAY!
THAT VOICE! IT'S...
CAP!!
I WAS THE ONE WHO CALLED YOU HERE, WASN'T I... OR DON'T YOU REMEMBER?
I'VE HEARD OF "OUT OF SIGHT, OUT OF MIND" ...BUT THIS IS RIDICULOUS!
4.

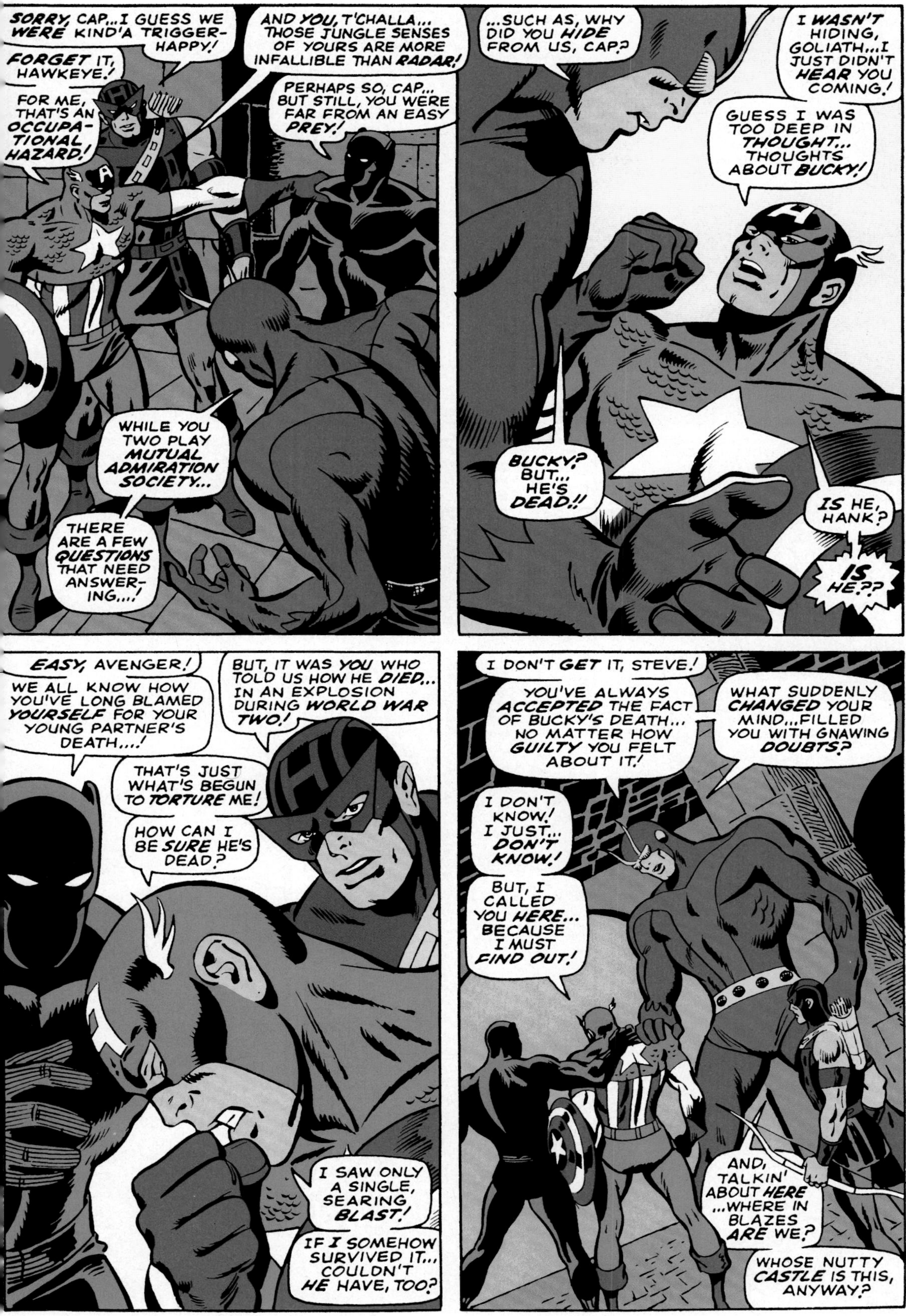
SORRY, CAP... I GUESS WE WERE KIND'A TRIGGER-HAPPY!
FORGET IT, HAWKEYE!
FOR ME, THAT'S AN OCCUPA-TIONAL HAZARD!
AND YOU, T'CHALLA... THOSE JUNGLE SENSES OF YOURS ARE MORE INFALLIBLE THAN RADAR!
PERHAPS SO, CAP... BUT STILL, YOU WERE FAR FROM AN EASY PREY!
WHILE YOU TWO PLAY MUTUAL ADMIRATION SOCIETY...
THERE ARE A FEW QUESTIONS THAT NEED ANSWER-ING....!
...SUCH AS, WHY DID YOU HIDE FROM US, CAP?
I WASN'T HIDING, GOLIATH... I JUST DIDN'T HEAR YOU COMING!
GUESS I WAS TOO DEEP IN THOUGHT... THOUGHTS ABOUT BUCKY!
BUCKY? BUT... HE'S DEAD!!
IS HE, HANK?
IS HE??
EASY, AVENGER!
WE ALL KNOW HOW YOU'VE LONG BLAMED YOURSELF FOR YOUR YOUNG PARTNER'S DEATH....!
BUT, IT WAS YOU WHO TOLD US HOW HE DIED... IN AN EXPLOSION DURING WORLD WAR TWO!
THAT'S JUST WHAT'S BEGUN TO TORTURE ME!
HOW CAN I BE SURE HE'S DEAD?
I SAW ONLY A SINGLE, SEARING BLAST!
IF I SOMEHOW SURVIVED IT... COULDN'T HE HAVE, TOO?
I DON'T GET IT, STEVE!
YOU'VE ALWAYS ACCEPTED THE FACT OF BUCKY'S DEATH... NO MATTER HOW GUILTY YOU FELT ABOUT IT!
WHAT SUDDENLY CHANGED YOUR MIND... FILLED YOU WITH GNAWING DOUBTS?
I DON'T KNOW! I JUST... DON'T KNOW!
BUT, I CALLED YOU HERE... BECAUSE I MUST FIND OUT!
AND, TALKIN' ABOUT HERE ...WHERE IN BLAZES ARE WE?
WHOSE NUTTY CASTLE IS THIS, ANYWAY?

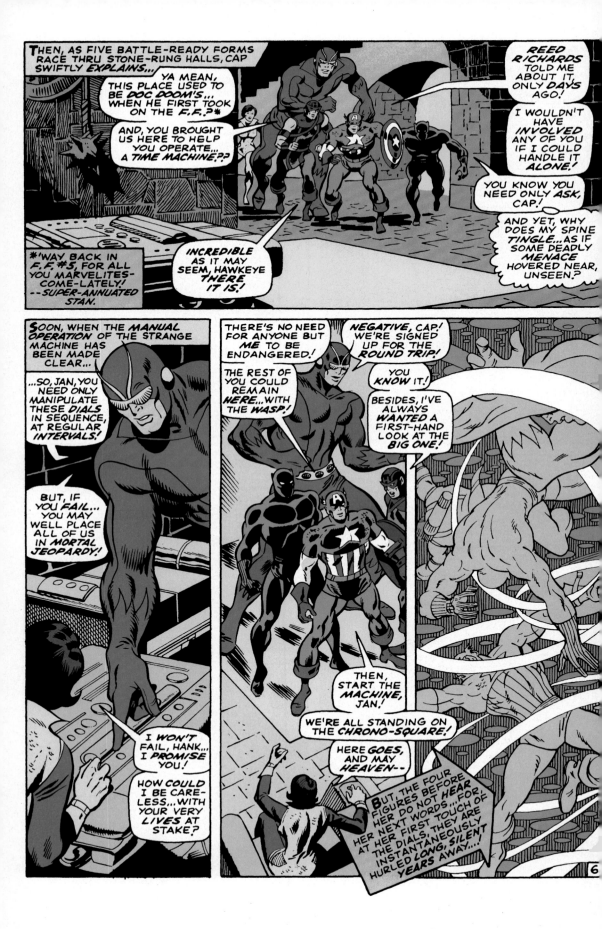

THEN, AS FIVE BATTLE-READY FORMS RACE THRU STONE-RUNG HALLS, CAP SWIFTLY *EXPLAINS*...

YA MEAN, THIS PLACE USED TO BE *DOC DOOM'S*... WHEN HE FIRST TOOK ON THE *F.F.?**

AND, YOU BROUGHT US HERE TO HELP YOU OPERATE... A *TIME MACHINE??*

*'WAY BACK IN *F.F. #5*, FOR ALL YOU MARVELITES-- COME-LATELY! --SUPER-ANNUATED STAN.

INCREDIBLE AS IT MAY SEEM, HAWKEYE *THERE* IT IS!

REED RICHARDS TOLD ME ABOUT IT, ONLY *DAYS* AGO!

I WOULDN'T HAVE *INVOLVED* ANY OF YOU IF I COULD HANDLE IT *ALONE!*

YOU KNOW YOU NEED ONLY *ASK*, CAP!

AND YET, WHY DOES MY SPINE *TINGLE*...AS IF SOME DEADLY MENACE HOVERED NEAR, UNSEEN?

SOON, WHEN THE *MANUAL OPERATION* OF THE STRANGE MACHINE HAS BEEN MADE CLEAR...

...SO, JAN, YOU NEED ONLY MANIPULATE THESE *DIALS* IN SEQUENCE, AT REGULAR *INTERVALS!*

BUT, IF YOU *FAIL*... YOU MAY WELL PLACE ALL OF US IN *MORTAL JEOPARDY!*

I *WON'T* FAIL, HANK... I *PROMISE* YOU!

HOW *COULD* I BE CARE- LESS...WITH YOUR VERY *LIVES* AT STAKE?

THERE'S NO NEED FOR ANYONE BUT *ME* TO BE ENDANGERED!

THE REST OF YOU COULD REMAIN *HERE*...WITH THE *WASP!*

NEGATIVE, CAP! WE'RE SIGNED UP FOR THE *ROUND TRIP!*

YOU *KNOW* IT!

BESIDES, I'VE ALWAYS *WANTED* A FIRST-HAND LOOK AT THE *BIG ONE!*

THEN, START THE *MACHINE*, JAN!

WE'RE ALL STANDING ON THE *CHRONO-SQUARE!*

HERE *GOES*, AND MAY *HEAVEN*--

BUT, THE FOUR FIGURES BEFORE HER DO NOT *HEAR* HER NEXT WORDS...FOR, AT HER FIRST TOUCH OF THE DIALS, THEY ARE INSTANTANEOUSLY HURLED *LONG, SILENT YEARS AWAY*...!

6

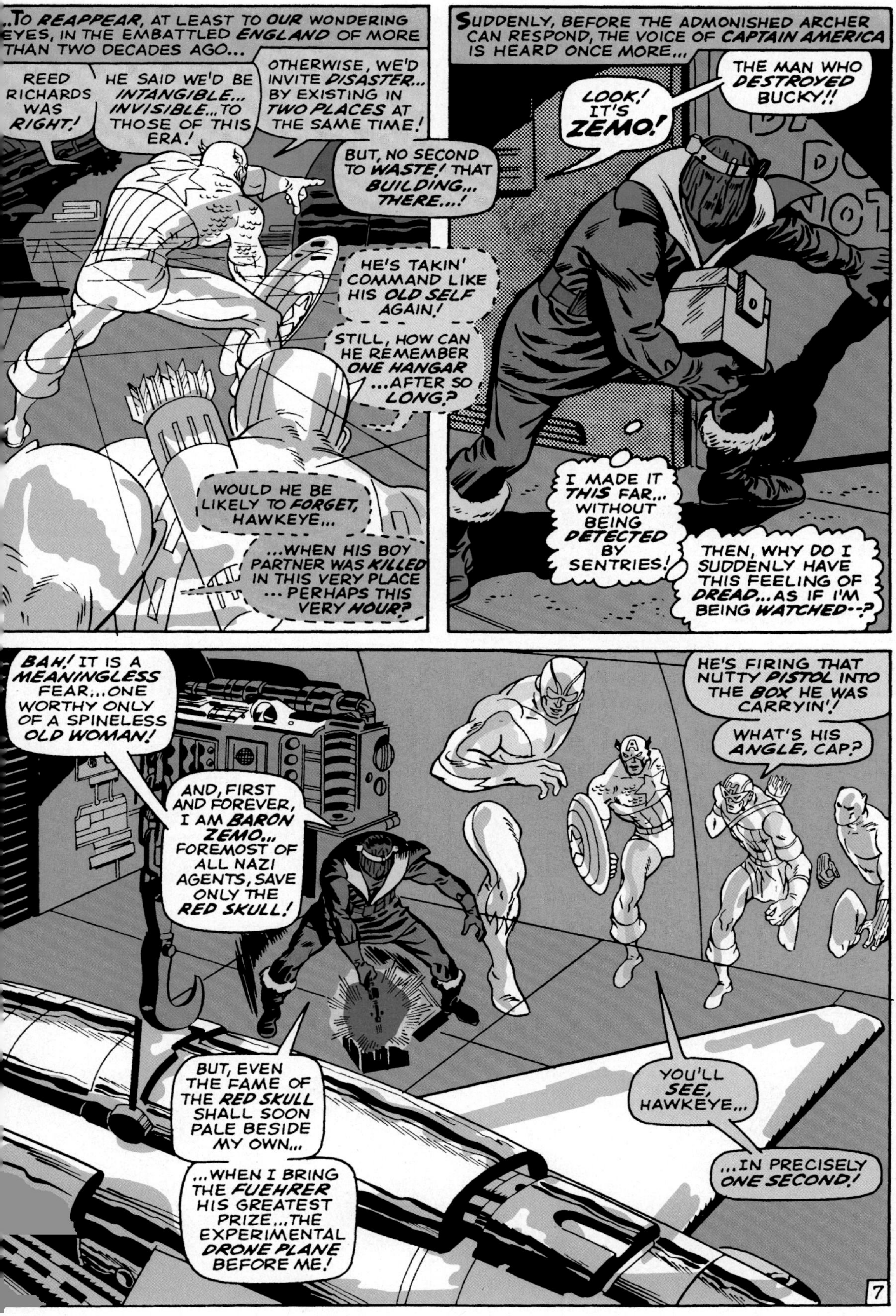

..TO REAPPEAR, AT LEAST TO OUR WONDERING EYES, IN THE EMBATTLED ENGLAND OF MORE THAN TWO DECADES AGO...
REED RICHARDS WAS RIGHT!
HE SAID WE'D BE INTANGIBLE... INVISIBLE...TO THOSE OF THIS ERA!
OTHERWISE, WE'D INVITE DISASTER... BY EXISTING IN TWO PLACES AT THE SAME TIME!
BUT, NO SECOND TO WASTE! THAT BUILDING... THERE...!
HE'S TAKIN' COMMAND LIKE HIS OLD SELF AGAIN!
STILL, HOW CAN HE REMEMBER ONE HANGAR ...AFTER SO LONG?
WOULD HE BE LIKELY TO FORGET, HAWKEYE...
...WHEN HIS BOY PARTNER WAS KILLED IN THIS VERY PLACE ... PERHAPS THIS VERY HOUR?
SUDDENLY, BEFORE THE ADMONISHED ARCHER CAN RESPOND, THE VOICE OF CAPTAIN AMERICA IS HEARD ONCE MORE...
LOOK! IT'S ZEMO!
THE MAN WHO DESTROYED BUCKY!!
I MADE IT THIS FAR... WITHOUT BEING DETECTED BY SENTRIES!
THEN, WHY DO I SUDDENLY HAVE THIS FEELING OF DREAD...AS IF I'M BEING WATCHED--?
BAH! IT IS A MEANINGLESS FEAR...ONE WORTHY ONLY OF A SPINELESS OLD WOMAN!
AND, FIRST AND FOREVER, I AM BARON ZEMO... FOREMOST OF ALL NAZI AGENTS, SAVE ONLY THE RED SKULL!
BUT, EVEN THE FAME OF THE RED SKULL SHALL SOON PALE BESIDE MY OWN...
...WHEN I BRING THE FUEHRER HIS GREATEST PRIZE...THE EXPERIMENTAL DRONE PLANE BEFORE ME!
HE'S FIRING THAT NUTTY PISTOL INTO THE BOX HE WAS CARRYIN'!
WHAT'S HIS ANGLE, CAP?
YOU'LL SEE, HAWKEYE...
...IN PRECISELY ONE SECOND!

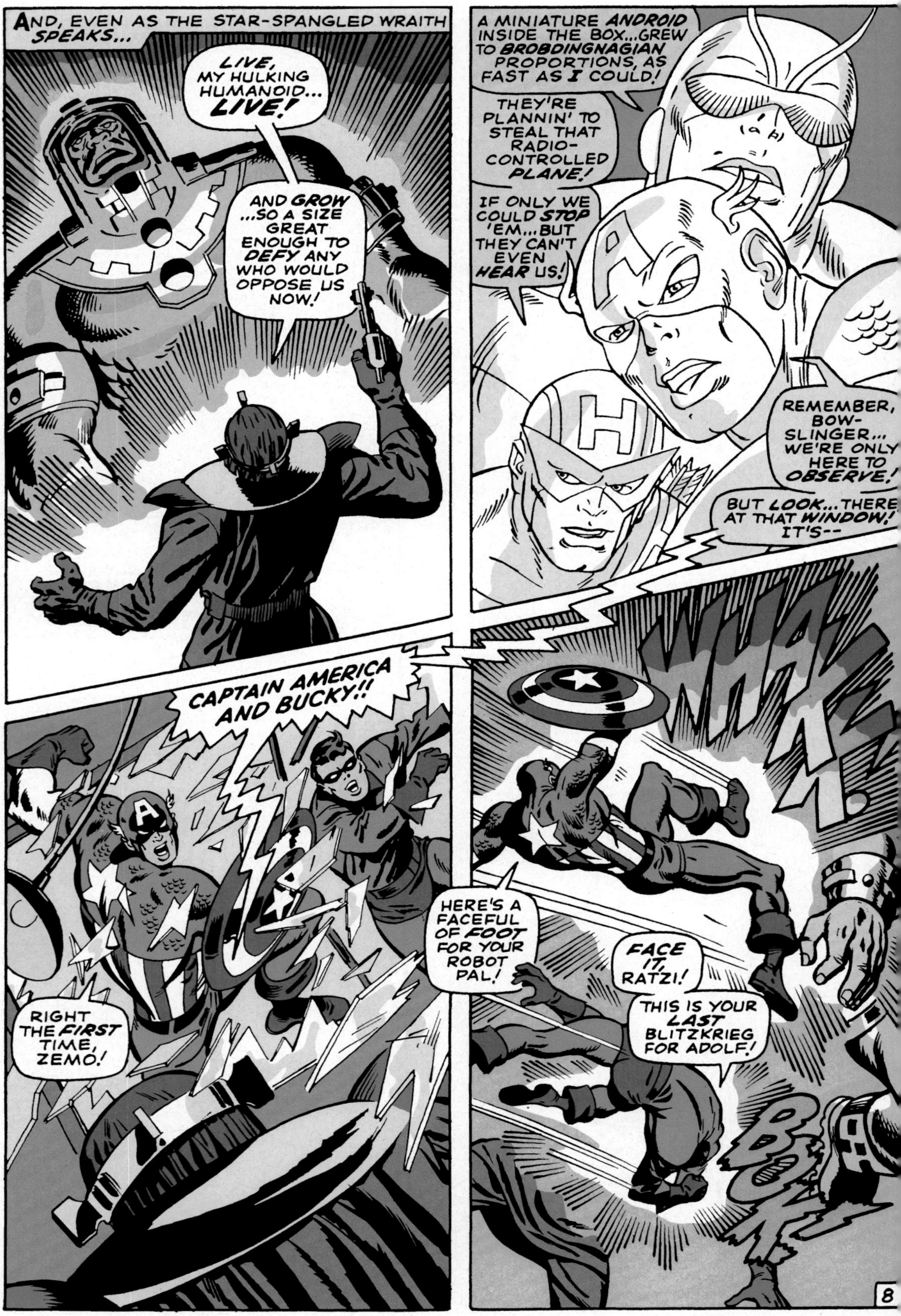
AND, EVEN AS THE STAR-SPANGLED WRAITH SPEAKS...
LIVE, MY HULKING HUMANOID... LIVE!
AND GROW ...SO A SIZE GREAT ENOUGH TO DEFY ANY WHO WOULD OPPOSE US NOW!
A MINIATURE ANDROID INSIDE THE BOX...GREW TO BROBDINGNAGIAN PROPORTIONS, AS FAST AS I COULD!
THEY'RE PLANNIN' TO STEAL THAT RADIO-CONTROLLED PLANE!
IF ONLY WE COULD STOP 'EM...BUT THEY CAN'T EVEN HEAR US!
REMEMBER, BOW-SLINGER... WE'RE ONLY HERE TO OBSERVE!
BUT LOOK...THERE AT THAT WINDOW! IT'S--
CAPTAIN AMERICA AND BUCKY!!
RIGHT THE FIRST TIME, ZEMO!
WHAK!
HERE'S A FACEFUL OF FOOT FOR YOUR ROBOT PAL!
FACE IT, RATZI!
THIS IS YOUR LAST BLITZKRIEG FOR ADOLF!
BOK!
8

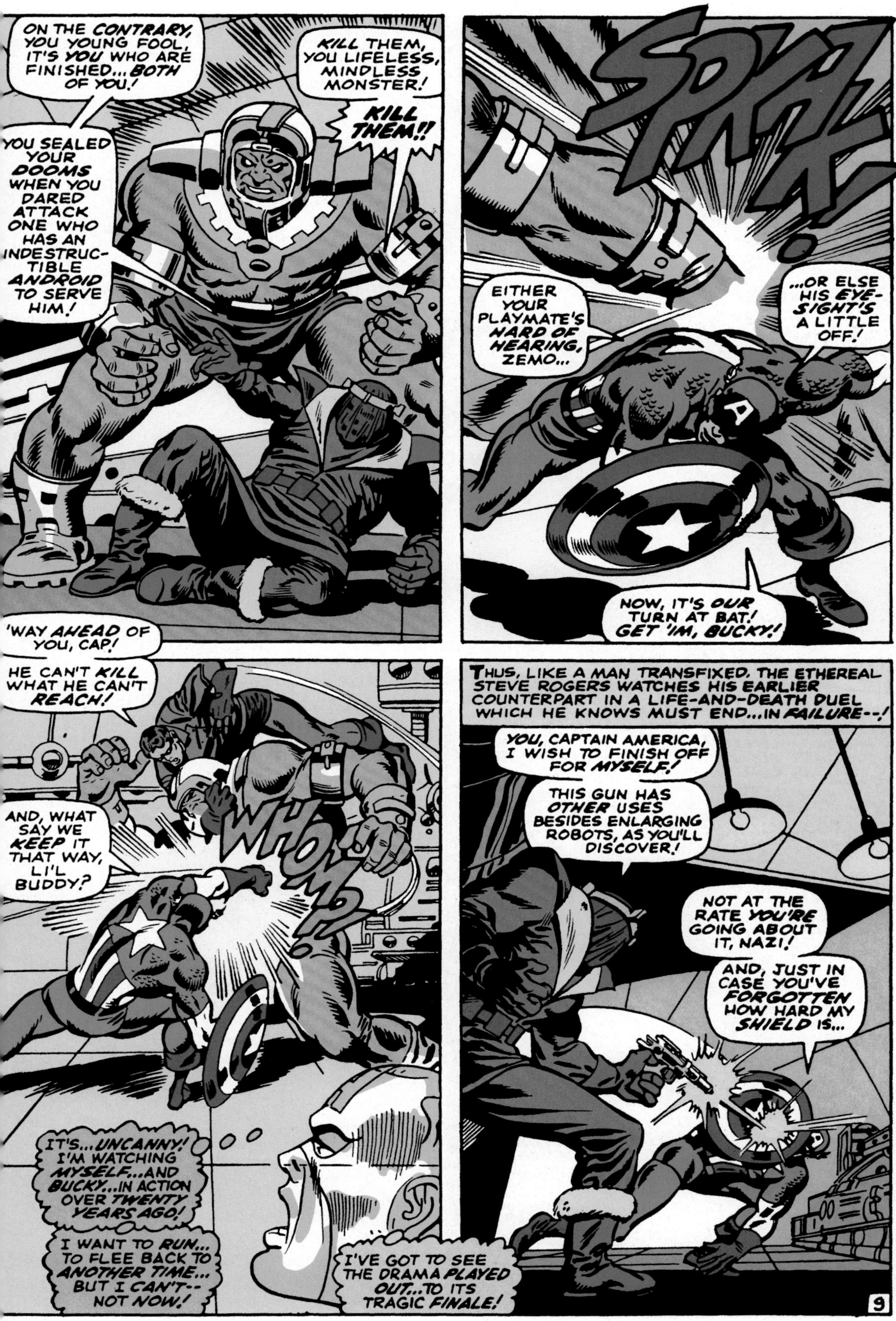
ON THE CONTRARY, YOU YOUNG FOOL, IT'S YOU WHO ARE FINISHED... BOTH OF YOU!
KILL THEM, YOU LIFELESS, MINDLESS MONSTER!
KILL THEM!!
YOU SEALED YOUR DOOMS WHEN YOU DARED ATTACK ONE WHO HAS AN INDESTRUCTIBLE ANDROID TO SERVE HIM!
SPAK!
EITHER YOUR PLAYMATE'S HARD OF HEARING, ZEMO...
...OR ELSE HIS EYE-SIGHT'S A LITTLE OFF!
NOW, IT'S OUR TURN AT BAT! GET 'IM, BUCKY!
'WAY AHEAD OF YOU, CAP!
HE CAN'T KILL WHAT HE CAN'T REACH!
AND, WHAT SAY WE KEEP IT THAT WAY, LI'L BUDDY?
WHOMP!
IT'S... UNCANNY! I'M WATCHING MYSELF... AND BUCKY... IN ACTION OVER TWENTY YEARS AGO!
I WANT TO RUN... TO FLEE BACK TO ANOTHER TIME... BUT I CAN'T-- NOT NOW!
I'VE GOT TO SEE THE DRAMA PLAYED OUT... TO ITS TRAGIC FINALE!
THUS, LIKE A MAN TRANSFIXED, THE ETHEREAL STEVE ROGERS WATCHES HIS EARLIER COUNTERPART IN A LIFE-AND-DEATH DUEL WHICH HE KNOWS MUST END... IN FAILURE--!
YOU, CAPTAIN AMERICA, I WISH TO FINISH OFF FOR MYSELF!
THIS GUN HAS OTHER USES BESIDES ENLARGING ROBOTS, AS YOU'LL DISCOVER!
NOT AT THE RATE YOU'RE GOING ABOUT IT, NAZI!
AND, JUST IN CASE YOU'VE FORGOTTEN HOW HARD MY SHIELD IS...

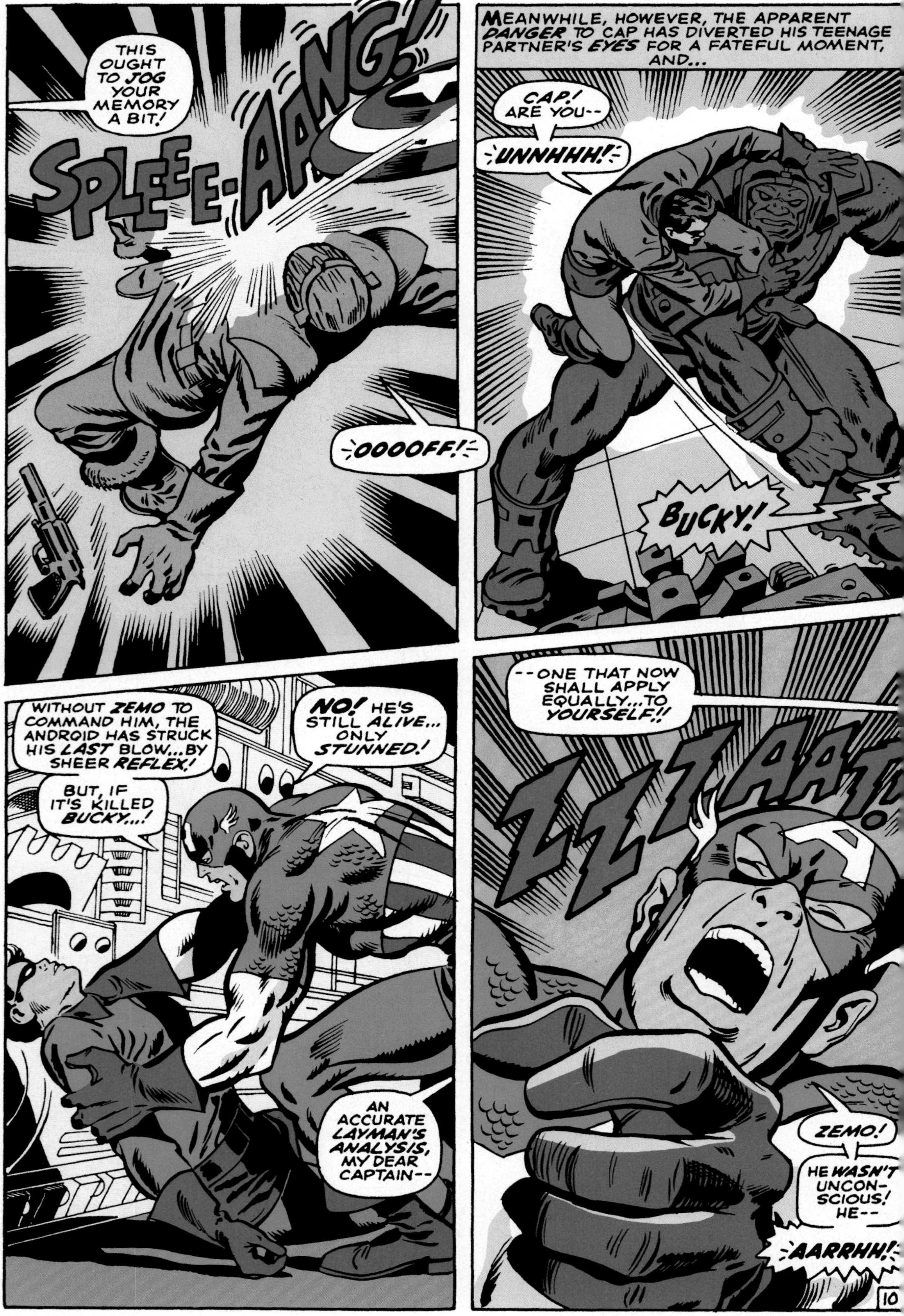
THIS OUGHT TO JOG YOUR MEMORY A BIT!
SPLEE-E-AAANG!
OOOOFF!
MEANWHILE, HOWEVER, THE APPARENT DANGER TO CAP HAS DIVERTED HIS TEENAGE PARTNER'S EYES FOR A FATEFUL MOMENT, AND...
CAP! ARE YOU--
UNNHHH!
BUCKY!
WITHOUT ZEMO TO COMMAND HIM, THE ANDROID HAS STRUCK HIS LAST BLOW...BY SHEER REFLEX!
BUT, IF IT'S KILLED BUCKY...!
NO! HE'S STILL ALIVE... ONLY STUNNED!
AN ACCURATE LAYMAN'S ANALYSIS, MY DEAR CAPTAIN--
--ONE THAT NOW SHALL APPLY EQUALLY...TO YOURSELF!!
ZZZAAT!
ZEMO!
HE WASN'T UNCONSCIOUS! HE--
AARRHH!

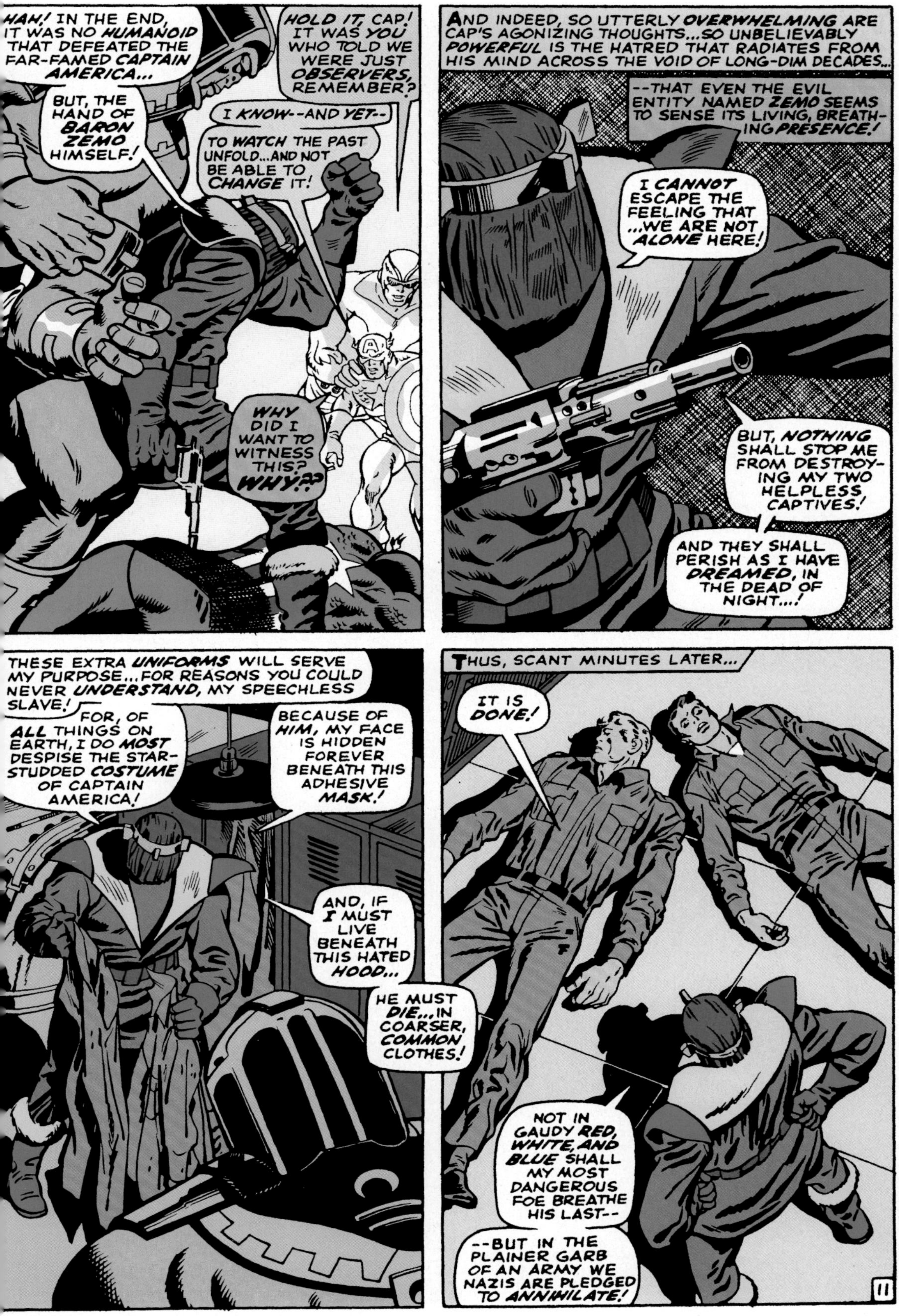
HAH! IN THE END, IT WAS NO HUMANOID THAT DEFEATED THE FAR-FAMED CAPTAIN AMERICA...
BUT, THE HAND OF BARON ZEMO HIMSELF!
HOLD IT, CAP! IT WAS YOU WHO TOLD WE WERE JUST OBSERVERS, REMEMBER?
I KNOW--AND YET--
TO WATCH THE PAST UNFOLD...AND NOT BE ABLE TO CHANGE IT!
WHY DID I WANT TO WITNESS THIS? WHY??
AND INDEED, SO UTTERLY OVERWHELMING ARE CAP'S AGONIZING THOUGHTS...SO UNBELIEVABLY POWERFUL IS THE HATRED THAT RADIATES FROM HIS MIND ACROSS THE VOID OF LONG-DIM DECADES...
--THAT EVEN THE EVIL ENTITY NAMED ZEMO SEEMS TO SENSE ITS LIVING, BREATHING PRESENCE!
I CANNOT ESCAPE THE FEELING THAT ...WE ARE NOT ALONE HERE!
BUT, NOTHING SHALL STOP ME FROM DESTROYING MY TWO HELPLESS CAPTIVES!
AND THEY SHALL PERISH AS I HAVE DREAMED, IN THE DEAD OF NIGHT...!
THESE EXTRA UNIFORMS WILL SERVE MY PURPOSE...FOR REASONS YOU COULD NEVER UNDERSTAND, MY SPEECHLESS SLAVE!
FOR, OF ALL THINGS ON EARTH, I DO MOST DESPISE THE STAR-STUDDED COSTUME OF CAPTAIN AMERICA!
BECAUSE OF HIM, MY FACE IS HIDDEN FOREVER BENEATH THIS ADHESIVE MASK!
AND, IF I MUST LIVE BENEATH THIS HATED HOOD...
HE MUST DIE...IN COARSER, COMMON CLOTHES!
THUS, SCANT MINUTES LATER...
IT IS DONE!
NOT IN GAUDY RED, WHITE, AND BLUE SHALL MY MOST DANGEROUS FOE BREATHE HIS LAST--
--BUT IN THE PLAINER GARB OF AN ARMY WE NAZIS ARE PLEDGED TO ANNIHILATE!
11

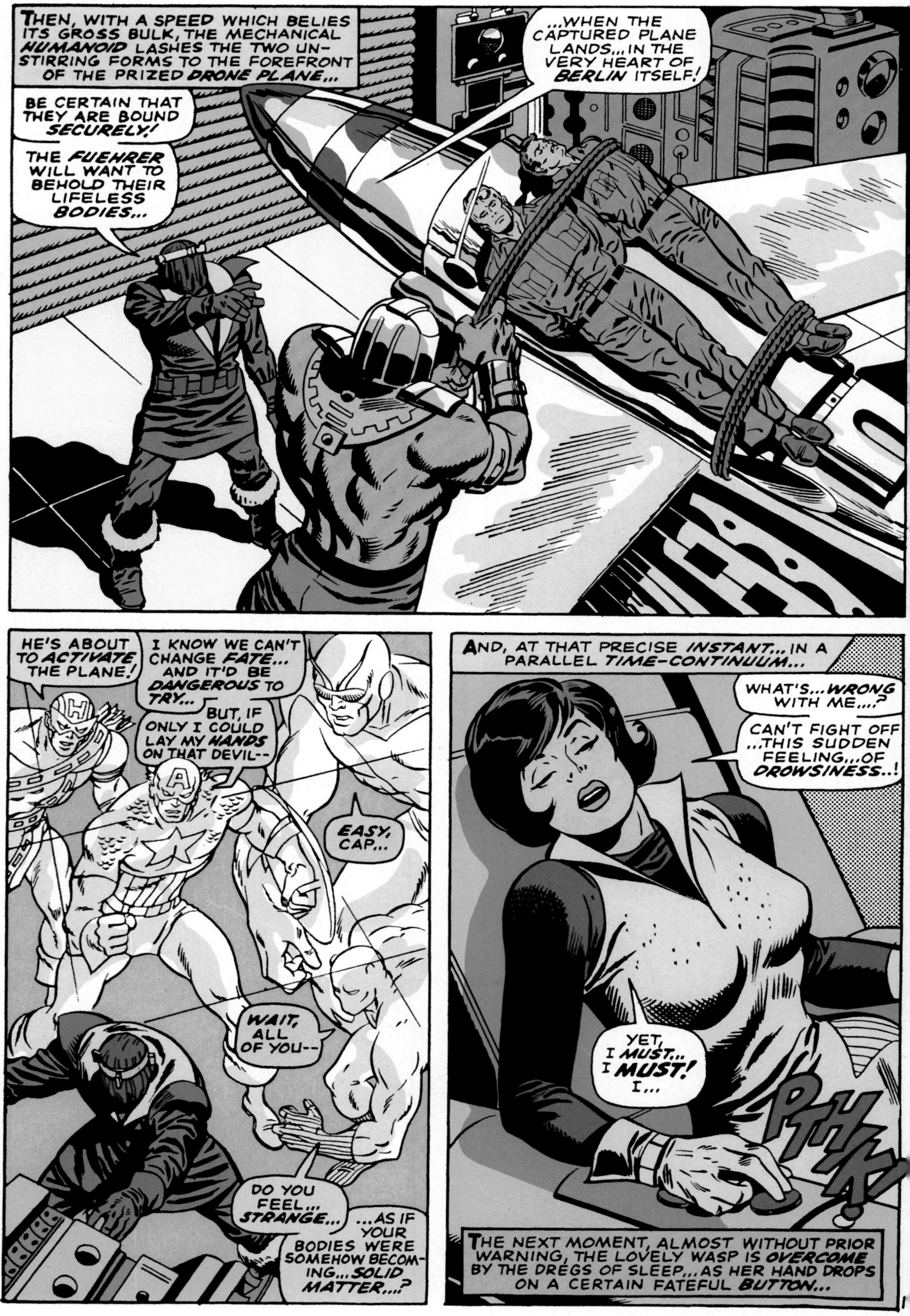
THEN, WITH A SPEED WHICH BELIES ITS GROSS BULK, THE MECHANICAL HUMANOID LASHES THE TWO UN-STIRRING FORMS TO THE FOREFRONT OF THE PRIZED DRONE PLANE...
BE CERTAIN THAT THEY ARE BOUND SECURELY!
THE FUEHRER WILL WANT TO BEHOLD THEIR LIFELESS BODIES...
...WHEN THE CAPTURED PLANE LANDS... IN THE VERY HEART OF BERLIN ITSELF!
HE'S ABOUT TO ACTIVATE THE PLANE!
I KNOW WE CAN'T CHANGE FATE... AND IT'D BE DANGEROUS TO TRY...
BUT, IF ONLY I COULD LAY MY HANDS ON THAT DEVIL--
EASY, CAP...
WAIT, ALL OF YOU--
DO YOU FEEL... STRANGE...
...AS IF YOUR BODIES WERE SOMEHOW BECOMING... SOLID MATTER...?
AND, AT THAT PRECISE INSTANT... IN A PARALLEL TIME-CONTINUUM...
WHAT'S... WRONG WITH ME...?
CAN'T FIGHT OFF ...THIS SUDDEN FEELING... OF DROWSINESS..!
YET, I MUST... I MUST! I...
PHHK!
THE NEXT MOMENT, ALMOST WITHOUT PRIOR WARNING, THE LOVELY WASP IS OVERCOME BY THE DREGS OF SLEEP... AS HER HAND DROPS ON A CERTAIN FATEFUL BUTTON...

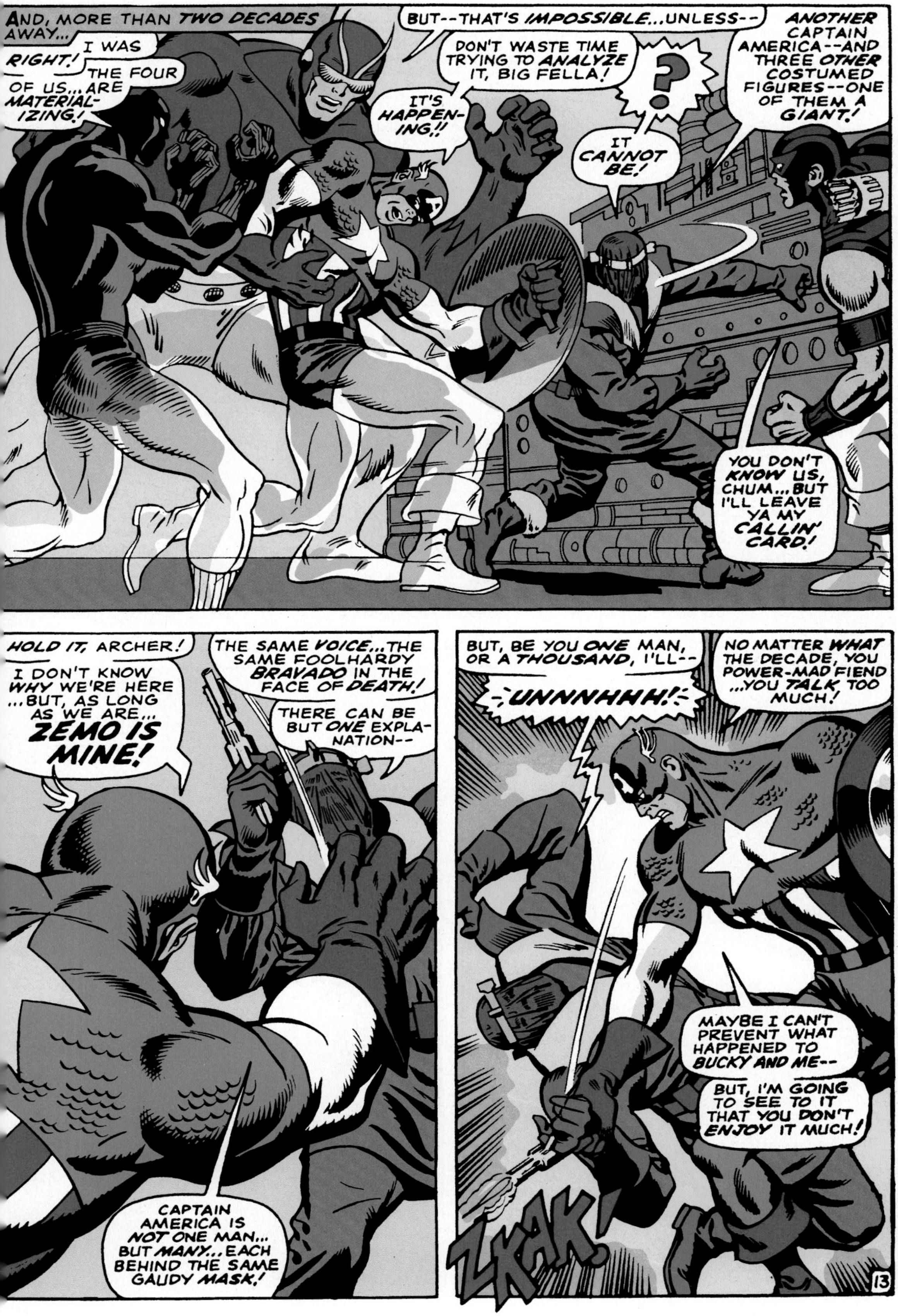

AND, MORE THAN TWO DECADES AWAY...
I WAS RIGHT!
THE FOUR OF US... ARE MATERIAL-IZING!
BUT--THAT'S IMPOSSIBLE...UNLESS--
DON'T WASTE TIME TRYING TO ANALYZE IT, BIG FELLA!
IT'S HAPPEN-ING!!
?
IT CANNOT BE!
ANOTHER CAPTAIN AMERICA--AND THREE OTHER COSTUMED FIGURES--ONE OF THEM A GIANT!
YOU DON'T KNOW US, CHUM... BUT I'LL LEAVE YA MY CALLIN' CARD!
HOLD IT, ARCHER!
I DON'T KNOW WHY WE'RE HERE ...BUT, AS LONG AS WE ARE... ZEMO IS MINE!
THE SAME VOICE... THE SAME FOOLHARDY BRAVADO IN THE FACE OF DEATH!
THERE CAN BE BUT ONE EXPLA-NATION--
CAPTAIN AMERICA IS NOT ONE MAN... BUT MANY... EACH BEHIND THE SAME GAUDY MASK!
BUT, BE YOU ONE MAN, OR A THOUSAND, I'LL--
UNNNHHH!
NO MATTER WHAT THE DECADE, YOU POWER-MAD FIEND ...YOU TALK TOO MUCH!
MAYBE I CAN'T PREVENT WHAT HAPPENED TO BUCKY AND ME--
BUT, I'M GOING TO SEE TO IT THAT YOU DON'T ENJOY IT MUCH!
ZKAK!
13

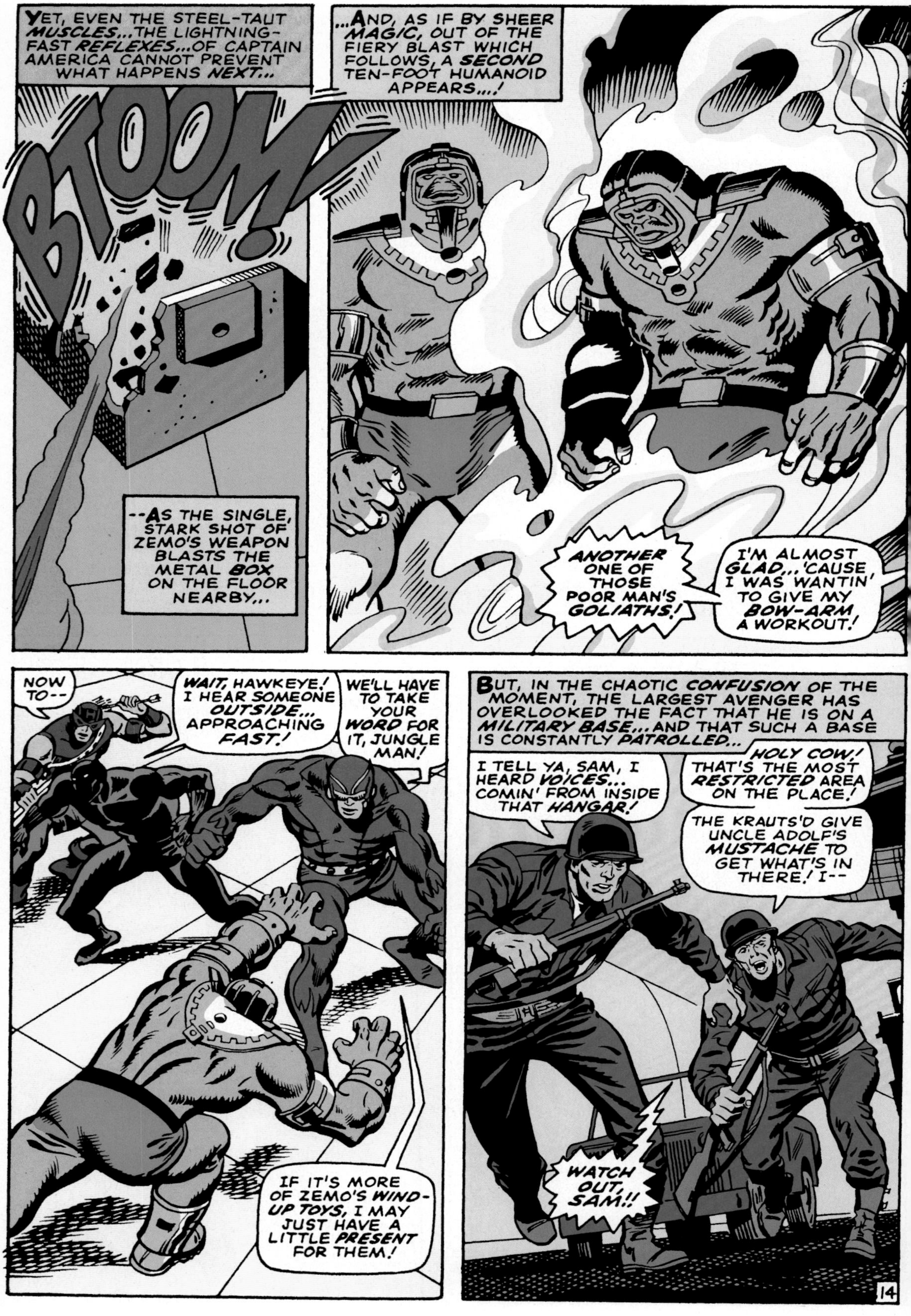
YET, EVEN THE STEEL-TAUT MUSCLES... THE LIGHTNING-FAST REFLEXES... OF CAPTAIN AMERICA CANNOT PREVENT WHAT HAPPENS NEXT...
BTOOM!
--AS THE SINGLE, STARK SHOT OF ZEMO'S WEAPON BLASTS THE METAL BOX ON THE FLOOR NEARBY...
...AND, AS IF BY SHEER MAGIC, OUT OF THE FIERY BLAST WHICH FOLLOWS, A SECOND TEN-FOOT HUMANOID APPEARS...!
ANOTHER ONE OF THOSE POOR MAN'S GOLIATHS!
I'M ALMOST GLAD... 'CAUSE, I WAS WANTIN' TO GIVE MY BOW-ARM A WORKOUT!
NOW TO--
WAIT, HAWKEYE! I HEAR SOMEONE OUTSIDE... APPROACHING FAST!
WE'LL HAVE TO TAKE YOUR WORD FOR IT, JUNGLE MAN!
IF IT'S MORE OF ZEMO'S WIND-UP TOYS, I MAY JUST HAVE A LITTLE PRESENT FOR THEM!
BUT, IN THE CHAOTIC CONFUSION OF THE MOMENT, THE LARGEST AVENGER HAS OVERLOOKED THE FACT THAT HE IS ON A MILITARY BASE... AND THAT SUCH A BASE IS CONSTANTLY PATROLLED...
I TELL YA, SAM, I HEARD VOICES... COMIN' FROM INSIDE THAT HANGAR!
HOLY COW! THAT'S THE MOST RESTRICTED AREA ON THE PLACE!
THE KRAUTS'D GIVE UNCLE ADOLF'S MUSTACHE TO GET WHAT'S IN THERE! I--
WATCH OUT, SAM!!

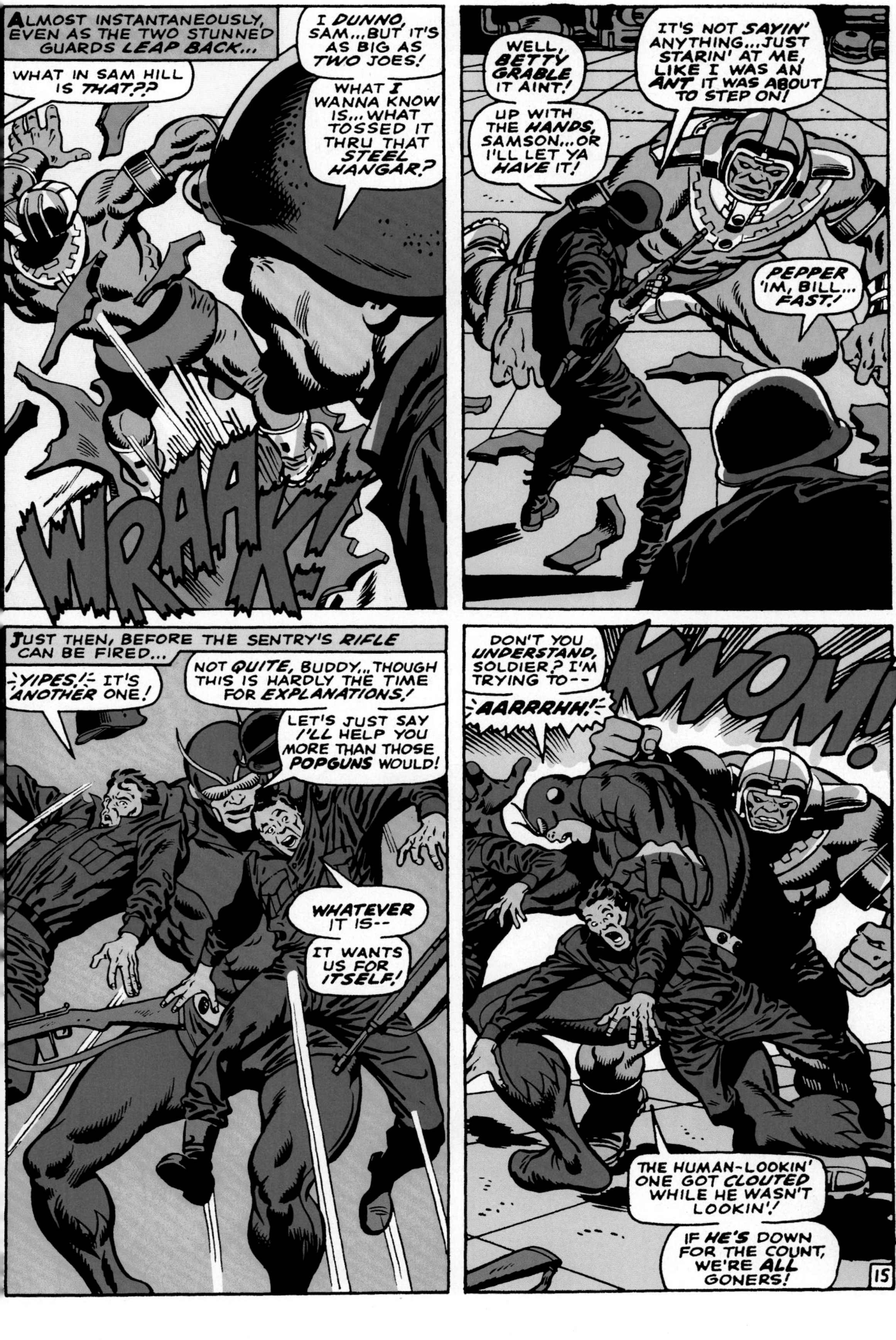
ALMOST INSTANTANEOUSLY, EVEN AS THE TWO STUNNED GUARDS LEAP BACK...
WHAT IN SAM HILL IS THAT??
I DUNNO, SAM...BUT IT'S AS BIG AS TWO JOES!
WHAT I WANNA KNOW IS...WHAT TOSSED IT THRU THAT STEEL HANGAR?
WRAAK!
WELL, BETTY GRABLE IT AINT!
IT'S NOT SAYIN' ANYTHING...JUST STARIN' AT ME, LIKE I WAS AN ANT IT WAS ABOUT TO STEP ON!
UP WITH THE HANDS, SAMSON...OR I'LL LET YA HAVE IT!
PEPPER 'IM, BILL... FAST!
JUST THEN, BEFORE THE SENTRY'S RIFLE CAN BE FIRED...
YIPES! IT'S ANOTHER ONE!
NOT QUITE, BUDDY...THOUGH THIS IS HARDLY THE TIME FOR EXPLANATIONS!
LET'S JUST SAY I'LL HELP YOU MORE THAN THOSE POPGUNS WOULD!
WHATEVER IT IS--
IT WANTS US FOR ITSELF!
DON'T YOU UNDERSTAND, SOLDIER? I'M TRYING TO--
KNOM!
AARRRHH!
THE HUMAN-LOOKIN' ONE GOT CLOUTED WHILE HE WASN'T LOOKIN'!
IF HE'S DOWN FOR THE COUNT, WE'RE ALL GONERS!
15

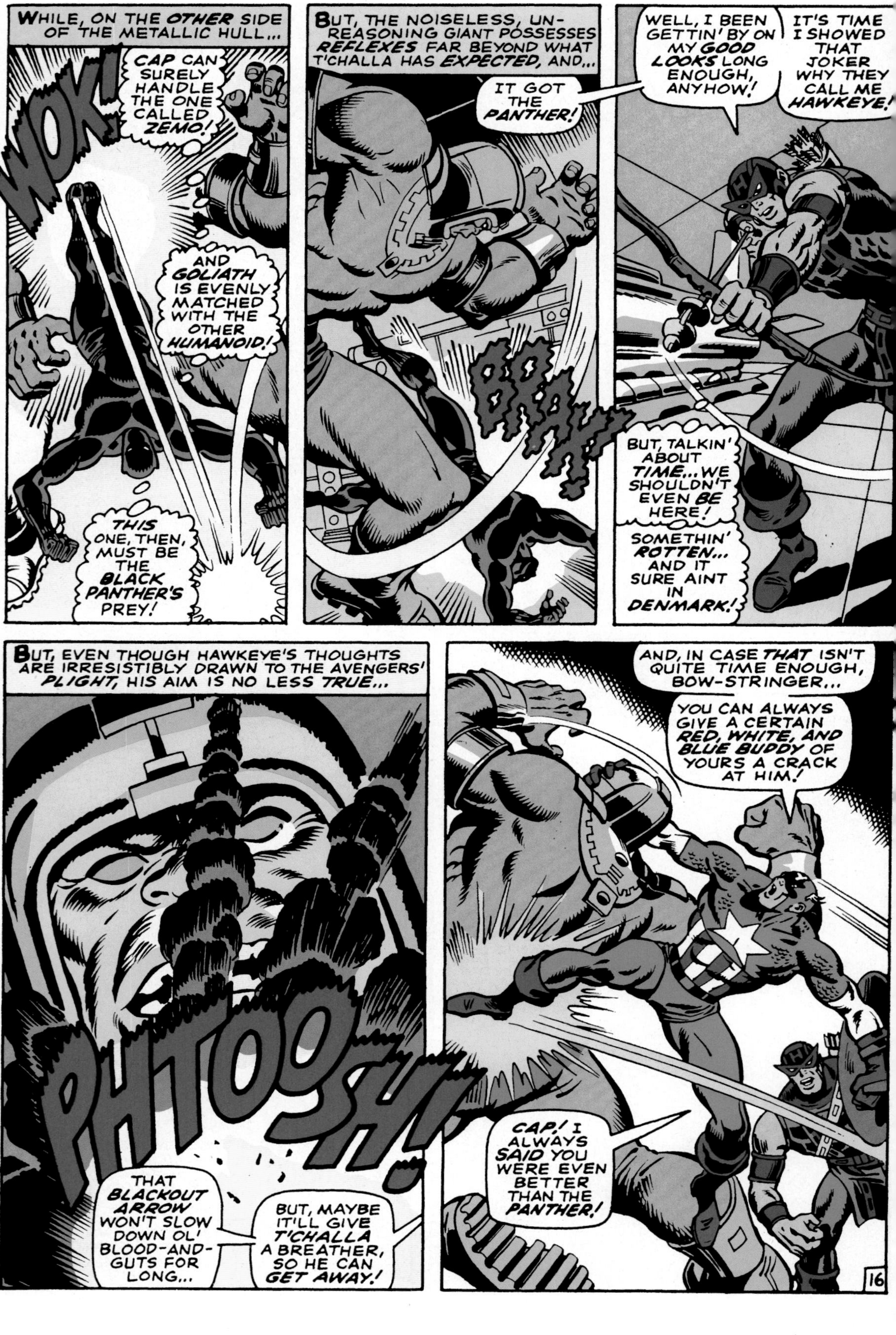
WHILE, ON THE OTHER SIDE OF THE METALLIC HULL...
WOK!
CAP CAN SURELY HANDLE THE ONE CALLED ZEMO!
AND GOLIATH IS EVENLY MATCHED WITH THE OTHER HUMANOID!
THIS ONE, THEN, MUST BE THE BLACK PANTHER'S PREY!
BUT, THE NOISELESS, UN-REASONING GIANT POSSESSES REFLEXES FAR BEYOND WHAT T'CHALLA HAS EXPECTED, AND...
IT GOT THE PANTHER!
BRAK
WELL, I BEEN GETTIN' BY ON MY GOOD LOOKS LONG ENOUGH, ANYHOW!
IT'S TIME I SHOWED THAT JOKER WHY THEY CALL ME HAWKEYE!
BUT, TALKIN' ABOUT TIME... WE SHOULDN'T EVEN BE HERE!
SOMETHIN' ROTTEN... AND IT SURE AINT IN DENMARK!
BUT, EVEN THOUGH HAWKEYE'S THOUGHTS ARE IRRESISTIBLY DRAWN TO THE AVENGERS' PLIGHT, HIS AIM IS NO LESS TRUE...
PHTOOSH!
THAT BLACKOUT ARROW WON'T SLOW DOWN OL' BLOOD-AND-GUTS FOR LONG...
BUT, MAYBE IT'LL GIVE T'CHALLA A BREATHER, SO HE CAN GET AWAY!
AND, IN CASE THAT ISN'T QUITE TIME ENOUGH, BOW-STRINGER...
YOU CAN ALWAYS GIVE A CERTAIN RED, WHITE, AND BLUE BUDDY OF YOURS A CRACK AT HIM!
CAP! I ALWAYS SAID YOU WERE EVEN BETTER THAN THE PANTHER!
16

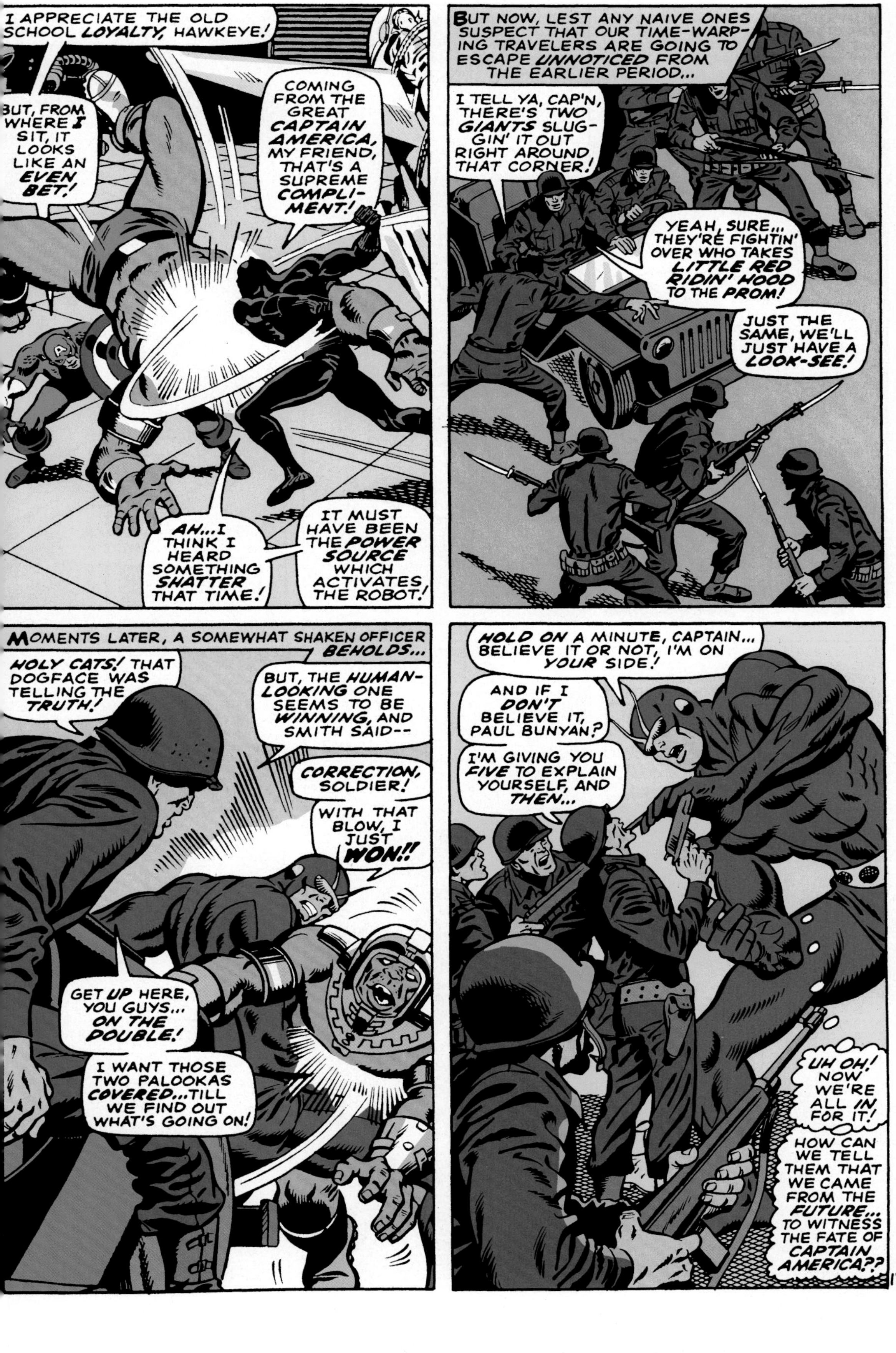
I APPRECIATE THE OLD SCHOOL LOYALTY, HAWKEYE!
BUT, FROM WHERE I SIT, IT LOOKS LIKE AN EVEN BET!
COMING FROM THE GREAT CAPTAIN AMERICA, MY FRIEND, THAT'S A SUPREME COMPLIMENT!
AH...I THINK I HEARD SOMETHING SHATTER THAT TIME!
IT MUST HAVE BEEN THE POWER SOURCE WHICH ACTIVATES THE ROBOT!
BUT NOW, LEST ANY NAIVE ONES SUSPECT THAT OUR TIME-WARPING TRAVELERS ARE GOING TO ESCAPE UNNOTICED FROM THE EARLIER PERIOD...
I TELL YA, CAP'N, THERE'S TWO GIANTS SLUGGIN' IT OUT RIGHT AROUND THAT CORNER!
YEAH, SURE... THEY'RE FIGHTIN' OVER WHO TAKES LITTLE RED RIDIN' HOOD TO THE PROM!
JUST THE SAME, WE'LL JUST HAVE A LOOK-SEE!
MOMENTS LATER, A SOMEWHAT SHAKEN OFFICER BEHOLDS...
HOLY CATS! THAT DOGFACE WAS TELLING THE TRUTH!
BUT, THE HUMAN-LOOKING ONE SEEMS TO BE WINNING, AND SMITH SAID--
CORRECTION, SOLDIER!
WITH THAT BLOW, I JUST WON!!
GET UP HERE, YOU GUYS... ON THE DOUBLE!
I WANT THOSE TWO PALOOKAS COVERED...TILL WE FIND OUT WHAT'S GOING ON!
HOLD ON A MINUTE, CAPTAIN... BELIEVE IT OR NOT, I'M ON YOUR SIDE!
AND IF I DON'T BELIEVE IT, PAUL BUNYAN?
I'M GIVING YOU FIVE TO EXPLAIN YOURSELF, AND THEN...
UH OH! NOW WE'RE ALL IN FOR IT!
HOW CAN WE TELL THEM THAT WE CAME FROM THE FUTURE... TO WITNESS THE FATE OF CAPTAIN AMERICA??

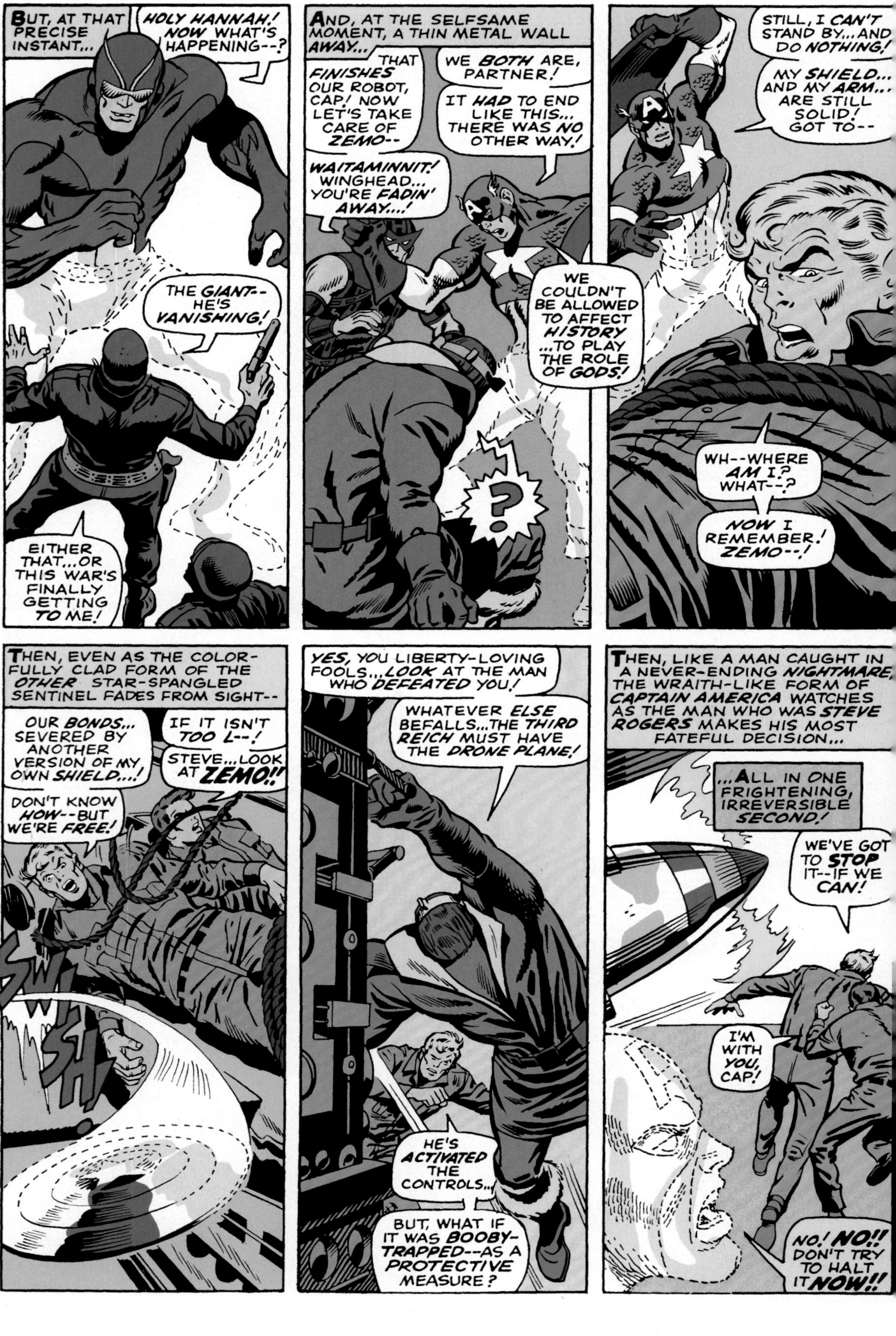
BUT, AT THAT PRECISE INSTANT...
HOLY HANNAH! NOW WHAT'S HAPPENING--?
THE GIANT--HE'S VANISHING!
EITHER THAT...OR THIS WAR'S FINALLY GETTING TO ME!
AND, AT THE SELFSAME MOMENT, A THIN METAL WALL AWAY...
THAT FINISHES OUR ROBOT, CAP! NOW LET'S TAKE CARE OF ZEMO--
WE BOTH ARE, PARTNER!
IT HAD TO END LIKE THIS... THERE WAS NO OTHER WAY!
WAITAMINNIT! WINGHEAD... YOU'RE FADIN' AWAY...!
WE COULDN'T BE ALLOWED TO AFFECT HISTORY ...TO PLAY THE ROLE OF GODS!
?
STILL, I CAN'T STAND BY...AND DO NOTHING!
MY SHIELD... AND MY ARM... ARE STILL SOLID! GOT TO--
WH--WHERE AM I? WHAT--?
NOW I REMEMBER! ZEMO--!
THEN, EVEN AS THE COLORFULLY CLAD FORM OF THE OTHER STAR-SPANGLED SENTINEL FADES FROM SIGHT--
OUR BONDS... SEVERED BY ANOTHER VERSION OF MY OWN SHIELD...!
IF IT ISN'T TOO L--!
STEVE...LOOK AT ZEMO!!
DON'T KNOW HOW--BUT WE'RE FREE!
SWSH
YES, YOU LIBERTY-LOVING FOOLS...LOOK AT THE MAN WHO DEFEATED YOU!
WHATEVER ELSE BEFALLS...THE THIRD REICH MUST HAVE THE DRONE PLANE!
HE'S ACTIVATED THE CONTROLS...
BUT, WHAT IF IT WAS BOOBY-TRAPPED--AS A PROTECTIVE MEASURE?
THEN, LIKE A MAN CAUGHT IN A NEVER-ENDING NIGHTMARE, THE WRAITH-LIKE FORM OF CAPTAIN AMERICA WATCHES AS THE MAN WHO WAS STEVE ROGERS MAKES HIS MOST FATEFUL DECISION...
...ALL IN ONE FRIGHTENING, IRREVERSIBLE SECOND!
WE'VE GOT TO STOP IT--IF WE CAN!
I'M WITH YOU, CAP!
NO! NO!! DON'T TRY TO HALT IT NOW!!

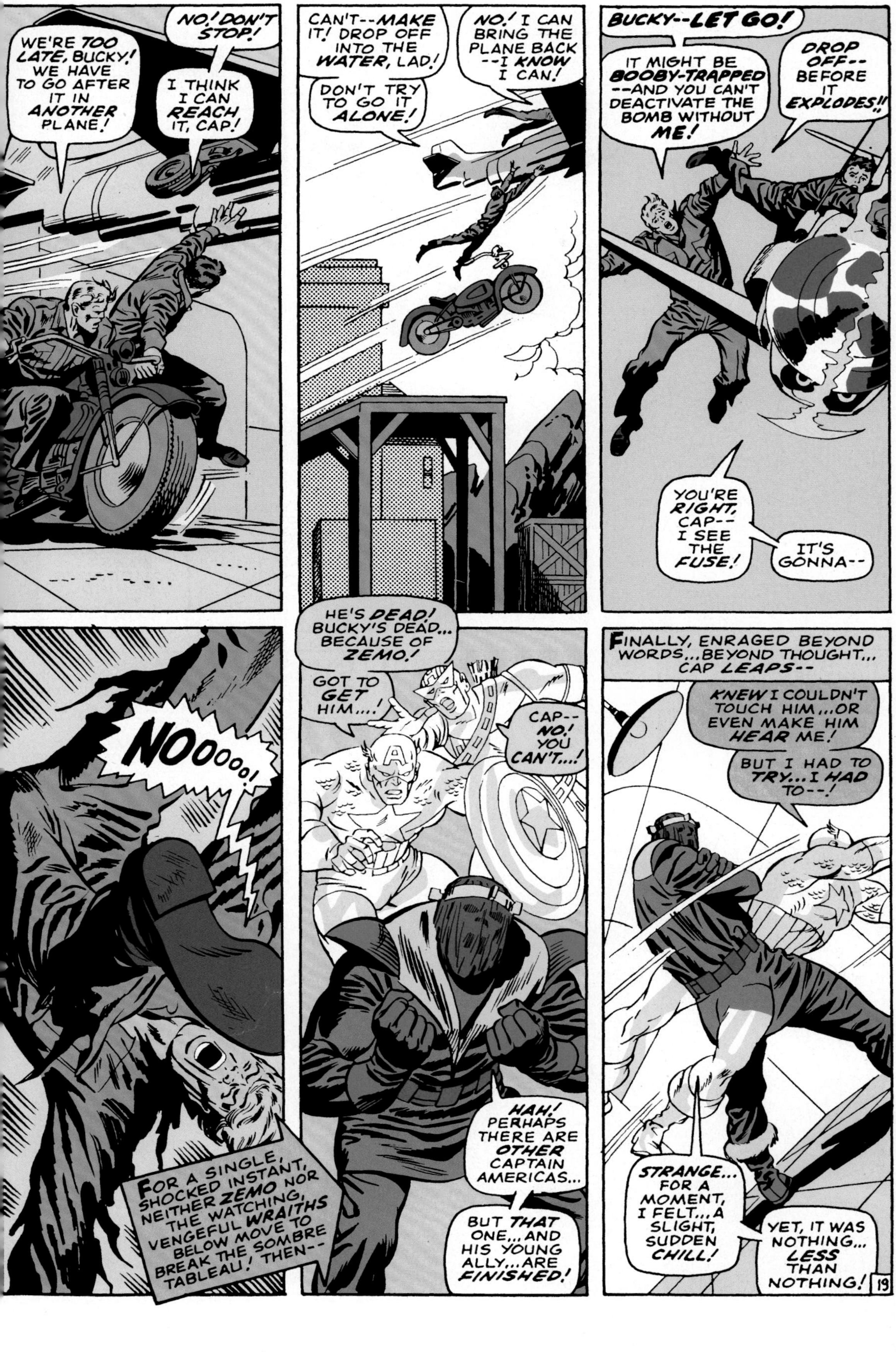
WE'RE TOO LATE, BUCKY! WE HAVE TO GO AFTER IT IN ANOTHER PLANE!
NO! DON'T STOP!
I THINK I CAN REACH IT, CAP!
CAN'T--MAKE IT! DROP OFF INTO THE WATER, LAD!
DON'T TRY TO GO IT ALONE!
NO! I CAN BRING THE PLANE BACK --I KNOW I CAN!
BUCKY--LET GO!
IT MIGHT BE BOOBY-TRAPPED --AND YOU CAN'T DEACTIVATE THE BOMB WITHOUT ME!
DROP OFF-- BEFORE IT EXPLODES!!
YOU'RE RIGHT, CAP-- I SEE THE FUSE!
IT'S GONNA--
NOOOoo!
FOR A SINGLE, SHOCKED INSTANT, NEITHER ZEMO NOR THE WATCHING, VENGEFUL WRAITHS BELOW MOVE TO BREAK THE SOMBRE TABLEAU! THEN--
HE'S DEAD! BUCKY'S DEAD... BECAUSE OF ZEMO!
GOT TO GET HIM...!
CAP-- NO! YOU CAN'T...!
HAH! PERHAPS THERE ARE OTHER CAPTAIN AMERICAS...
BUT THAT ONE... AND HIS YOUNG ALLY... ARE FINISHED!
FINALLY, ENRAGED BEYOND WORDS... BEYOND THOUGHT... CAP LEAPS--
KNEW I COULDN'T TOUCH HIM... OR EVEN MAKE HIM HEAR ME!
BUT I HAD TO TRY... I HAD TO--!
STRANGE... FOR A MOMENT, I FELT... A SLIGHT, SUDDEN CHILL!
YET, IT WAS NOTHING... LESS THAN NOTHING!
19

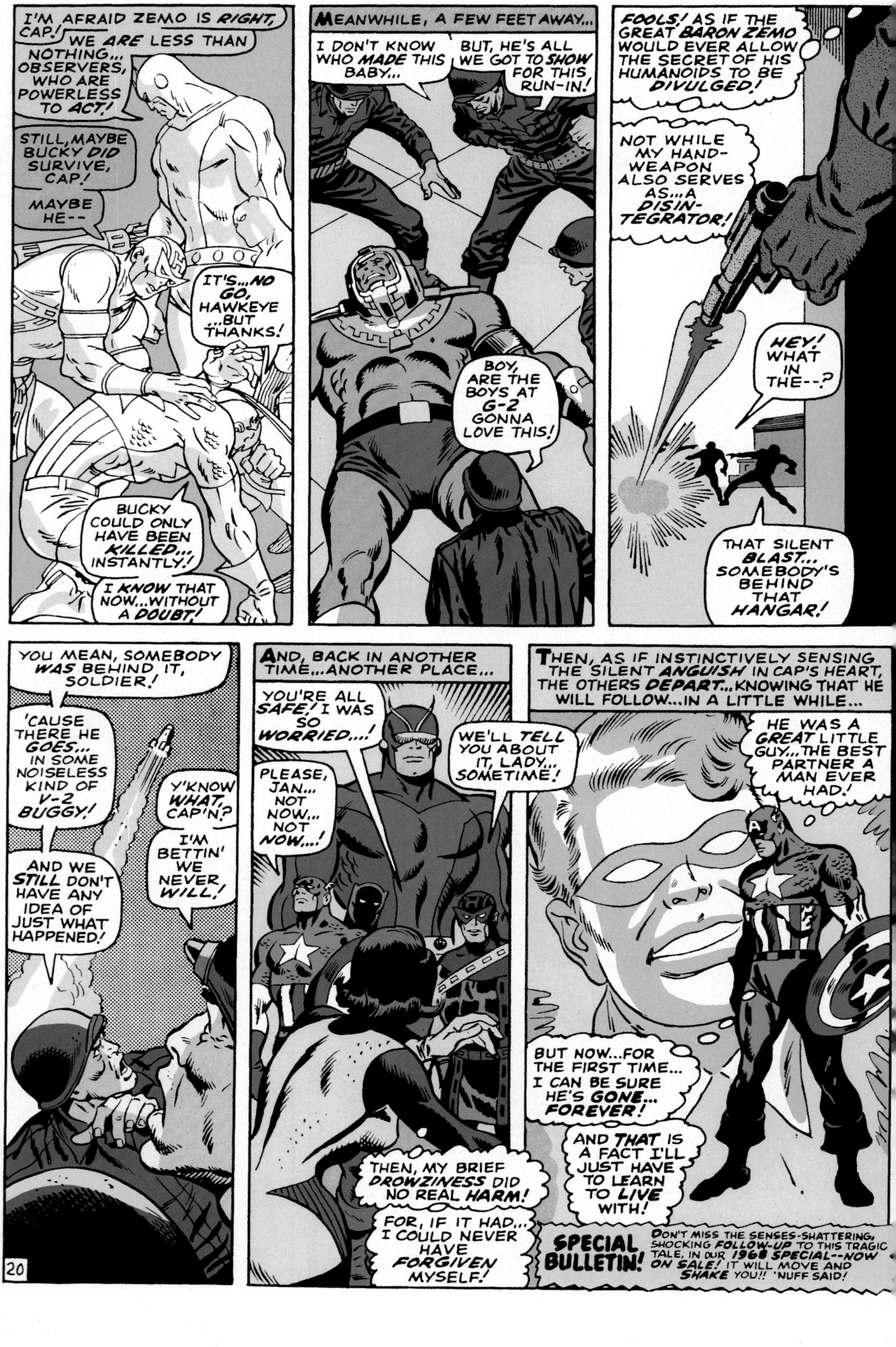

I'M AFRAID ZEMO IS RIGHT, CAP!
WE ARE LESS THAN NOTHING... OBSERVERS, WHO ARE POWERLESS TO ACT!
STILL, MAYBE BUCKY DID SURVIVE, CAP!
MAYBE HE--
IT'S...NO GO, HAWKEYE ...BUT THANKS!
BUCKY COULD ONLY HAVE BEEN KILLED... INSTANTLY!
I KNOW THAT NOW...WITHOUT A DOUBT!
MEANWHILE, A FEW FEET AWAY...
I DON'T KNOW WHO MADE THIS BABY...
BUT, HE'S ALL WE GOT TO SHOW FOR THIS RUN-IN!
BOY, ARE THE BOYS AT G-2 GONNA LOVE THIS!
FOOLS! AS IF THE GREAT BARON ZEMO WOULD EVER ALLOW THE SECRET OF HIS HUMANOIDS TO BE DIVULGED!
NOT WHILE MY HAND-WEAPON ALSO SERVES AS...A DISIN-TEGRATOR!
HEY! WHAT IN THE--?
THAT SILENT BLAST... SOMEBODY'S BEHIND THAT HANGAR!
YOU MEAN, SOMEBODY WAS BEHIND IT, SOLDIER!
'CAUSE THERE HE GOES... IN SOME NOISELESS KIND OF V-2 BUGGY!
Y'KNOW WHAT, CAP'N?
I'M BETTIN' WE NEVER WILL!
AND WE STILL DON'T HAVE ANY IDEA OF JUST WHAT HAPPENED!
AND, BACK IN ANOTHER TIME...ANOTHER PLACE...
YOU'RE ALL SAFE! I WAS SO WORRIED...!
WE'LL TELL YOU ABOUT IT, LADY... SOMETIME!
PLEASE, JAN... NOT NOW... NOT NOW...!
THEN, MY BRIEF DROWZINESS DID NO REAL HARM!
FOR, IF IT HAD... I COULD NEVER HAVE FORGIVEN MYSELF!
THEN, AS IF INSTINCTIVELY SENSING THE SILENT ANGUISH IN CAP'S HEART, THE OTHERS DEPART...KNOWING THAT HE WILL FOLLOW...IN A LITTLE WHILE...
HE WAS A GREAT LITTLE GUY... THE BEST PARTNER A MAN EVER HAD!
BUT NOW...FOR THE FIRST TIME... I CAN BE SURE HE'S GONE... FOREVER!
AND THAT IS A FACT I'LL JUST HAVE TO LEARN TO LIVE WITH!
SPECIAL BULLETIN!
DON'T MISS THE SENSES-SHATTERING, SHOCKING FOLLOW-UP TO THIS TRAGIC TALE, IN OUR 1968 SPECIAL--NOW ON SALE! IT WILL MOVE AND SHAKE YOU!! 'NUFF SAID!

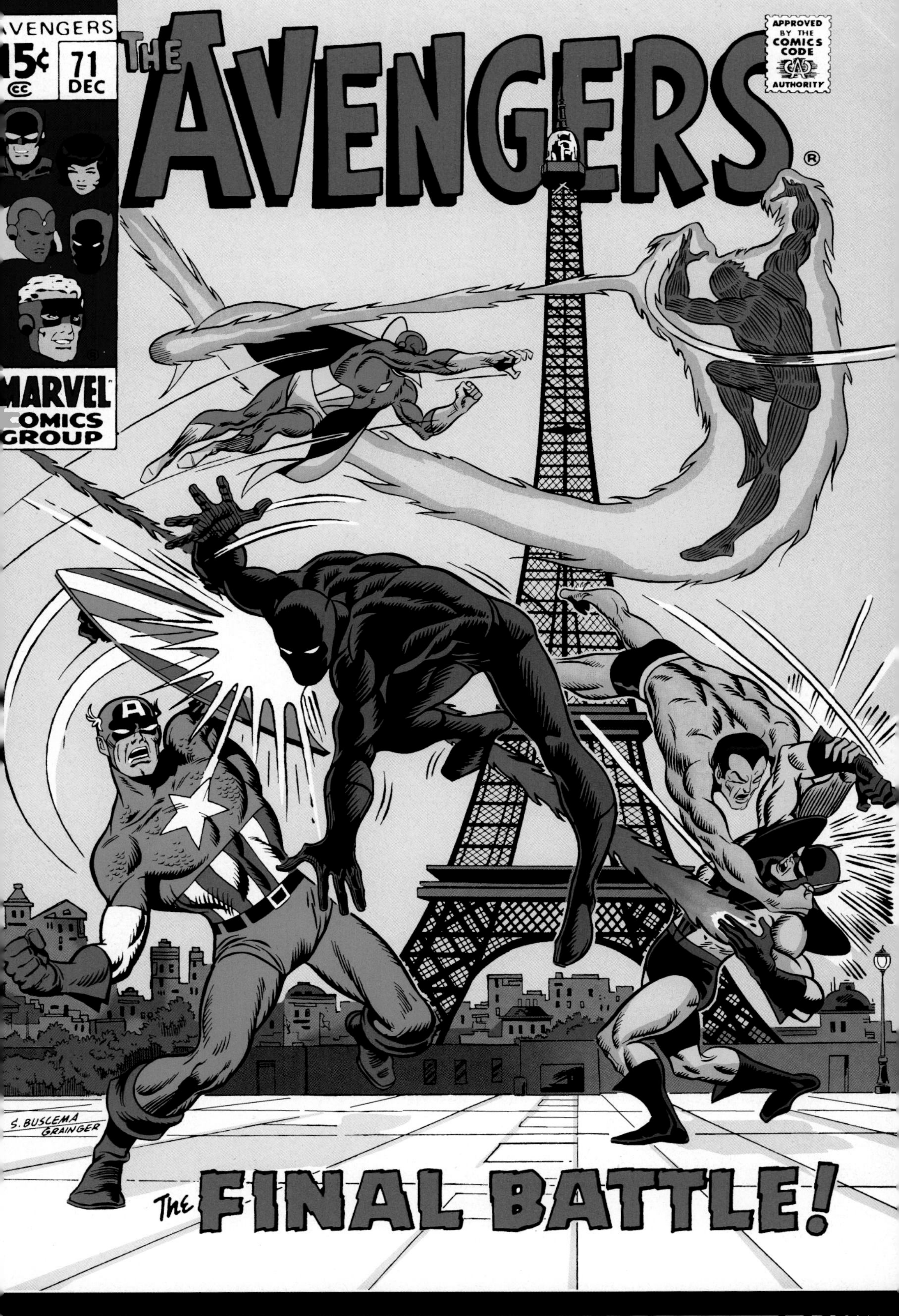
AVENGERS
15¢
71
DEC
THE AVENGERS
APPROVED BY THE COMICS CODE AUTHORITY
MARVEL COMICS GROUP
S. BUSCEMA
GRAINGER
THE FINAL BATTLE!

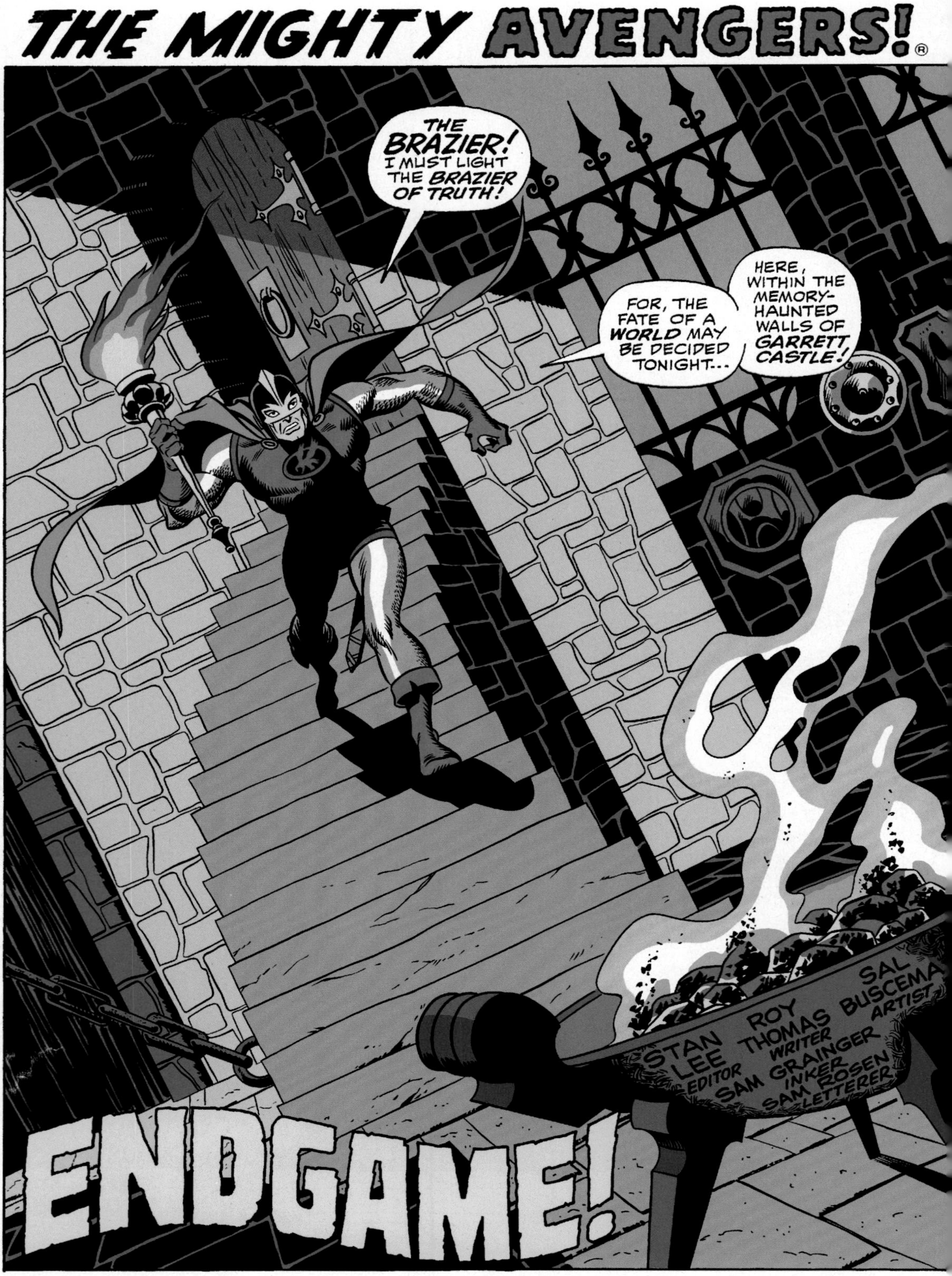

THE MIGHTY AVENGERS!®
THE BRAZIER! I MUST LIGHT THE BRAZIER OF TRUTH!
FOR, THE FATE OF A WORLD MAY BE DECIDED TONIGHT...
HERE, WITHIN THE MEMORY-HAUNTED WALLS OF GARRETT CASTLE!
STAN LEE EDITOR
ROY THOMAS WRITER
SAL BUSCEMA ARTIST
SAM GRAINGER INKER
SAM ROSEN LETTERER
ENDGAME!

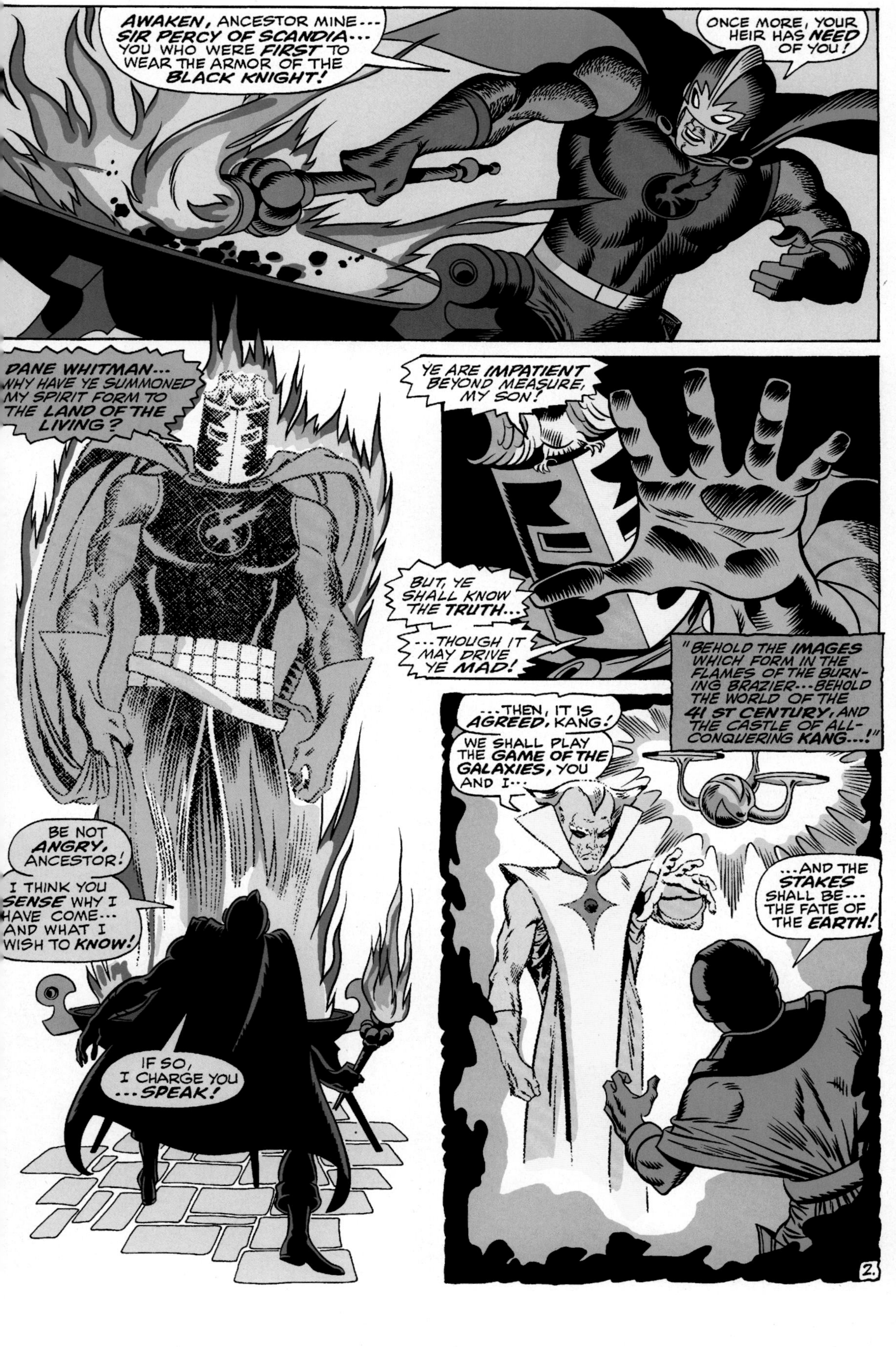

AWAKEN, ANCESTOR MINE... SIR PERCY OF SCANDIA... YOU WHO WERE FIRST TO WEAR THE ARMOR OF THE BLACK KNIGHT!
ONCE MORE, YOUR HEIR HAS NEED OF YOU!
DANE WHITMAN... WHY HAVE YE SUMMONED MY SPIRIT FORM TO THE LAND OF THE LIVING?
BE NOT ANGRY, ANCESTOR!
I THINK YOU SENSE WHY I HAVE COME... AND WHAT I WISH TO KNOW!
IF SO, I CHARGE YOU ...SPEAK!
YE ARE IMPATIENT BEYOND MEASURE, MY SON!
BUT, YE SHALL KNOW THE TRUTH...
...THOUGH IT MAY DRIVE YE MAD!
"BEHOLD THE IMAGES WHICH FORM IN THE FLAMES OF THE BURNING BRAZIER... BEHOLD THE WORLD OF THE 41 ST CENTURY, AND THE CASTLE OF ALL-CONQUERING KANG...!"
...THEN, IT IS AGREED, KANG!
WE SHALL PLAY THE GAME OF THE GALAXIES, YOU AND I...
...AND THE STAKES SHALL BE... THE FATE OF THE EARTH!
2.

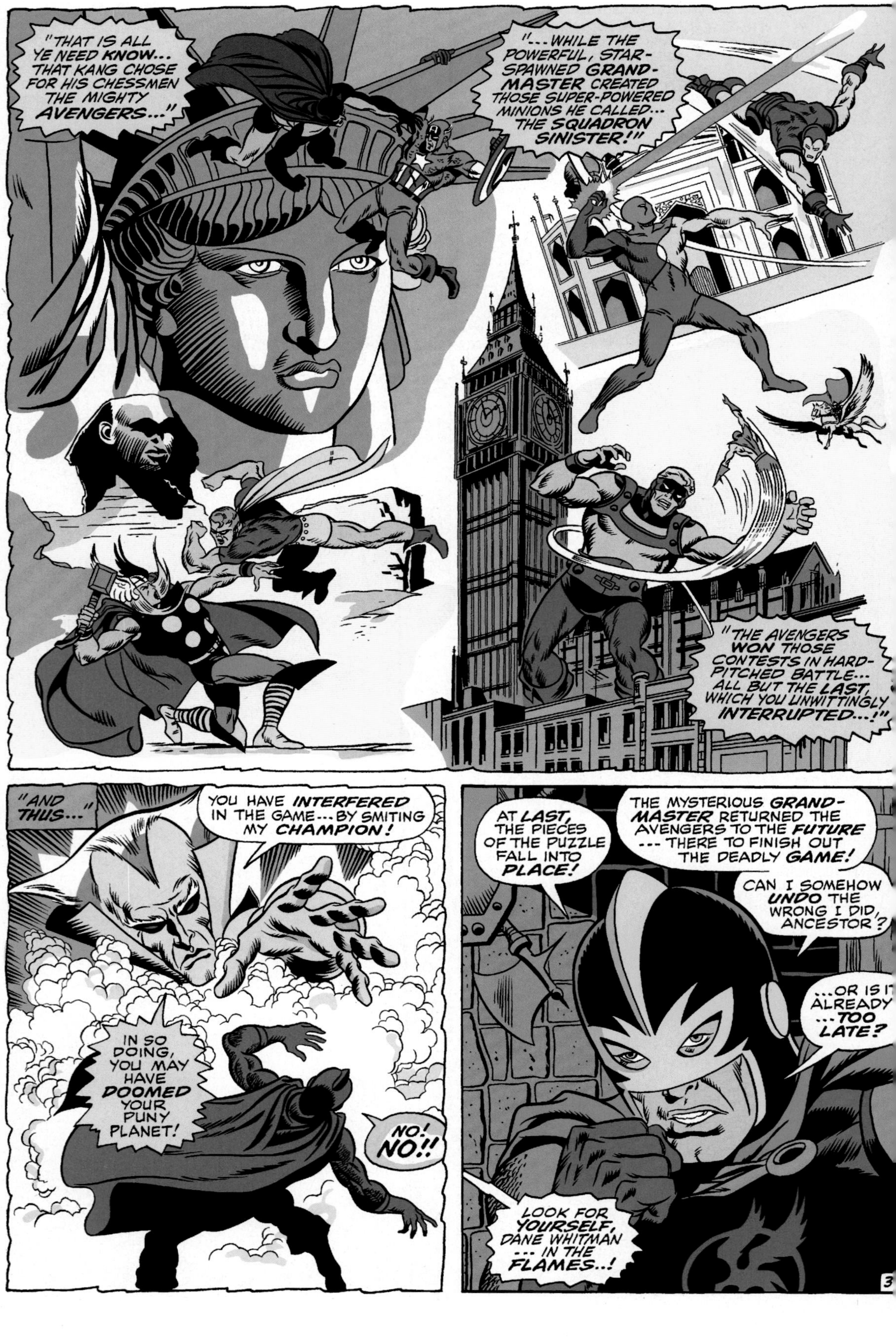

"THAT IS ALL YE NEED KNOW... THAT KANG CHOSE FOR HIS CHESSMEN THE MIGHTY AVENGERS..."
"...WHILE THE POWERFUL, STAR-SPAWNED GRANDMASTER CREATED THOSE SUPER-POWERED MINIONS HE CALLED... THE SQUADRON SINISTER!"
"THE AVENGERS WON THOSE CONTESTS IN HARD-PITCHED BATTLE... ALL BUT THE LAST, WHICH YOU UNWITTINGLY INTERRUPTED...!"
"AND THUS..."
YOU HAVE INTERFERED IN THE GAME--- BY SMITING MY CHAMPION!
IN SO DOING, YOU MAY HAVE DOOMED YOUR PUNY PLANET!
NO! NO!!
AT LAST, THE PIECES OF THE PUZZLE FALL INTO PLACE!
THE MYSTERIOUS GRANDMASTER RETURNED THE AVENGERS TO THE FUTURE --- THERE TO FINISH OUT THE DEADLY GAME!
CAN I SOMEHOW UNDO THE WRONG I DID, ANCESTOR?
...OR IS IT ALREADY ...TOO LATE?
LOOK FOR YOURSELF, DANE WHITMAN ... IN THE FLAMES..!
3

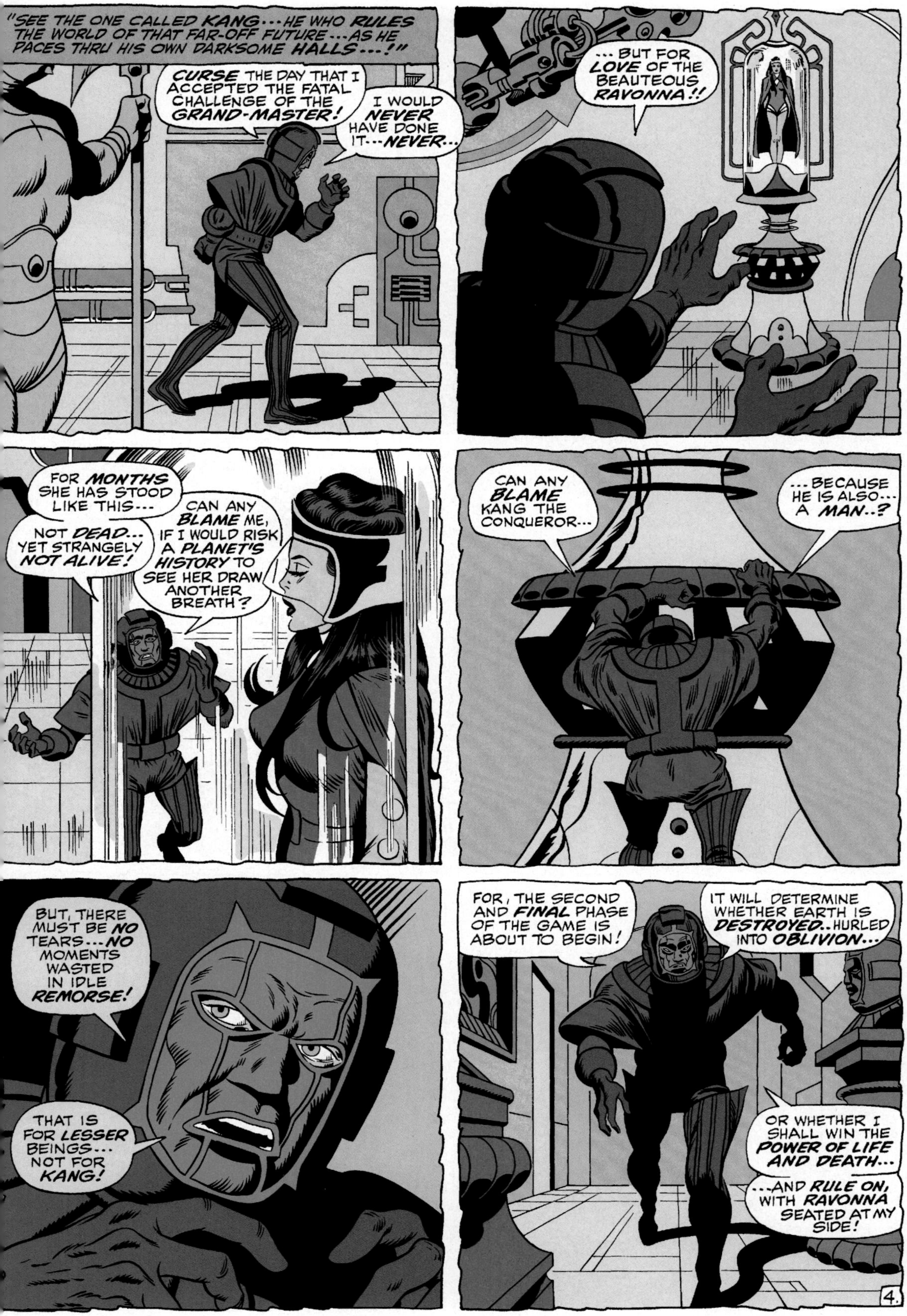
"SEE THE ONE CALLED KANG... HE WHO RULES THE WORLD OF THAT FAR-OFF FUTURE... AS HE PACES THRU HIS OWN DARKSOME HALLS...!"
CURSE THE DAY THAT I ACCEPTED THE FATAL CHALLENGE OF THE GRAND-MASTER!
I WOULD NEVER HAVE DONE IT--NEVER...
...BUT FOR LOVE OF THE BEAUTEOUS RAVONNA!!
FOR MONTHS SHE HAS STOOD LIKE THIS---
NOT DEAD... YET STRANGELY NOT ALIVE!
CAN ANY BLAME ME, IF I WOULD RISK A PLANET'S HISTORY TO SEE HER DRAW ANOTHER BREATH?
CAN ANY BLAME KANG THE CONQUEROR...
...BECAUSE HE IS ALSO... A MAN..?
BUT, THERE MUST BE NO TEARS...NO MOMENTS WASTED IN IDLE REMORSE!
THAT IS FOR LESSER BEINGS... NOT FOR KANG!
FOR, THE SECOND AND FINAL PHASE OF THE GAME IS ABOUT TO BEGIN!
IT WILL DETERMINE WHETHER EARTH IS DESTROYED..HURLED INTO OBLIVION...
OR WHETHER I SHALL WIN THE POWER OF LIFE AND DEATH...
...AND RULE ON, WITH RAVONNA SEATED AT MY SIDE!
4.

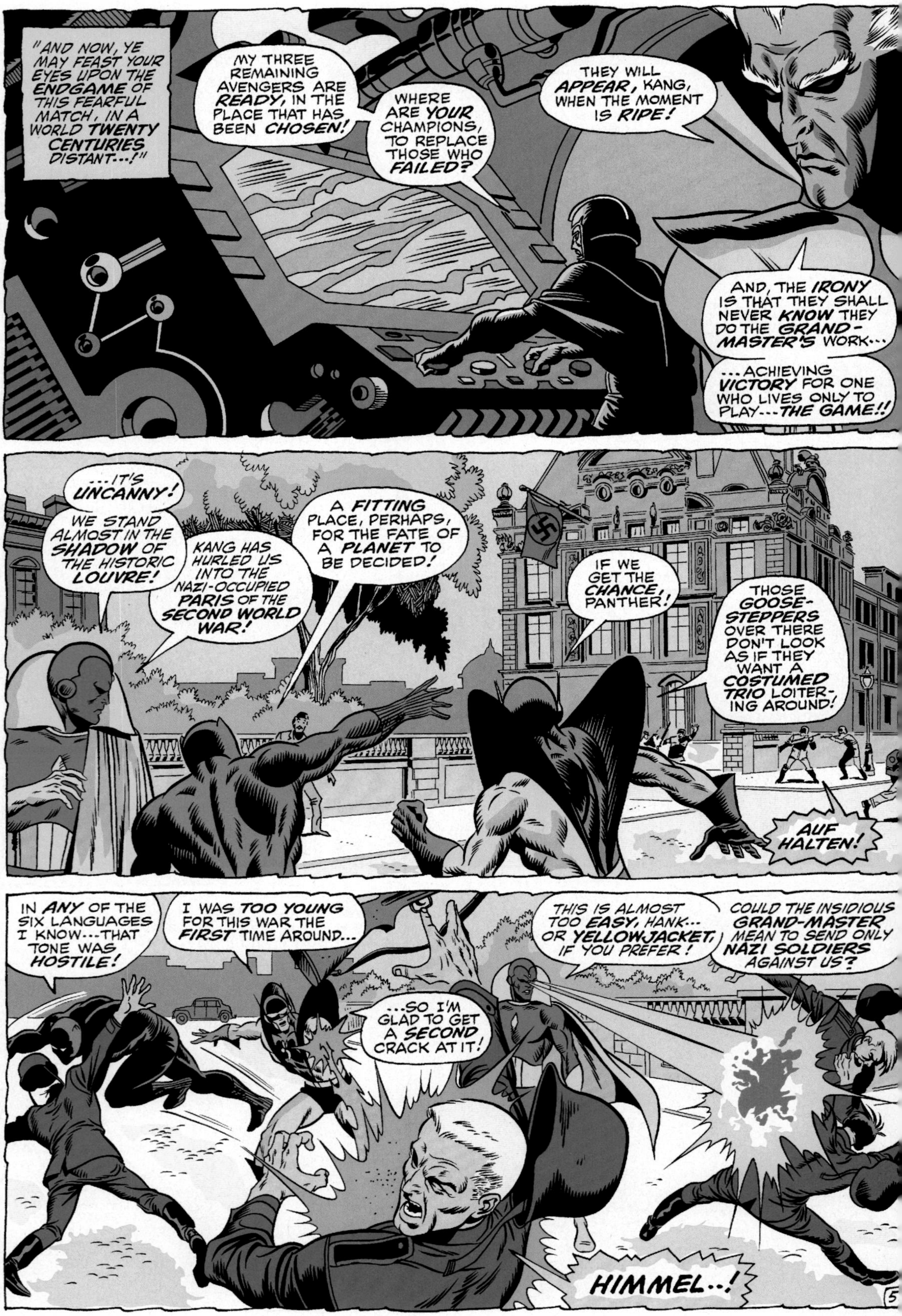
"AND NOW, YE MAY FEAST YOUR EYES UPON THE ENDGAME OF THIS FEARFUL MATCH, IN A WORLD TWENTY CENTURIES DISTANT...!"
MY THREE REMAINING AVENGERS ARE READY, IN THE PLACE THAT HAS BEEN CHOSEN!
WHERE ARE YOUR CHAMPIONS, TO REPLACE THOSE WHO FAILED?
THEY WILL APPEAR, KANG, WHEN THE MOMENT IS RIPE!
AND, THE IRONY IS THAT THEY SHALL NEVER KNOW THEY DO THE GRAND-MASTER'S WORK...
...ACHIEVING VICTORY FOR ONE WHO LIVES ONLY TO PLAY---THE GAME!!
...IT'S UNCANNY!
WE STAND ALMOST IN THE SHADOW OF THE HISTORIC LOUVRE!
KANG HAS HURLED US INTO THE NAZI-OCCUPIED PARIS OF THE SECOND WORLD WAR!
A FITTING PLACE, PERHAPS, FOR THE FATE OF A PLANET TO BE DECIDED!
IF WE GET THE CHANCE, PANTHER!
THOSE GOOSE-STEPPERS OVER THERE DON'T LOOK AS IF THEY WANT A COSTUMED TRIO LOITER-ING AROUND!
AUF HALTEN!
IN ANY OF THE SIX LANGUAGES I KNOW---THAT TONE WAS HOSTILE!
I WAS TOO YOUNG FOR THIS WAR THE FIRST TIME AROUND...
...SO I'M GLAD TO GET A SECOND CRACK AT IT!
THIS IS ALMOST TOO EASY, HANK... OR YELLOWJACKET, IF YOU PREFER!
COULD THE INSIDIOUS GRAND-MASTER MEAN TO SEND ONLY NAZI SOLDIERS AGAINST US?
HIMMEL..!

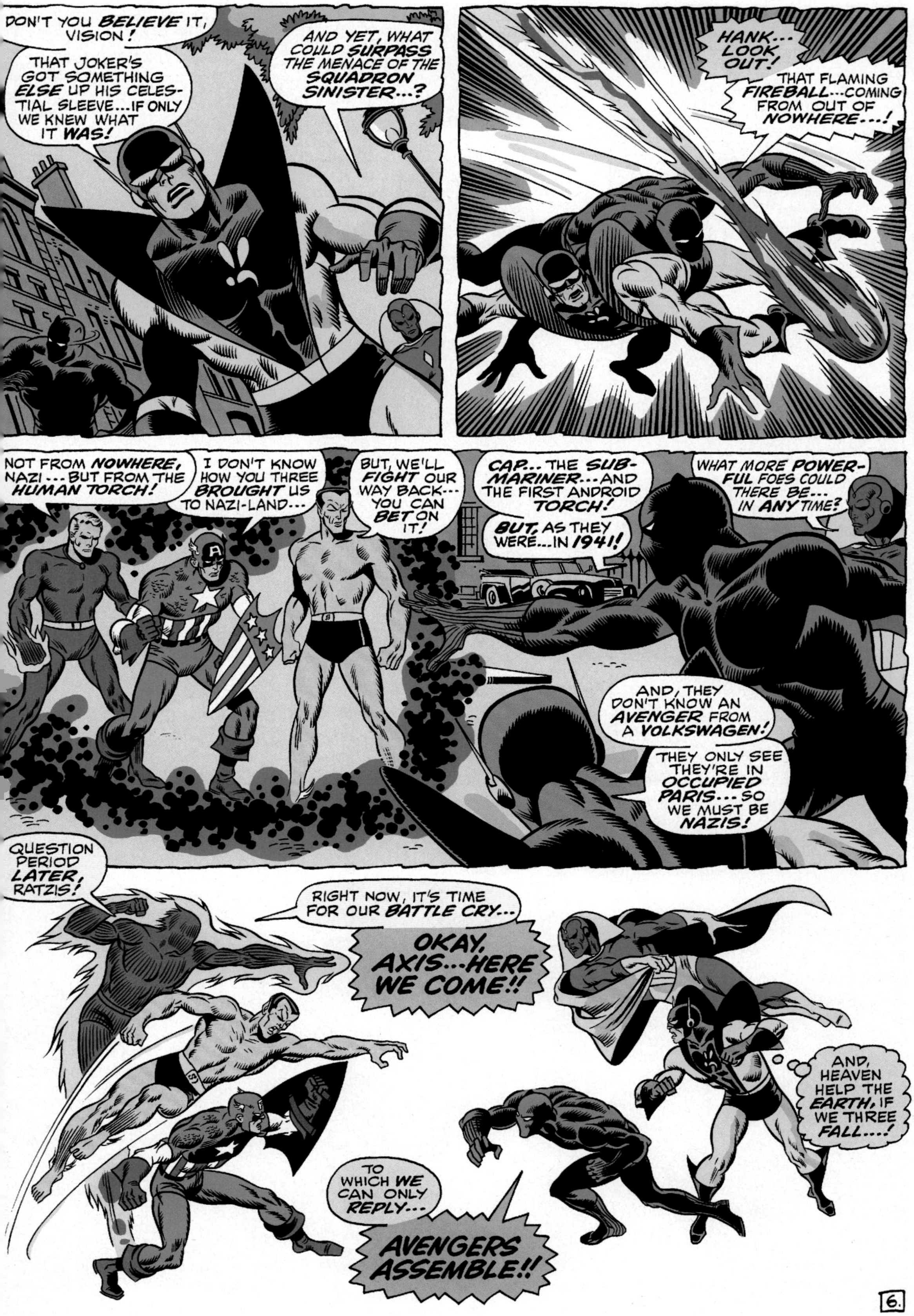
DON'T YOU BELIEVE IT, VISION!
THAT JOKER'S GOT SOMETHING ELSE UP HIS CELESTIAL SLEEVE...IF ONLY WE KNEW WHAT IT WAS!
AND YET, WHAT COULD SURPASS THE MENACE OF THE SQUADRON SINISTER...?
HANK... LOOK OUT!
THAT FLAMING FIREBALL...COMING FROM OUT OF NOWHERE...!
NOT FROM NOWHERE, NAZI... BUT FROM THE HUMAN TORCH!
I DON'T KNOW HOW YOU THREE BROUGHT US TO NAZI-LAND...
BUT, WE'LL FIGHT OUR WAY BACK--- YOU CAN BET ON IT!
CAP... THE SUB-MARINER... AND THE FIRST ANDROID TORCH!
BUT, AS THEY WERE...IN 1941!
WHAT MORE POWERFUL FOES COULD THERE BE... IN ANY TIME?
AND, THEY DON'T KNOW AN AVENGER FROM A VOLKSWAGEN!
THEY ONLY SEE THEY'RE IN OCCUPIED PARIS... SO WE MUST BE NAZIS!
QUESTION PERIOD LATER, RATZIS!
RIGHT NOW, IT'S TIME FOR OUR BATTLE CRY...
OKAY, AXIS...HERE WE COME!!
AND, HEAVEN HELP THE EARTH, IF WE THREE FALL...!
TO WHICH WE CAN ONLY REPLY...
AVENGERS ASSEMBLE!!

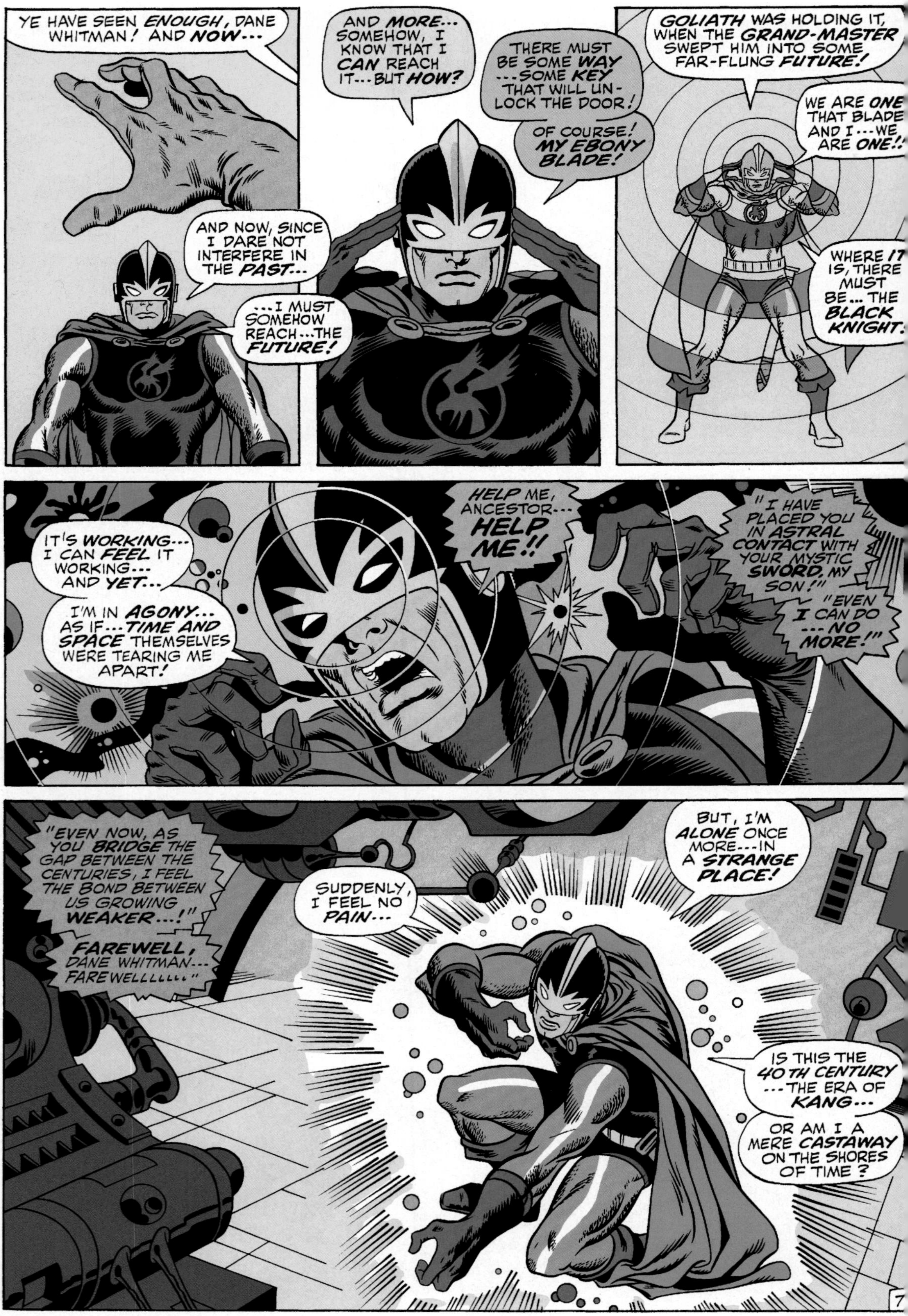

YE HAVE SEEN ENOUGH, DANE WHITMAN! AND NOW---
AND NOW, SINCE I DARE NOT INTERFERE IN THE PAST...
...I MUST SOMEHOW REACH---THE FUTURE!
AND MORE... SOMEHOW, I KNOW THAT I CAN REACH IT--- BUT HOW?
THERE MUST BE SOME WAY ---SOME KEY THAT WILL UN-LOCK THE DOOR!
OF COURSE! MY EBONY BLADE!
GOLIATH WAS HOLDING IT, WHEN THE GRAND-MASTER SWEPT HIM INTO SOME FAR-FLUNG FUTURE!
WE ARE ONE THAT BLADE AND I---WE ARE ONE!!
WHERE IT IS, THERE MUST BE... THE BLACK KNIGHT!
IT'S WORKING--- I CAN FEEL IT WORKING--- AND YET...
I'M IN AGONY... AS IF---TIME AND SPACE THEMSELVES WERE TEARING ME APART!
HELP ME, ANCESTOR--- HELP ME!!
"I HAVE PLACED YOU IN ASTRAL CONTACT WITH YOUR MYSTIC SWORD, MY SON!"
"EVEN I CAN DO ---NO MORE!"
"EVEN NOW, AS YOU BRIDGE THE GAP BETWEEN THE CENTURIES, I FEEL THE BOND BETWEEN US GROWING WEAKER---!"
FAREWELL, DANE WHITMAN--- FAREWELLLLLL..."
SUDDENLY, I FEEL NO PAIN---
BUT, I'M ALONE ONCE MORE---IN A STRANGE PLACE!
IS THIS THE 40TH CENTURY ---THE ERA OF KANG...
OR AM I A MERE CASTAWAY ON THE SHORES OF TIME?

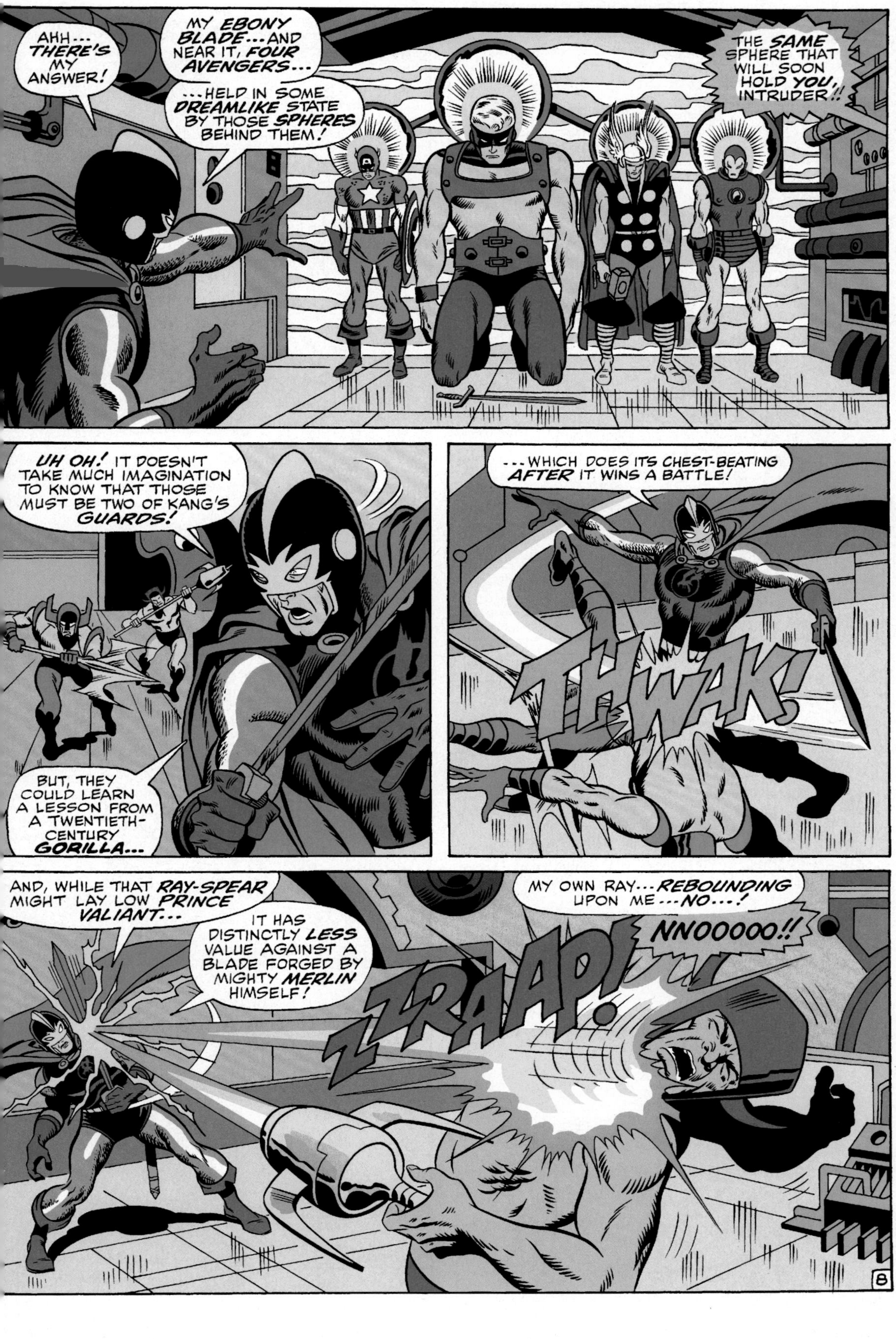
AHH... THERE'S MY ANSWER!
MY EBONY BLADE... AND NEAR IT, FOUR AVENGERS...
...HELD IN SOME DREAMLIKE STATE BY THOSE SPHERES BEHIND THEM!
THE SAME SPHERE THAT WILL SOON HOLD YOU, INTRUDER!!
UH OH! IT DOESN'T TAKE MUCH IMAGINATION TO KNOW THAT THOSE MUST BE TWO OF KANG'S GUARDS!
BUT, THEY COULD LEARN A LESSON FROM A TWENTIETH-CENTURY GORILLA...
...WHICH DOES ITS CHEST-BEATING AFTER IT WINS A BATTLE!
THWAK!
AND, WHILE THAT RAY-SPEAR MIGHT LAY LOW PRINCE VALIANT...
IT HAS DISTINCTLY LESS VALUE AGAINST A BLADE FORGED BY MIGHTY MERLIN HIMSELF!
MY OWN RAY...REBOUNDING UPON ME...NO...!
NNOOOOO!!
ZZRAAAP!
8

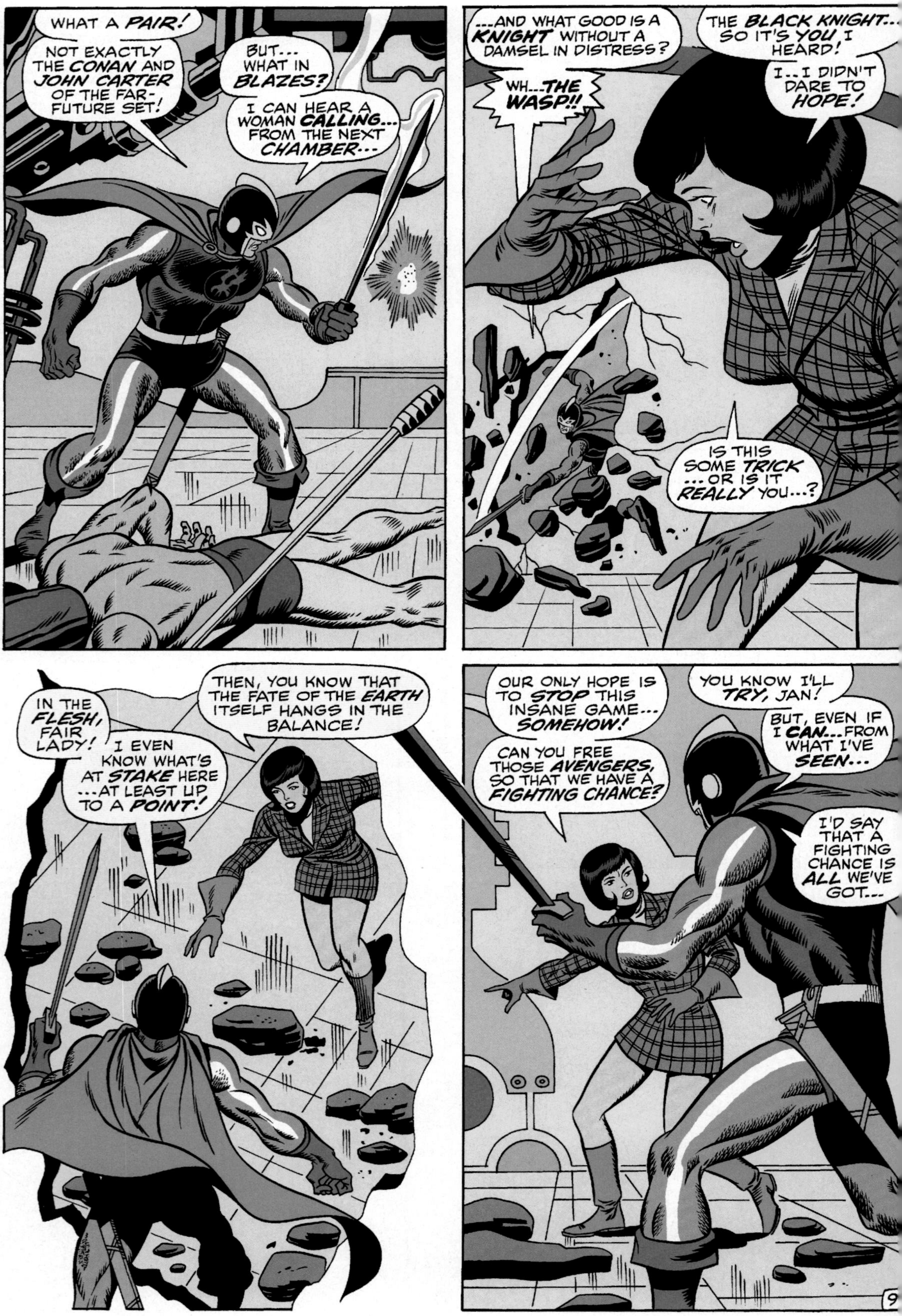
WHAT A PAIR!
NOT EXACTLY THE CONAN AND JOHN CARTER OF THE FAR-FUTURE SET!
BUT... WHAT IN BLAZES?
I CAN HEAR A WOMAN CALLING... FROM THE NEXT CHAMBER...
...AND WHAT GOOD IS A KNIGHT WITHOUT A DAMSEL IN DISTRESS?
WH...THE WASP!!
THE BLACK KNIGHT... SO IT'S YOU, I HEARD!
I...I DIDN'T DARE TO HOPE!
IS THIS SOME TRICK ...OR IS IT REALLY YOU...?
IN THE FLESH, FAIR LADY!
I EVEN KNOW WHAT'S AT STAKE HERE ...AT LEAST UP TO A POINT!
THEN, YOU KNOW THAT THE FATE OF THE EARTH ITSELF HANGS IN THE BALANCE!
OUR ONLY HOPE IS TO STOP THIS INSANE GAME... SOMEHOW!
CAN YOU FREE THOSE AVENGERS, SO THAT WE HAVE A FIGHTING CHANCE?
YOU KNOW I'LL TRY, JAN!
BUT, EVEN IF I CAN...FROM WHAT I'VE SEEN...
I'D SAY THAT A FIGHTING CHANCE IS ALL WE'VE GOT...
9

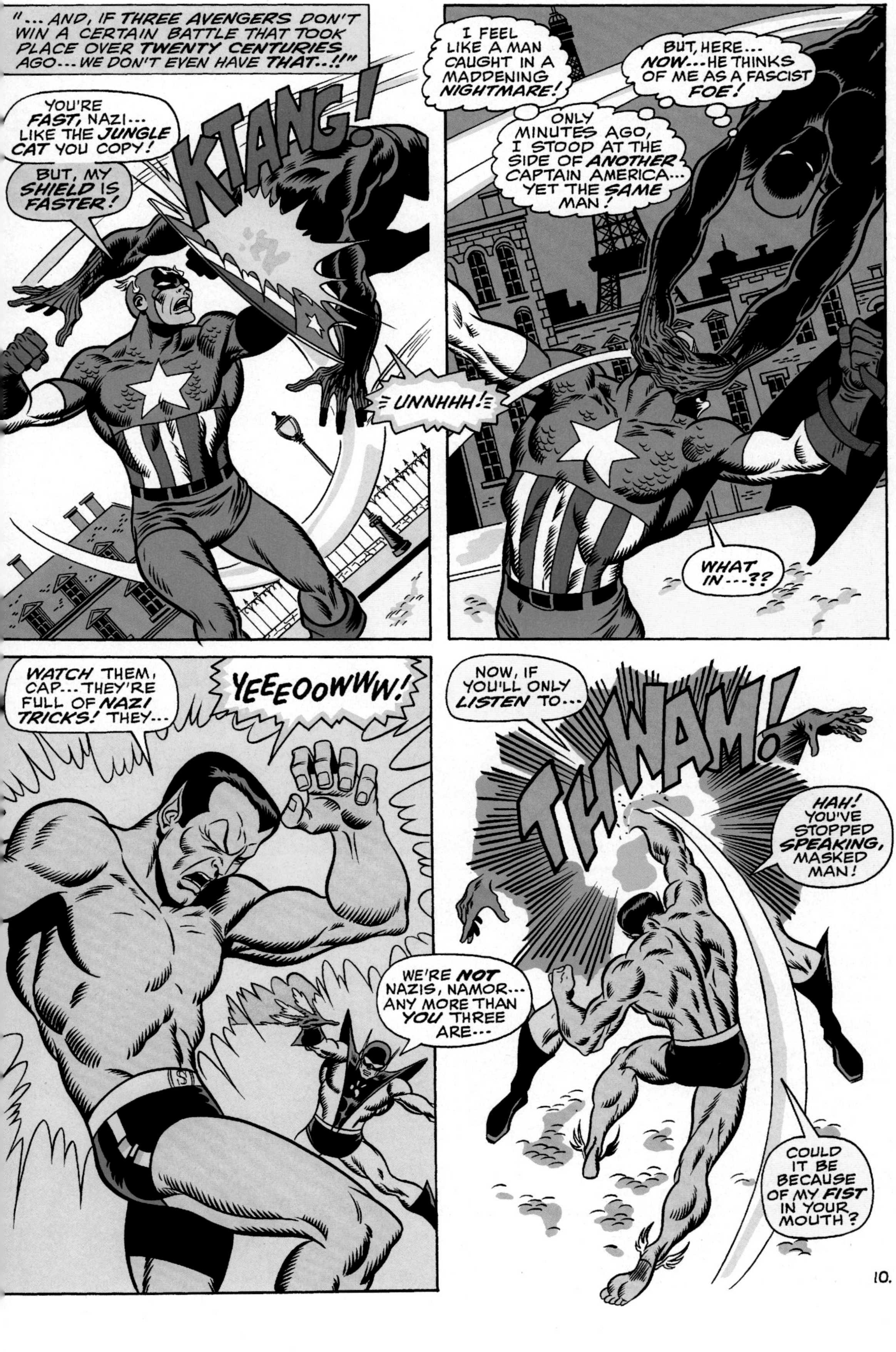
"... AND, IF THREE AVENGERS DON'T WIN A CERTAIN BATTLE THAT TOOK PLACE OVER TWENTY CENTURIES AGO... WE DON'T EVEN HAVE THAT..!!"
YOU'RE FAST, NAZI... LIKE THE JUNGLE CAT YOU COPY!
BUT, MY SHIELD IS FASTER!
KTANG!
UNNHHH!
I FEEL LIKE A MAN CAUGHT IN A MADDENING NIGHTMARE!
BUT, HERE... NOW... HE THINKS OF ME AS A FASCIST FOE!
ONLY MINUTES AGO, I STOOD AT THE SIDE OF ANOTHER CAPTAIN AMERICA... YET THE SAME MAN!
WHAT IN---??
WATCH THEM, CAP... THEY'RE FULL OF NAZI TRICKS! THEY...
YEEEOOWWW!
WE'RE NOT NAZIS, NAMOR... ANY MORE THAN YOU THREE ARE...
NOW, IF YOU'LL ONLY LISTEN TO...
THWAM!
HAH! YOU'VE STOPPED SPEAKING, MASKED MAN!
COULD IT BE BECAUSE OF MY FIST IN YOUR MOUTH?

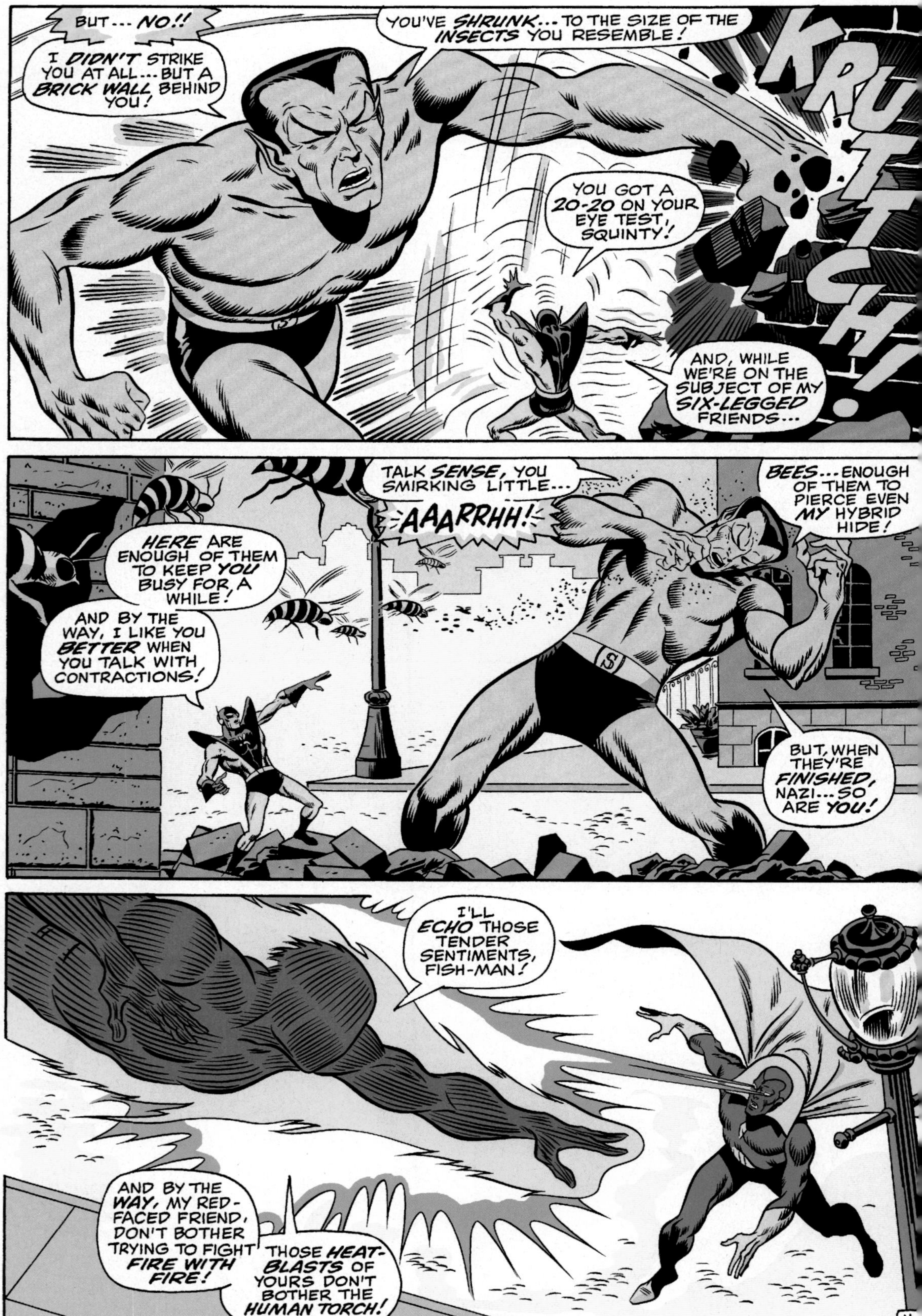
BUT... NO!!
I DIDN'T STRIKE YOU AT ALL... BUT A BRICK WALL BEHIND YOU!
YOU'VE SHRUNK... TO THE SIZE OF THE INSECTS YOU RESEMBLE!
KRUTTCH!!
YOU GOT A 20-20 ON YOUR EYE TEST, SQUINTY!
AND, WHILE WE'RE ON THE SUBJECT OF MY SIX-LEGGED FRIENDS...
HERE ARE ENOUGH OF THEM TO KEEP YOU BUSY FOR A WHILE!
AND BY THE WAY, I LIKE YOU BETTER WHEN YOU TALK WITH CONTRACTIONS!
TALK SENSE, YOU SMIRKING LITTLE...
AAARRHH!
BEES... ENOUGH OF THEM TO PIERCE EVEN MY HYBRID HIDE!
BUT, WHEN THEY'RE FINISHED, NAZI... SO ARE YOU!
I'LL ECHO THOSE TENDER SENTIMENTS, FISH-MAN!
AND BY THE WAY, MY RED-FACED FRIEND, DON'T BOTHER TRYING TO FIGHT FIRE WITH FIRE!
THOSE HEAT-BLASTS OF YOURS DON'T BOTHER THE HUMAN TORCH!

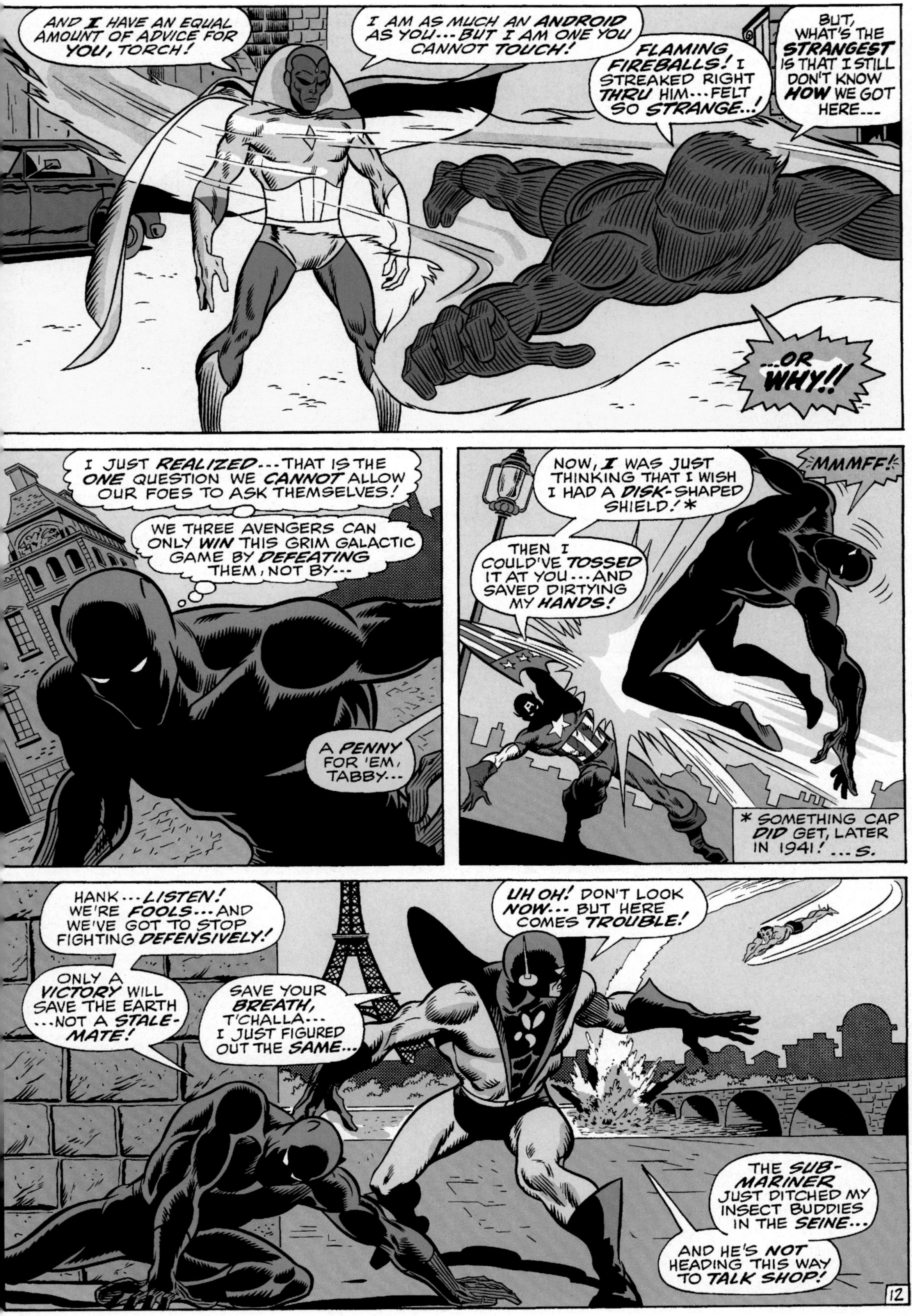
AND I HAVE AN EQUAL AMOUNT OF ADVICE FOR YOU, TORCH!
I AM AS MUCH AN ANDROID AS YOU... BUT I AM ONE YOU CANNOT TOUCH!
FLAMING FIREBALLS! I STREAKED RIGHT THRU HIM... FELT SO STRANGE...!
BUT, WHAT'S THE STRANGEST IS THAT I STILL DON'T KNOW HOW WE GOT HERE...
...OR WHY!!
I JUST REALIZED... THAT IS THE ONE QUESTION WE CANNOT ALLOW OUR FOES TO ASK THEMSELVES!
WE THREE AVENGERS CAN ONLY WIN THIS GRIM GALACTIC GAME BY DEFEATING THEM, NOT BY---
A PENNY FOR 'EM, TABBY...
NOW, I WAS JUST THINKING THAT I WISH I HAD A DISK-SHAPED SHIELD! *
MMMFF!
THEN I COULD'VE TOSSED IT AT YOU... AND SAVED DIRTYING MY HANDS!
* SOMETHING CAP DID GET, LATER IN 1941! ...S.
HANK... LISTEN! WE'RE FOOLS... AND WE'VE GOT TO STOP FIGHTING DEFENSIVELY!
ONLY A VICTORY WILL SAVE THE EARTH ...NOT A STALE-MATE!
SAVE YOUR BREATH, T'CHALLA... I JUST FIGURED OUT THE SAME...
UH OH! DON'T LOOK NOW... BUT HERE COMES TROUBLE!
THE SUB-MARINER JUST DITCHED MY INSECT BUDDIES IN THE SEINE...
AND HE'S NOT HEADING THIS WAY TO TALK SHOP!
12

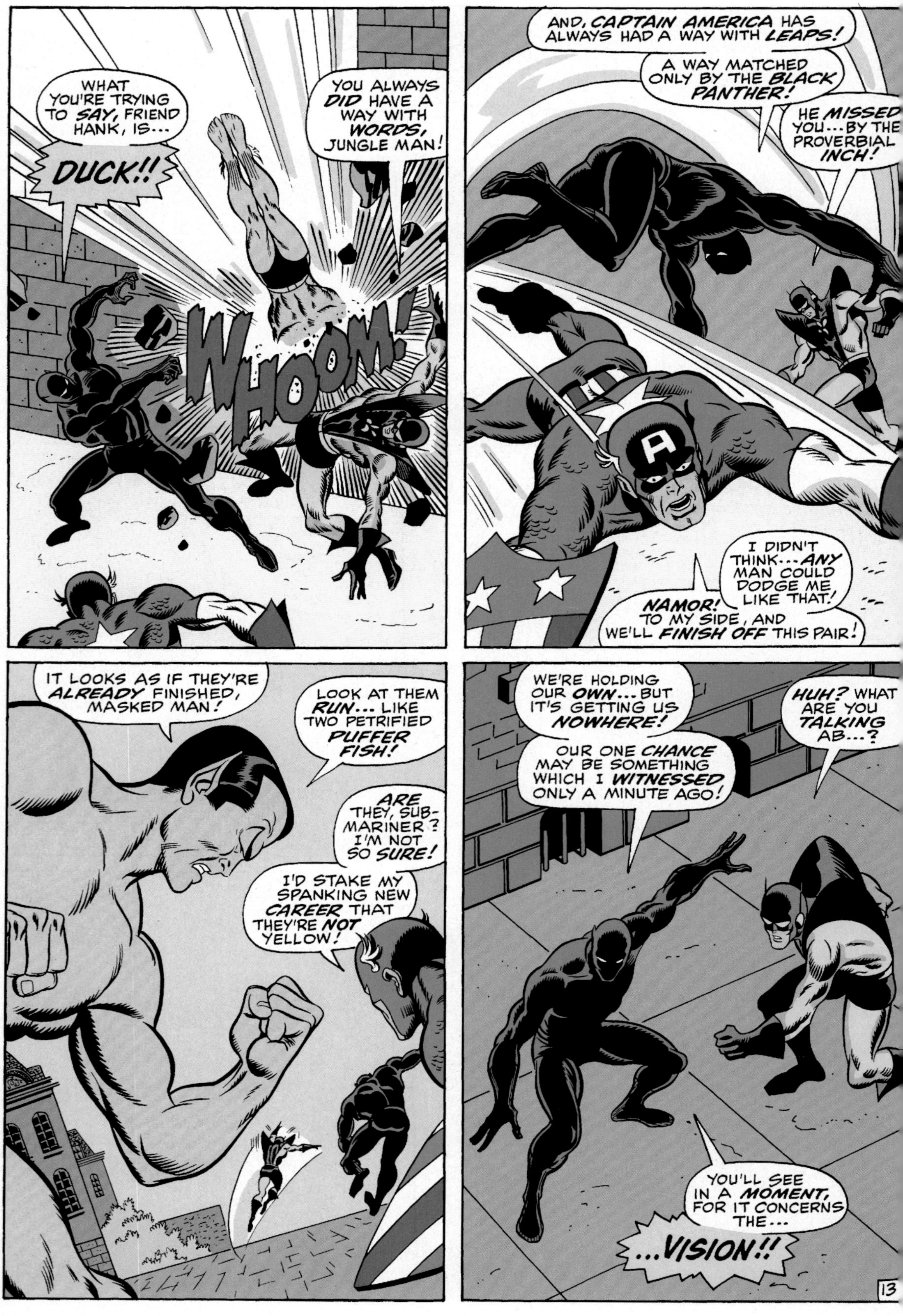

WHAT YOU'RE TRYING TO SAY, FRIEND HANK, IS...
DUCK!!
YOU ALWAYS DID HAVE A WAY WITH WORDS, JUNGLE MAN!
WHOOM!
AND, CAPTAIN AMERICA HAS ALWAYS HAD A WAY WITH LEAPS!
A WAY MATCHED ONLY BY THE BLACK PANTHER!
HE MISSED YOU...BY THE PROVERBIAL INCH!
I DIDN'T THINK...ANY MAN COULD DODGE ME, LIKE THAT!
NAMOR! TO MY SIDE, AND WE'LL FINISH OFF THIS PAIR!
IT LOOKS AS IF THEY'RE ALREADY FINISHED, MASKED MAN!
LOOK AT THEM RUN...LIKE TWO PETRIFIED PUFFER FISH!
ARE THEY, SUB-MARINER? I'M NOT SO SURE!
I'D STAKE MY SPANKING NEW CAREER THAT THEY'RE NOT YELLOW!
WE'RE HOLDING OUR OWN...BUT IT'S GETTING US NOWHERE!
OUR ONE CHANCE MAY BE SOMETHING WHICH I WITNESSED ONLY A MINUTE AGO!
HUH? WHAT ARE YOU TALKING AB...?
YOU'LL SEE IN A MOMENT, FOR IT CONCERNS THE...
...VISION!!

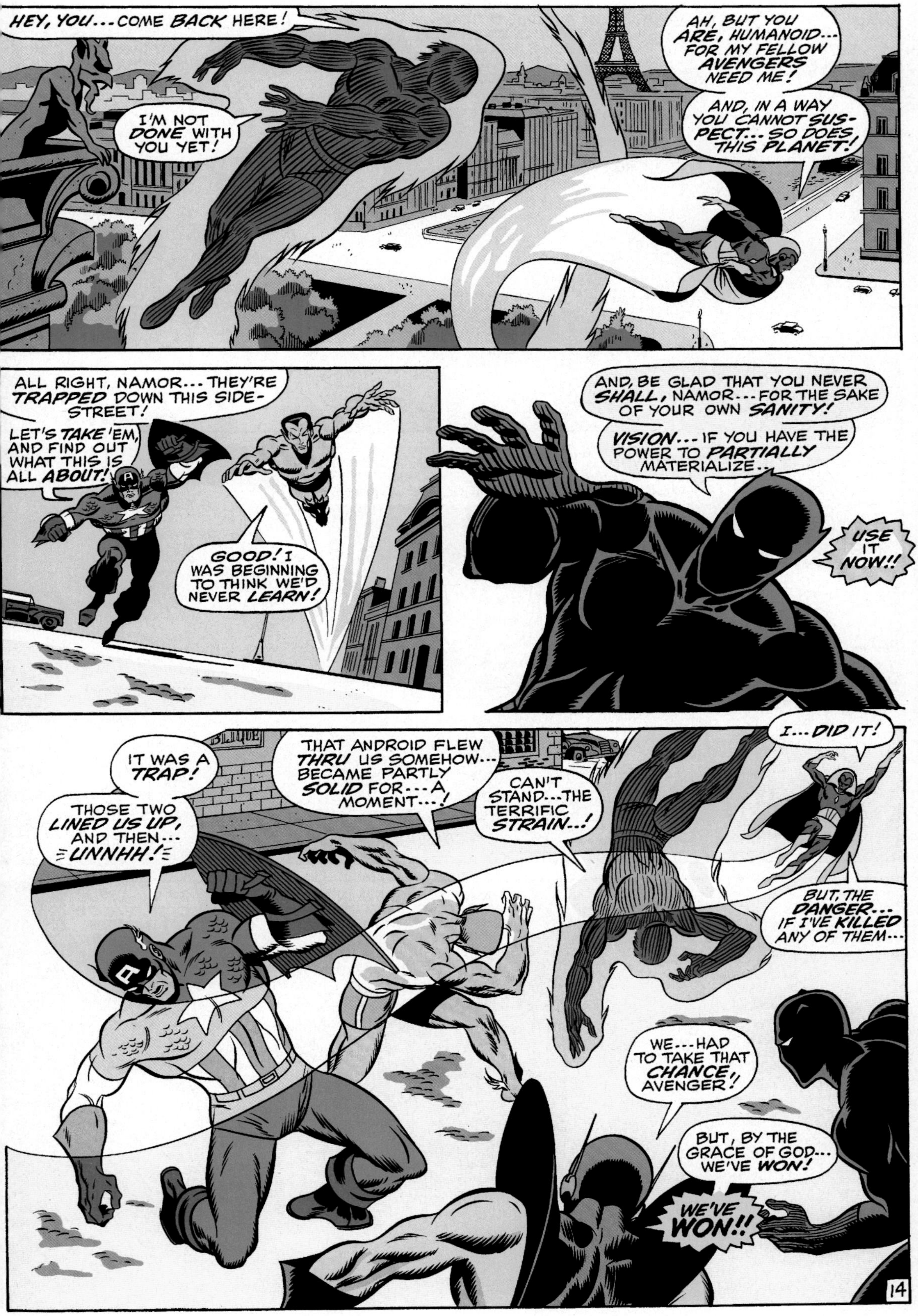
HEY, YOU... COME BACK HERE!
I'M NOT DONE WITH YOU YET!
AH, BUT YOU ARE, HUMANOID... FOR MY FELLOW AVENGERS NEED ME!
AND, IN A WAY YOU CANNOT SUS-PECT... SO DOES THIS PLANET!
ALL RIGHT, NAMOR... THEY'RE TRAPPED DOWN THIS SIDE-STREET!
LET'S TAKE 'EM, AND FIND OUT WHAT THIS IS ALL ABOUT!
GOOD! I WAS BEGINNING TO THINK WE'D NEVER LEARN!
AND, BE GLAD THAT YOU NEVER SHALL, NAMOR... FOR THE SAKE OF YOUR OWN SANITY!
VISION... IF YOU HAVE THE POWER TO PARTIALLY MATERIALIZE...
USE IT NOW!!
IT WAS A TRAP!
THOSE TWO LINED US UP, AND THEN... UNNHH!
THAT ANDROID FLEW THRU US SOMEHOW... BECAME PARTLY SOLID FOR... A MOMENT...!
CAN'T STAND... THE TERRIFIC STRAIN...!
I... DID IT!
BUT, THE DANGER... IF I'VE KILLED ANY OF THEM...
WE... HAD TO TAKE THAT CHANCE!! AVENGER!
BUT, BY THE GRACE OF GOD... WE'VE WON!
WE'VE WON!!
14

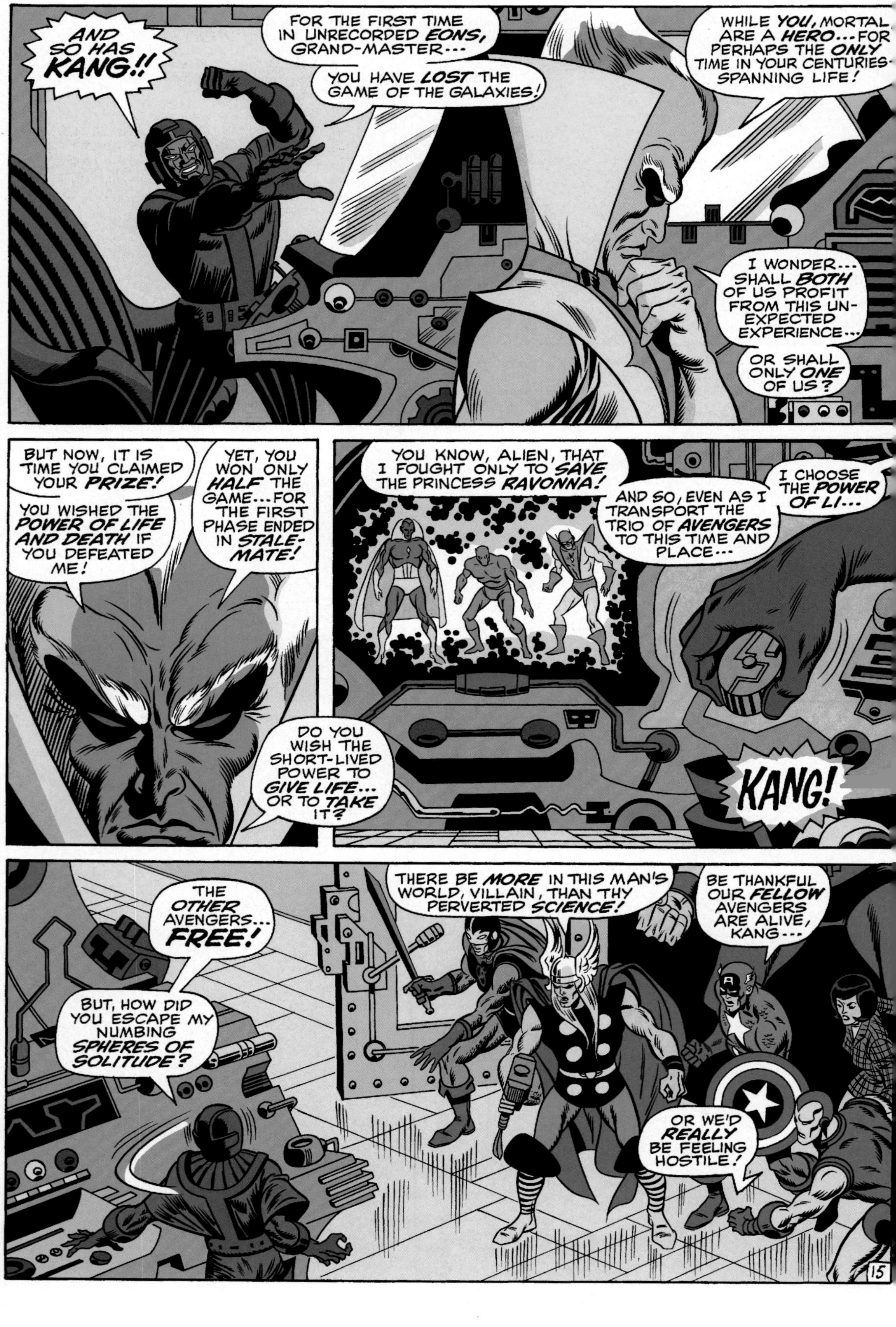
AND SO HAS KANG!!
FOR THE FIRST TIME IN UNRECORDED EONS, GRAND-MASTER---
YOU HAVE LOST THE GAME OF THE GALAXIES!
WHILE YOU, MORTAL ARE A HERO...FOR PERHAPS THE ONLY TIME IN YOUR CENTURIES-SPANNING LIFE!
I WONDER... SHALL BOTH OF US PROFIT FROM THIS UN-EXPECTED EXPERIENCE...
OR SHALL ONLY ONE OF US?
BUT NOW, IT IS TIME YOU CLAIMED YOUR PRIZE!
YOU WISHED THE POWER OF LIFE AND DEATH IF YOU DEFEATED ME!
YET, YOU WON ONLY HALF THE GAME...FOR THE FIRST PHASE ENDED IN STALE-MATE!
DO YOU WISH THE SHORT-LIVED POWER TO GIVE LIFE... OR TO TAKE IT?
YOU KNOW, ALIEN, THAT I FOUGHT ONLY TO SAVE THE PRINCESS RAVONNA!
AND SO, EVEN AS I TRANSPORT THE TRIO OF AVENGERS TO THIS TIME AND PLACE---
I CHOOSE THE POWER OF LI...
KANG!
THE OTHER AVENGERS... FREE!
BUT, HOW DID YOU ESCAPE MY NUMBING SPHERES OF SOLITUDE?
THERE BE MORE IN THIS MAN'S WORLD, VILLAIN, THAN THY PERVERTED SCIENCE!
BE THANKFUL OUR FELLOW AVENGERS ARE ALIVE, KANG---
OR WE'D REALLY BE FEELING HOSTILE!
15

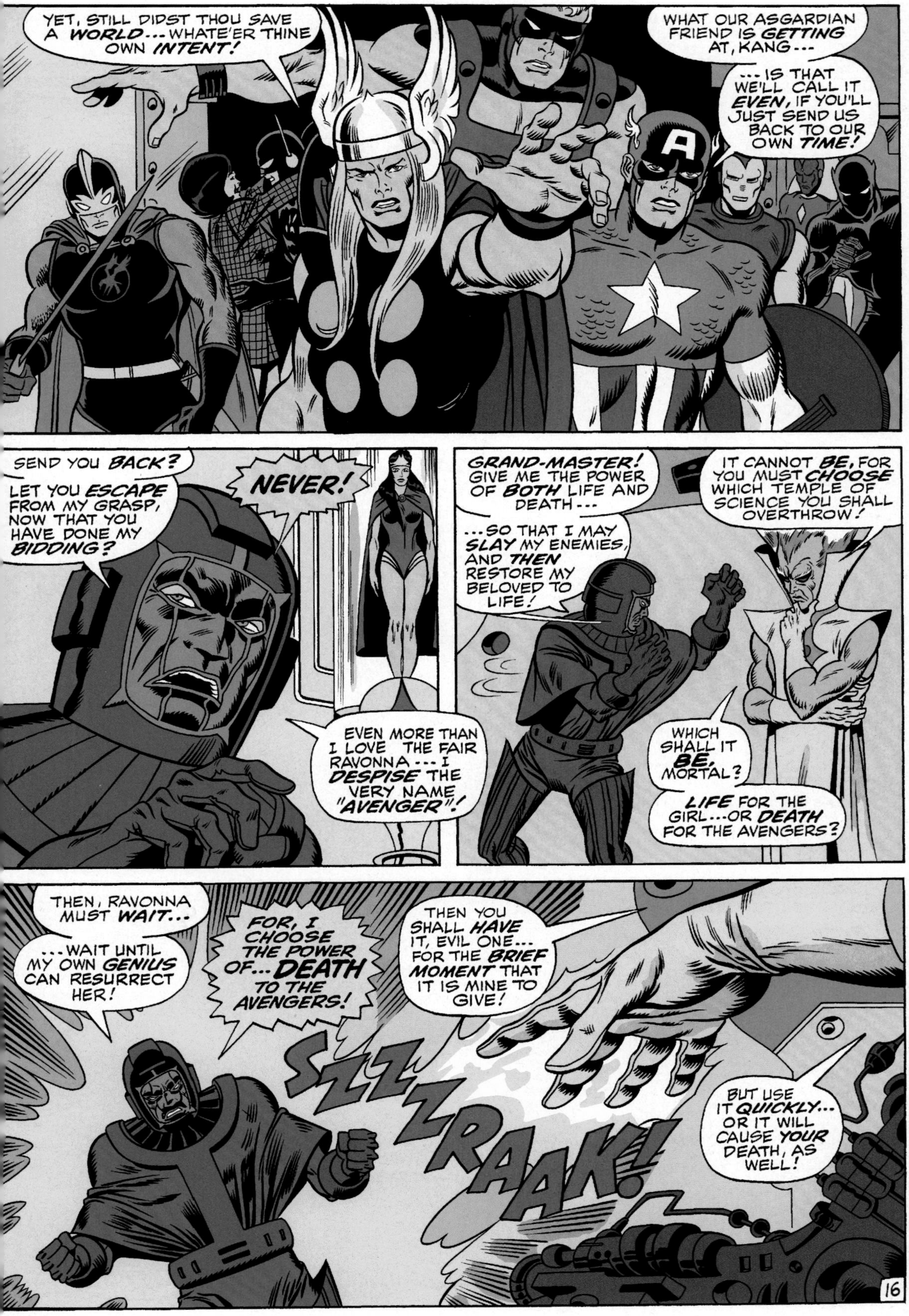
YET, STILL DIDST THOU SAVE A WORLD... WHATE'ER THINE OWN INTENT!
WHAT OUR ASGARDIAN FRIEND IS GETTING AT, KANG...
...IS THAT WE'LL CALL IT EVEN, IF YOU'LL JUST SEND US BACK TO OUR OWN TIME!
SEND YOU BACK?
LET YOU ESCAPE FROM MY GRASP, NOW THAT YOU HAVE DONE MY BIDDING?
NEVER!
EVEN MORE THAN I LOVE THE FAIR RAVONNA --- I DESPISE THE VERY NAME "AVENGER"!
GRAND-MASTER! GIVE ME THE POWER OF BOTH LIFE AND DEATH ---
...SO THAT I MAY SLAY MY ENEMIES, AND THEN RESTORE MY BELOVED TO LIFE!
IT CANNOT BE, FOR YOU MUST CHOOSE WHICH TEMPLE OF SCIENCE YOU SHALL OVERTHROW!
WHICH SHALL IT BE, MORTAL?
LIFE FOR THE GIRL...OR DEATH FOR THE AVENGERS?
THEN, RAVONNA MUST WAIT...
...WAIT UNTIL MY OWN GENIUS CAN RESURRECT HER!
FOR, I CHOOSE THE POWER OF... DEATH TO THE AVENGERS!
THEN YOU SHALL HAVE IT, EVIL ONE... FOR THE BRIEF MOMENT THAT IT IS MINE TO GIVE!
SZZZRAAK!
BUT USE IT QUICKLY... OR IT WILL CAUSE YOUR DEATH, AS WELL!
16

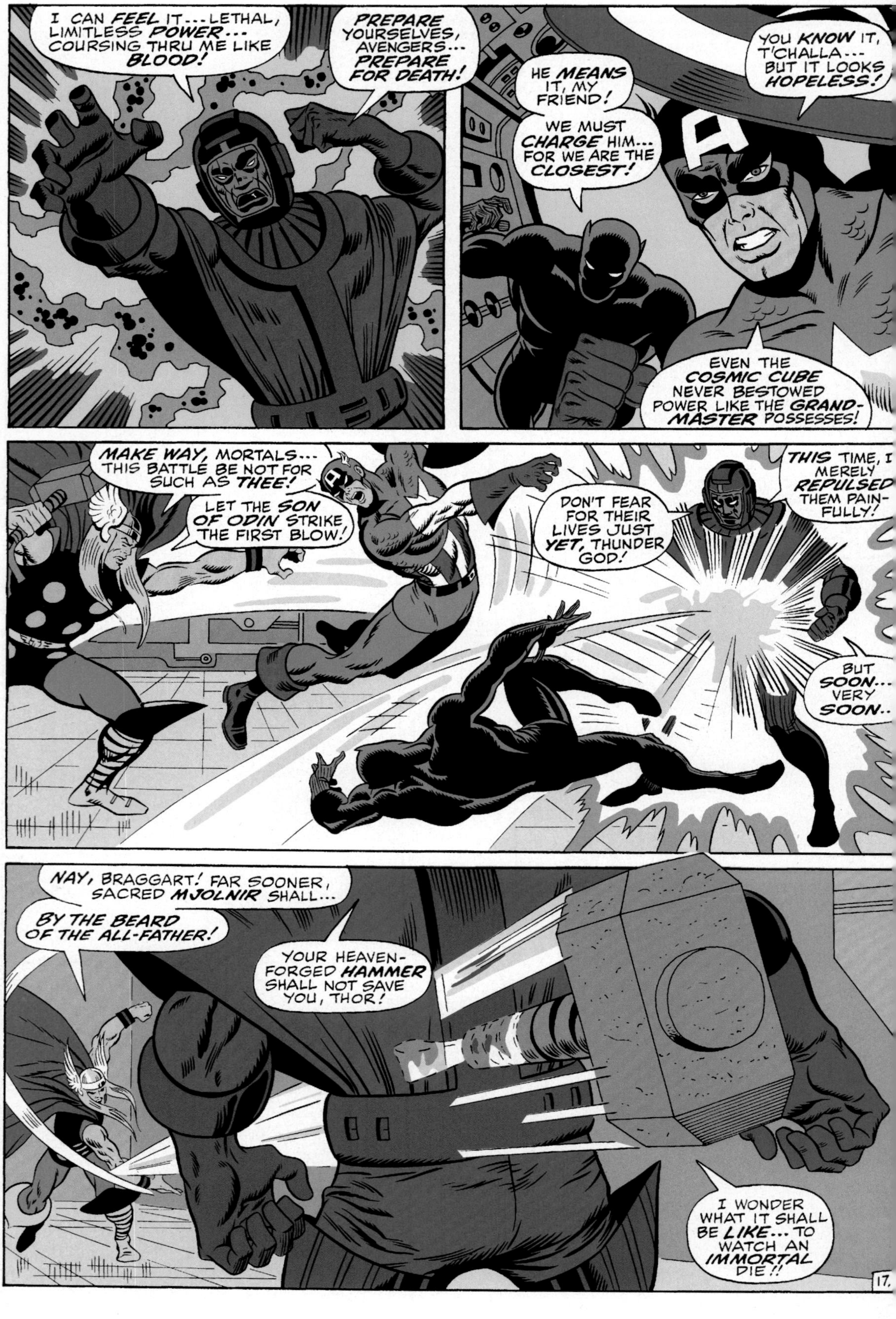
I CAN FEEL IT... LETHAL, LIMITLESS POWER... COURSING THRU ME LIKE BLOOD!
PREPARE YOURSELVES, AVENGERS... PREPARE FOR DEATH!
HE MEANS IT, MY FRIEND!
WE MUST CHARGE HIM... FOR WE ARE THE CLOSEST!
YOU KNOW IT, T'CHALLA... BUT IT LOOKS HOPELESS!
EVEN THE COSMIC CUBE NEVER BESTOWED POWER LIKE THE GRAND-MASTER POSSESSES!
MAKE WAY, MORTALS... THIS BATTLE BE NOT FOR SUCH AS THEE!
LET THE SON OF ODIN STRIKE THE FIRST BLOW!
DON'T FEAR FOR THEIR LIVES JUST YET, THUNDER GOD!
THIS TIME, I MERELY REPULSED THEM PAIN-FULLY!
BUT SOON... VERY SOON..
NAY, BRAGGART! FAR SOONER, SACRED MJOLNIR SHALL...
BY THE BEARD OF THE ALL-FATHER!
YOUR HEAVEN-FORGED HAMMER SHALL NOT SAVE YOU, THOR!
I WONDER WHAT IT SHALL BE LIKE... TO WATCH AN IMMORTAL DIE!!
17

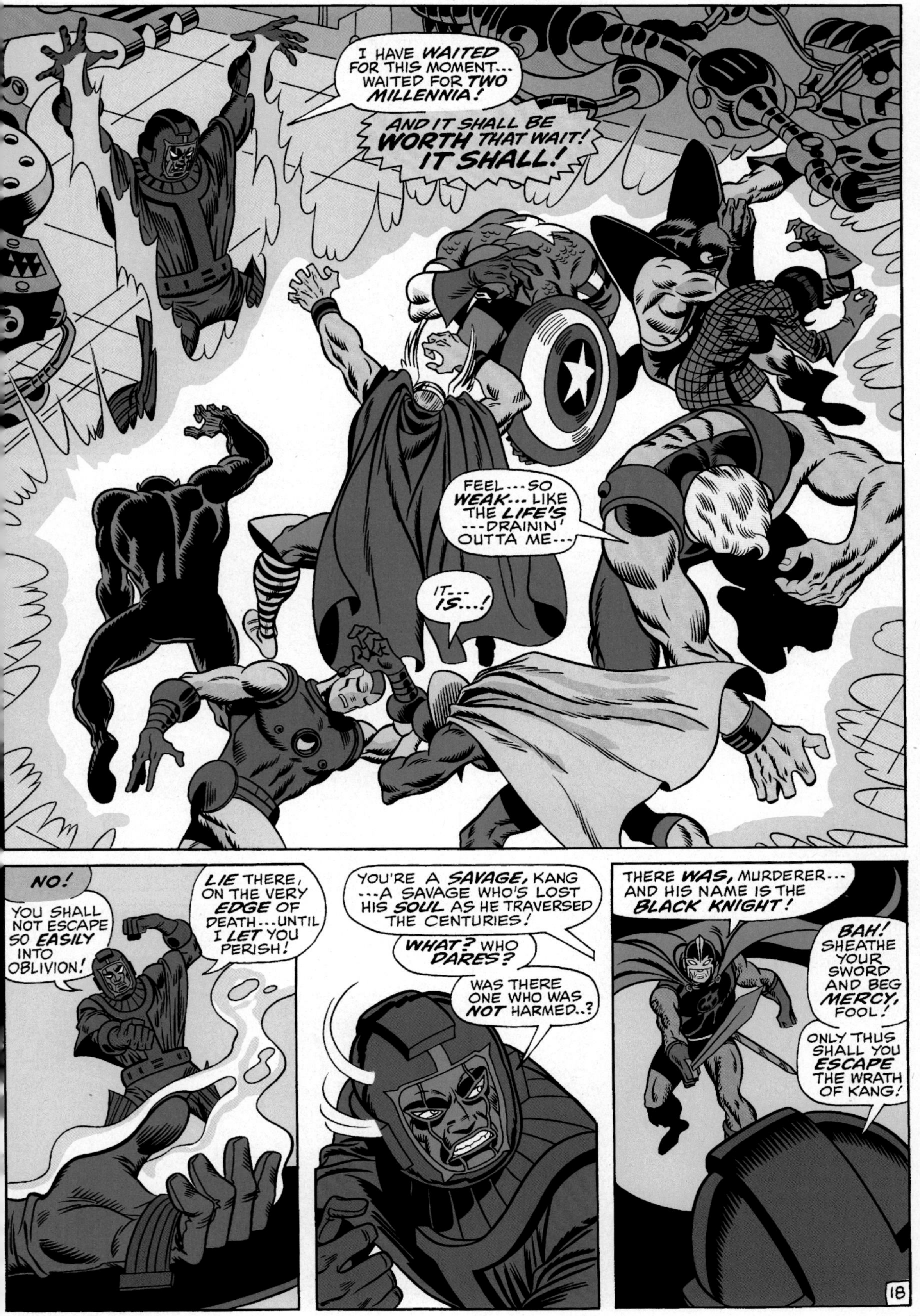
I HAVE WAITED FOR THIS MOMENT... WAITED FOR TWO MILLENNIA!
AND IT SHALL BE WORTH THAT WAIT! IT SHALL!
FEEL... SO WEAK... LIKE THE LIFE'S ...DRAININ' OUTTA ME...
IT... IS...!
NO!
YOU SHALL NOT ESCAPE SO EASILY INTO OBLIVION!
LIE THERE, ON THE VERY EDGE OF DEATH... UNTIL I LET YOU PERISH!
YOU'RE A SAVAGE, KANG ...A SAVAGE WHO'S LOST HIS SOUL AS HE TRAVERSED THE CENTURIES!
WHAT? WHO DARES?
WAS THERE ONE WHO WAS NOT HARMED..?
THERE WAS, MURDERER... AND HIS NAME IS THE BLACK KNIGHT!
BAH! SHEATHE YOUR SWORD AND BEG MERCY, FOOL!
ONLY THUS SHALL YOU ESCAPE THE WRATH OF KANG!
18

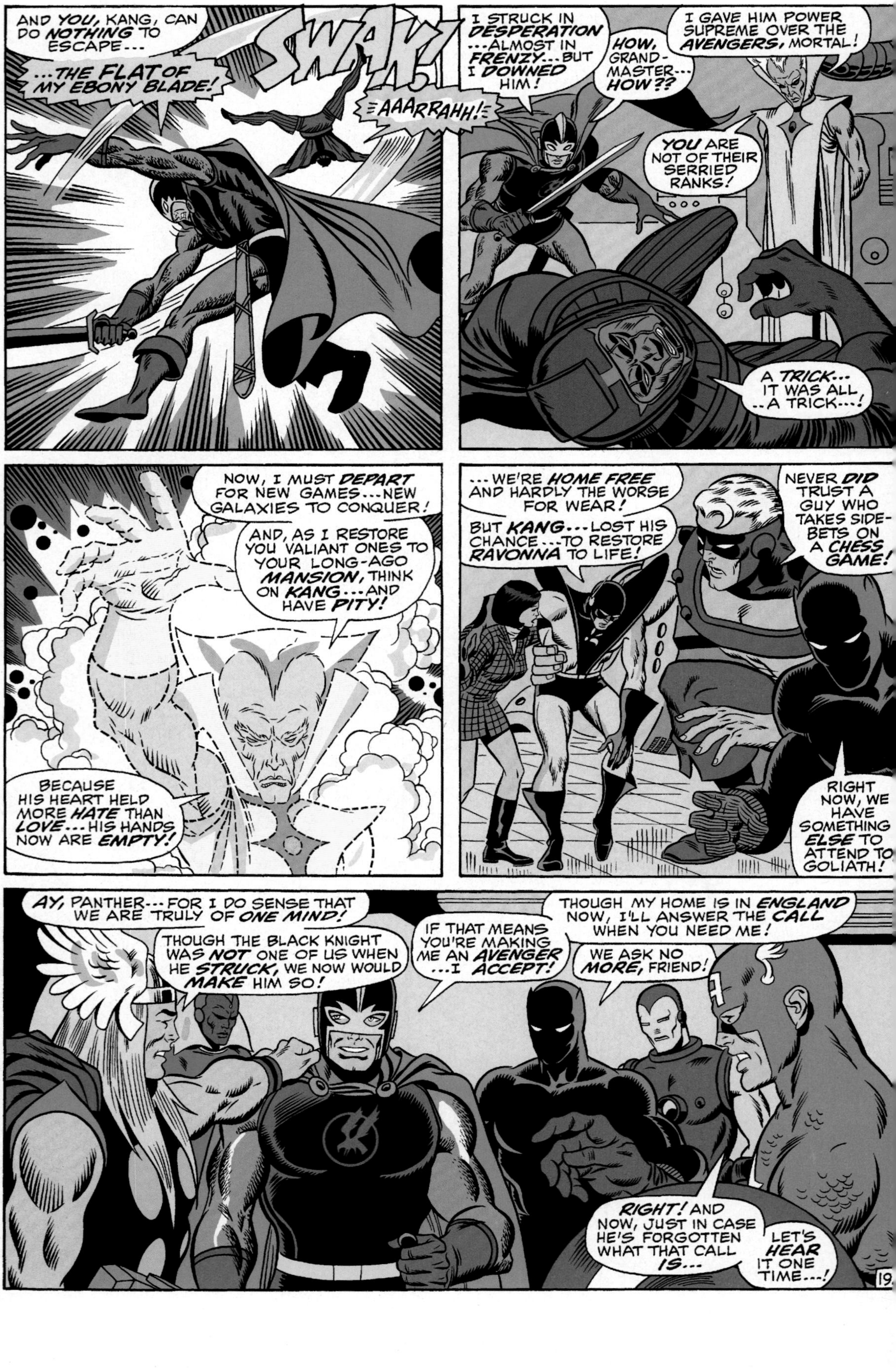
AND YOU, KANG, CAN DO NOTHING TO ESCAPE---
...THE FLAT OF MY EBONY BLADE!
SWAK!
AAARRAHH!
I STRUCK IN DESPERATION ---ALMOST IN FRENZY... BUT I DOWNED HIM!
HOW, GRAND-MASTER--- HOW??
I GAVE HIM POWER SUPREME OVER THE AVENGERS, MORTAL!
YOU ARE NOT OF THEIR SERRIED RANKS!
A TRICK... IT WAS ALL ..A TRICK---!
NOW, I MUST DEPART FOR NEW GAMES---NEW GALAXIES TO CONQUER!
AND, AS I RESTORE YOU VALIANT ONES TO YOUR LONG-AGO MANSION, THINK ON KANG---AND HAVE PITY!
BECAUSE HIS HEART HELD MORE HATE THAN LOVE---HIS HANDS NOW ARE EMPTY!
...WE'RE HOME FREE AND HARDLY THE WORSE FOR WEAR!
BUT KANG...LOST HIS CHANCE ...TO RESTORE RAVONNA TO LIFE!
NEVER DID TRUST A GUY WHO TAKES SIDE-BETS ON A CHESS GAME!
RIGHT NOW, WE HAVE SOMETHING ELSE TO ATTEND TO GOLIATH!
AY, PANTHER--- FOR I DO SENSE THAT WE ARE TRULY OF ONE MIND!
THOUGH THE BLACK KNIGHT WAS NOT ONE OF US WHEN HE STRUCK, WE NOW WOULD MAKE HIM SO!
IF THAT MEANS YOU'RE MAKING ME AN AVENGER ...I ACCEPT!
THOUGH MY HOME IS IN ENGLAND NOW, I'LL ANSWER THE CALL WHEN YOU NEED ME!
WE ASK NO MORE, FRIEND!
RIGHT! AND NOW, JUST IN CASE HE'S FORGOTTEN WHAT THAT CALL IS...
LET'S HEAR IT ONE TIME---!
19

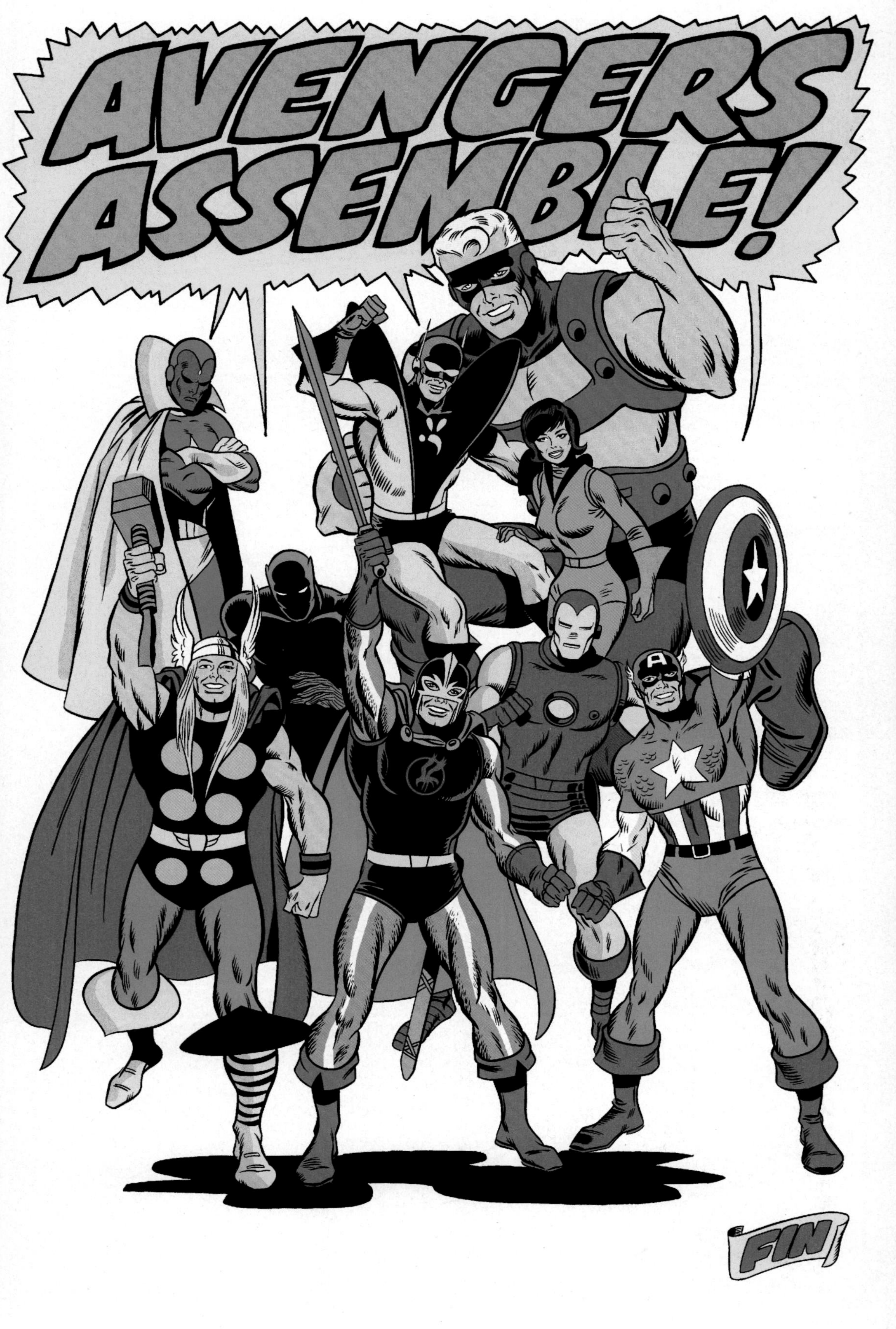
AVENGERS ASSEMBLE!
FIN

NFINITE COMIC STORYBOARDS BY MAST & GEO

nfinite Comics are Marvel's newest and boldest jump into the world of digital comics. Cr
specifically to be read on the Marvel Comics App, Infinite Comics take advantage of new storyt
opportunities the digital realm makes possible. This story has been restructured into tradit
print comics, but the original versions can be read on the Marvel Comics App to get the full e

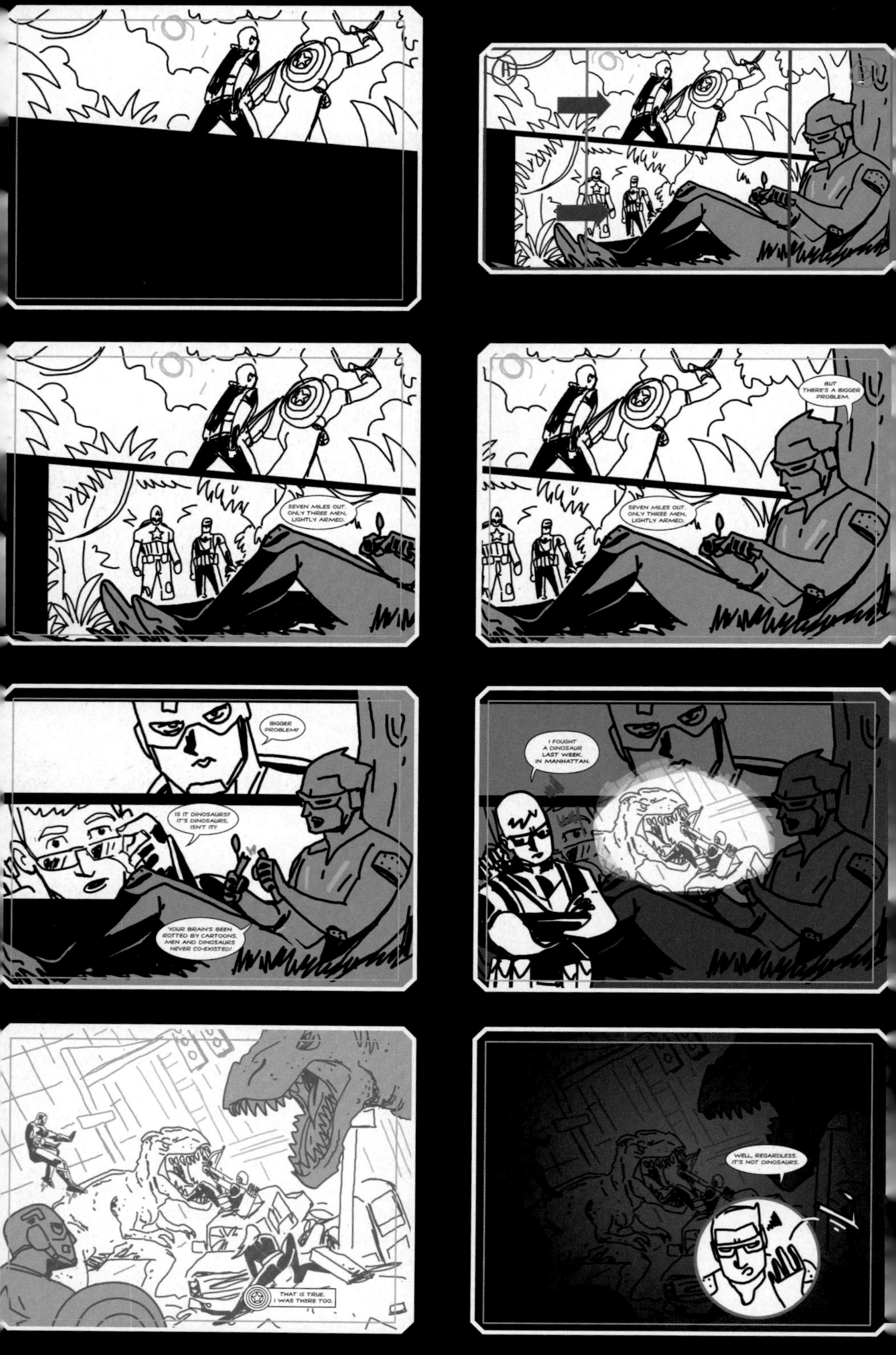

SEVEN MILES OUT. ONLY THREE MEN, LIGHTLY ARMED.
BUT THERE'S A BIGGER PROBLEM.
SEVEN MILES OUT. ONLY THREE MEN, LIGHTLY ARMED.
BIGGER PROBLEM?
IS IT DINOSAURS? IT'S DINOSAURS, ISN'T IT?
YOUR BRAIN'S BEEN ROTTED BY CARTOONS. MEN AND DINOSAURS NEVER CO-EXISTED!
I FOUGHT A DINOSAUR LAST WEEK. IN MANHATTAN.
THAT IS TRUE. I WAS THERE TOO.
WELL, REGARDLESS. IT'S NOT DINOSAURS.

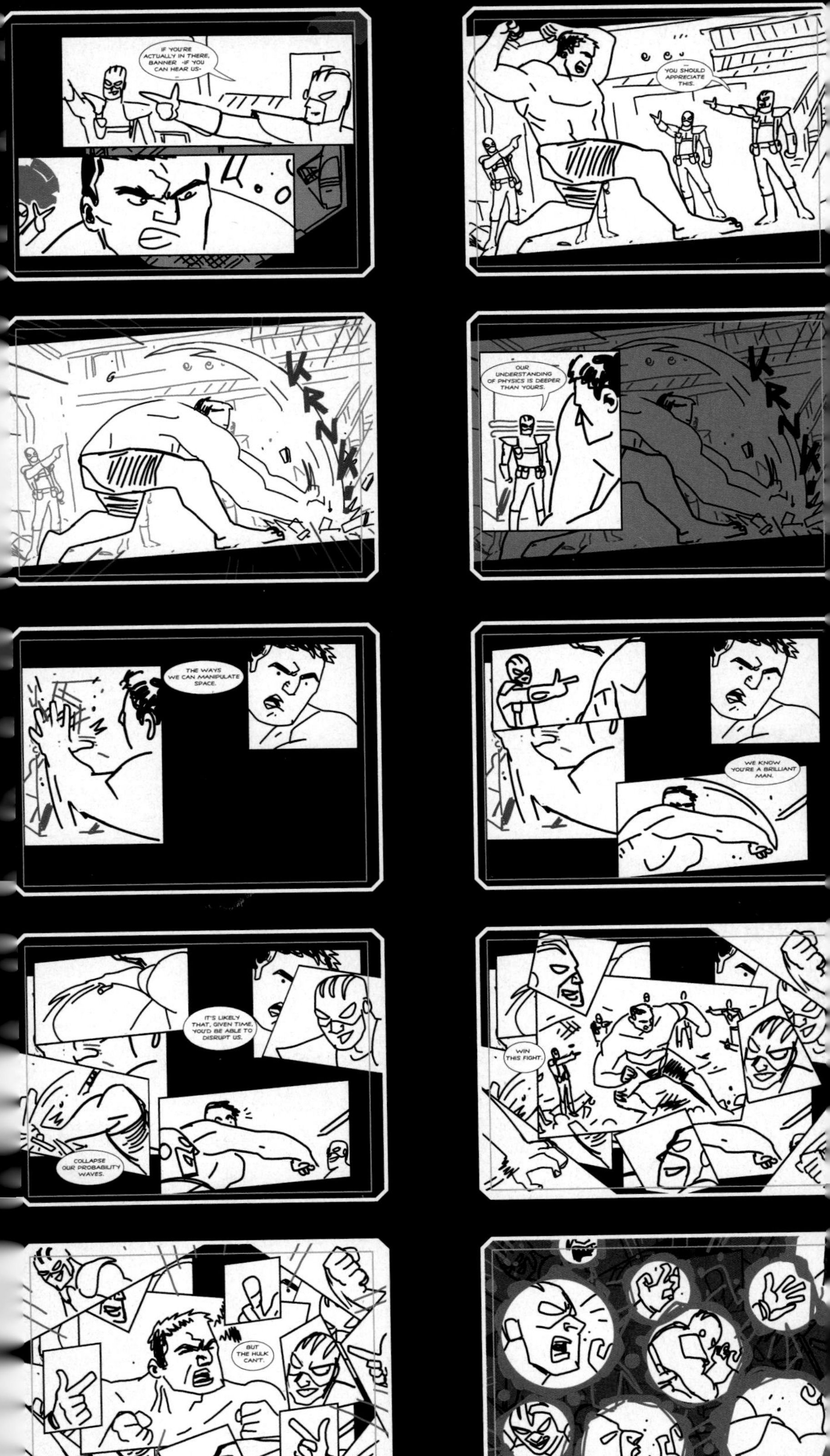
IF YOU'RE ACTUALLY IN THERE, BANNER -IF YOU CAN HEAR US-
YOU SHOULD APPRECIATE THIS.
KRNK
OUR UNDERSTANDING OF PHYSICS IS DEEPER THAN YOURS.
KRNK
THE WAYS WE CAN MANIPULATE SPACE.
WE KNOW YOU'RE A BRILLIANT MAN.
IT'S LIKELY THAT, GIVEN TIME, YOU'D BE ABLE TO DISRUPT US.
COLLAPSE OUR PROBABILITY WAVES.
WIN THIS FIGHT.
BUT THE HULK CAN'T.

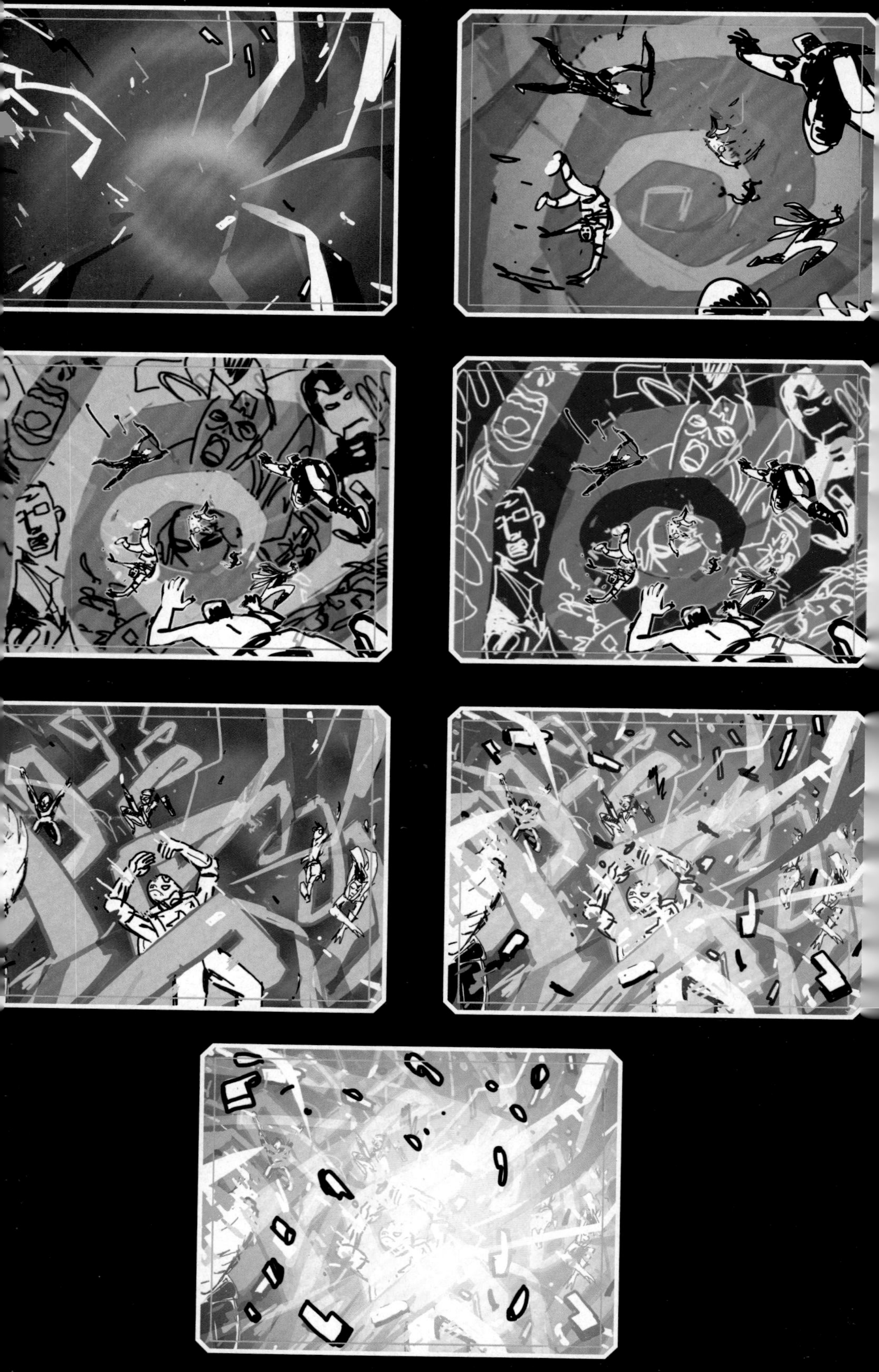